# The Workaholics Anonymous Book of Recovery

# The Workaholics Anonymous Book of Recovery

**Workaholics Anonymous
World Service Organization**

*Box 289 Menlo Park, California 94026
www.workaholics-anonymous.org*

All references to the Big Book of *Alcoholics Anonymous* refer to the
Third Edition, © 1976, Alcoholics Anonymous.

This is W.A. World Service Conference approved literature.

**First Edition, Fourth Printing, 2012**

We welcome your additional comments, suggestions, and
materials for other literature and for the revision of this book.

*Workaholics Anonymous World Services Organization*
PO Box 289 Menlo Park, California 94026-0289 USA
phone: 510-273-9253
email: wso@workaholics-anonymous. org
web: www.workaholics-anonymous.org

ISBN 13: 978-1-7325768-3-4

Library of Congress Cataloging Number 2005931980

Printed in the United States of America

# Table of Contents

# Foreword and Gratitude to Alcoholics Anonymous

We have a lot to be grateful for. We are in recovery. The old days of insanity, rushing, anxiety, toxic depletion, isolation, and self-hate are replaced with the sanity of a program of recovery. That program is described in this book of recovery from workaholism. We hope you will find in these pages the hope and guidance we have found in Workaholics Anonymous. The materials for this book were drawn from the personal experiences and writings of work addicted people in recovery. In addition, we are grateful to the writers of the Alcoholics Anonymous "Big Book" and the Twelve Steps and Twelve Traditions of Alcoholics Anonymous. They set the foundation of all the Twelve Step programs to follow. Each program adds to and deepens our understanding of addiction and recovery. We are thankful to them all for their contribution to our Workaholics Anonymous Book of Recovery.

A New York corporate financial planner, his spouse, and a schoolteacher started Workaholics Anonymous (W.A.) in April 1983. They founded W.A. based on the hoped-for success they knew in A.A. and Al-Anon. For many years our literature was written meeting by meeting or adapted from other programs. Much of the early literature was written by V.M. We wish to gratefully acknowledge those early leaders who kept this program going.

This book begins with describing the problem of workaholism and its many manifestations. Most of us come to W.A. not completely understanding our attraction to compulsive work or activity. Regularly reading literature and discussing our problems help us identify and free ourselves. It is the First Step of recovery: "We admitted we were powerless over work—that our lives had become unmanageable." The next section of this book describes the solution. It includes our tools and a guide to working the Twelve Steps of Recovery. It also includes a series of personal stories written by members in recovery. These are followed by articles written by members that describe recovering behaviors, thinking, and ways of being. We have chapters on how to contact us, how to find a meeting, and how to start a meeting. We wish to thank all of our authors, known and anonymous, who contributed to this book.

# ABOUT RECOVERY

Workaholics Anonymous is a fellowship and program of recovery that has successfully addressed the problems of work and activity addiction. We welcome you to join us on a journey to find balance and sanity in work and life. Many of us came to Workaholics Anonymous (W.A.) skeptical and defeated. We credit this program for bringing about a transformation that has enhanced our lives. It has worked for us and it can work for you. W.A. was adapted from the A.A. (Alcoholics Anonymous) program and Twelve Steps of recovery with their permission. We are very grateful to them.

**The W.A. Preamble** describes our fellowship:

"Workaholics Anonymous is a fellowship of individuals who share their experience, strength, and hope with each other that they may solve their common problems and help others to recover from workaholism.

The only requirement for membership is the desire to stop working compulsively. There are no dues or fees for W.A. membership; we are self-supporting through our own contributions. W.A. is not allied with any sect, denomination, politics, organization or institution; does not wish to engage in any controversy; neither endorses nor opposes any causes. Our primary purpose is to stop working compulsively and to carry the message of recovery to workaholics who still suffer."

We invite you to join in our healing process. Work addicts in recovery wrote this book to share their experience, strength and hope using the Twelve Steps of Workaholics Anonymous. This book includes our stories about how workaholism drove us to desperation and what recovery has given us. Because meetings are a source of support, we include information on how to contact us to find a meeting or how to start a meeting if there are none in your area.

Many of us, when we first heard of workaholism as an addiction, thought that it was some kind of joke. We had many reasons: Didn't everyone have issues around work? After all, we didn't work *that* much. We knew people who worked much more that we did. Isn't hard work how one succeeds? In uncertain economic times, people need to work long hours to keep jobs.

Others of us had periods when we hardly worked at all or when we actively avoided work. Some thought that we could not possibly be workaholics. In the beginning, most of us were ambivalent about recovery. After all, hard work is admired and rewarded. We were afraid we would be forced to quit, never attain goals or give up a good paycheck. Or we wanted to slow down and have a balanced life but the lure of the "rush," "intensity," and "self importance" were overpowering.

Workaholism is not strictly about the amount of work we do but rather about our emotional and spiritual relationship to work and activity and how it can negatively affect us and those around us—often without our knowing it. This includes our health, happiness and relationships. Workaholism involves both a substance addiction (adrenaline and other stress hormones) and a process addiction (compulsive doing or not doing) and is not limited to our paid work life. We have found that we have also been workaholic in hobbies, fitness, volunteering, or in trying to save the world. All of these seemed admirable at first but as we lost ourselves to incessant doing, we fell prey to compulsive work addiction.

Since this is a progressive disease, we became more driven until we hit bottom. Our unmanageability sometimes came in the form of burnout, a serious health problem, or sometimes an ultimatum from our partner or employer. At some point "workaholic" was no longer a label we prized. Because of the many misconceptions about workaholism, recognizing it sometimes took a long time. Slowly we came to understand the debilitating, progressive grip workaholism can have. We came to believe that, unchecked, it would prove fatal. Many of us had lost our family and health before we got into recovery.

If you are wondering if you or someone you care about could benefit from this program, the following 20 questions may help to evaluate the situation.

# The Twenty Questions

1. Do you get more excited about your work than about family or anything else?
2. Are there times when you can charge through your work and other times when you can't get anything done?
3. Do you take work with you to bed? On weekends? On vacation?
4. Is work the activity you like to do best and talk about most?
5. Do you work more than 40 hours a week?
6. Do you turn your hobbies into moneymaking ventures?
7. Do you take complete responsibility for the outcome of your work efforts?
8. Have your family or friends given up expecting you on time?

9. Do you take on extra work because you are concerned that it won't otherwise get done?
10. Do you underestimate how long a project will take and then rush to complete it?
11. Do you believe that it is okay to work long hours if you love what you are doing?
12. Do you get impatient with people who have other priorities besides work?
13. Are you afraid that if you don't work hard you will lose your job or be a failure?
14. Is the future a constant worry for you even when things are going very well?
15. Do you do things energetically and competitively including play?
16. Do you get irritated when people ask you to stop doing your work in order to do something else?
17. Have your long hours hurt your family or other relationships?
18. Do you think about your work while driving, falling asleep, or when others are talking?
19. Do you work or read during meals?
20. Do you believe that more money will solve the other problems in your life?

Three positive answers are considered an indicator there may be a problem with workaholism. After carefully considering your answers to the above questions and perhaps even talking about them with your family and friends, you may come to realize that there is a problem. Most of us were slow to fully comprehend the signs of our problem. Recovery began when we identified with workaholic behaviors. It was our first step. Awareness of our problem opens the door to possible solutions.

# The Problem: Characteristics of Workaholics

1. It is very difficult for us to relax. We often, if not always, feel the need to get just a few more tasks done before we can feel good about ourselves and allow ourselves to relax. When we do complete these tasks we find just a few more that we need to complete, and then a few more.... These uncontrollable desires often result in frantic, compulsive working. We are powerless to control this pattern.

2.   We are so used to doing what we are expected to do that we are often unable to know what it is that we really want to do and need to do for ourselves.

3.   We often feel that we must complete certain tasks, even though we do not want to, yet we are too scared to stop.

4.   We often feel resentment about *having* to complete tasks when we would rather relax or play. At these times we procrastinate, usually wallowing in self-pity and self-judgment. We become absorbed by our "stinking thinking," cannot concentrate on the task at hand, and yet are too scared to give up the task for a moment and allow ourselves the space we need.

5.   Our sense of self-esteem is based largely on our perceptions of how others judge our performance at work and in other areas of our lives.

6.   We often think of ourselves as either the most intelligent, capable people we know or the most incapable and worthless people we know.

7.   It is hard for us to see ourselves honestly and accept who we really are.

8.   We often betray ourselves by giving in to the demands of people whom we perceive as being in "authority."

9.   We operate out of the mini-crisis mode, using this as an escape from experiencing our true emotions.

10.  We do not often experience true serenity.

11.  We have an obsessive desire to understand everything in our lives, including our every emotion. We cannot allow ourselves to experience emotions that we do not understand, fearing our loss of control.

12.  We have an underlying fear that if we give up control and allow our emotions to surface, we will become raving lunatics for the rest of our lives.

13.  We judge ourselves by our accomplishments and hence have the illusion that we must always be in the process of accomplishing something worthwhile in order to feel good about ourselves.

14.  We cannot sit down and just be.

15.  We often go on intense work binges with the illusion that we need to get the praise of our fellow workers and bosses in order to feel OK.

16.  We have the illusion that people will like us more if we appear more competent than we actually are.

17.  Often when we are praised by others we tend to discount ourselves as not worthy of their praise.

18. We tend to schedule ourselves for more than we can handle, believing people will like us more if we can do more and do it faster.

19. We are often dishonest about our past experiences and our present capabilities, tending to not mention our failures and to exaggerate our successes. We believe that people will not respect us or like us just as we are.

20. We hurt inside.

# The Signposts of Workaholism

1. We find it hard to love and accept ourselves. Work has become our means of gaining approval, finding our identity and justifying our existence.

2. We use work to escape our feelings. Thus, we deprive ourselves of knowing what we truly want and need.

3. By overworking, we neglect our health, relationships, recreation and spirituality. Even when we are not working, we are thinking of our next task. Most of our activities are work-related. We deny ourselves the enjoyment of a balanced and varied life.

4. We use work as a way to deal with the uncertainties of life. We lie awake worrying; we over-plan and over-organize. By being unwilling to surrender control, we lose our spontaneity, creativity and flexibility.

5. Many of us grew up in chaotic homes. Stress and intensity feel normal to us. We seek out these conditions in the workplace. We create crises and get adrenaline highs by overworking to resolve them. Then we suffer withdrawals and become anxious and depressed. Such mood swings destroy our peace of mind.

6. Work has become an addiction. We lie to ourselves and to others about the amount we do. We hoard work to insure that we will always be busy and never bored. We fear free time and vacations and find them painful instead of refreshing.

7. Instead of being a haven, our home is an extension of our workplace. Our family and friends often arrange their time with us around our work, vainly hoping we will finish it and then can be with them.

8. We make unreasonable demands upon ourselves. We aren't aware of any difference between job-imposed and self-imposed pressure. By over-scheduling our lives, we become driven, racing to beat the clock, fearful that we will get behind, and binge-work in order to catch up. Our attention is fragmented by trying to do several things at

once. Our inability to pace ourselves leads to breakdown
and burnout. We rob ourselves of the enjoyment of
conclusion and rest.

9.    We tend to be perfectionistic. We don't accept mistakes
as part of being human and find it hard to ask for help.
Because we believe no one can meet our standards, we
have difficulty delegating and so do more than our share of
the work. Thinking ourselves indispensable often prevents
our progress. Unrealistic expectations often cheat us of
contentment.

10.   We tend to be over-serious and responsible. All activity
must be purposeful. We find it hard to relax and just be;
we feel guilty and restless when not working. Because we
often work at our play, we rarely experience re-creation
and renewal. We neglect our sense of humor and rarely
enjoy the healing power of laughter.

11.   Waiting is hard for us. We are more interested in results
than process, in quantity than quality. Our impatience
often distorts our work by not allowing it proper timing.

12.   Many of us are concerned with image. We think that
looking busy makes people think we are important and
gains their admiration. By seeking others' approval of us,
we lose ourselves.

# How Does Recovery Begin?

Realizing and admitting that we had a problem was our
first step of recovery. Most of us came to Workaholics
Anonymous (W.A.) not completely understanding our compulsive
attraction to—or avoidance of—work and activity. Regularly
reading program literature, attending meetings, and discussing our
problems helped us to identify with other workaholics and to free
ourselves. It was our First Step of recovery: **"We admitted we
were powerless over work—that our lives had become
unmanageable."**

For many of us Step One initially seemed counterintuitive
and even wrong. Powerless! Didn't powerless mean helpless and
therefore hopeless? In Workaholics Anonymous, we learned that
Step One meant that by ourselves we were powerless to solve our
problems with work. For a long time, we were in denial that we
needed help, and we assumed that intellect and hard work could
solve our problems. In practice, we found that our unaided efforts
were not sufficient. Over time our workaholism worsened, despite
our resolution and good intentions. We came to see how our
responses weren't working and how our lives were unmanageable.
We came to Workaholics Anonymous meetings having crossed a

mental barrier of pride and denial. We admitted something was wrong and that we needed help. It was a relief. We were not alone. We began to identify with our fellow members. Workaholics Anonymous offered us a fellowship and a program of recovery that helped us do what we could not do by ourselves alone.

# Meetings and Recovery

**Looking for your first meeting?** You can look up meetings at the Workaholics Anonymous web page www.workaholics-anonymous.org or by calling 510-273-9253.

When we first heard about Workaholics Anonymous meetings, many of us wondered how meetings could help. We were already too busy. We wondered how it could possibly help us to go to a meeting with other people who also had a problem with work and activity. What could other workaholics teach us? On the other hand, we were desperate. So we skeptically went to our first meeting. Although we did not feel that we completely understood everything that went on, we discovered to our immense relief that Workaholics Anonymous is not a cult. There is no belief in any dogma or religion. By going to meetings we discovered that Workaholics Anonymous itself could be a power greater than ourselves in the sense that members in meetings could do something that we could not do by ourselves: recover from workaholism.

Although not a religious organization, Workaholics Anonymous—and its members—had a deeply spiritual nature. The members spoke of how a "Higher Power" was an important part of their lives. We learned that a power greater than ourselves could restore us to sanity. This power can be God, as we understand God, or the W.A. Group. It is whatever our source of strength is. It is important to remind ourselves that our ego is not this Power. We came to believe that recovery from workaholism requires a spiritual basis that includes a Higher Power. We are free to define our Higher Power as we grow in experiencing it.

# Turning it Over

**"Step Two. Came to believe that a Power greater than ourselves could restore us to sanity."**

Step Two speaks of sanity because workaholism is a kind of insanity—the kind of insanity that includes repeating the same workaholic activity and somehow expecting different results. We began to recover by gradually removing our insane thinking and habits with the help of a power greater than ourselves.

A member writes: "I've had 27 years of setting unrealistic standards for myself, thinking I should be doing more, pushing myself past where I could go, thinking others wanted me to do things. I know how many painful problems compulsive busyness has caused me. But it is hard for me to remember how my attempts to control it have failed. I am starting to recognize times in the past that had been opportunities to cram one more thing into my life."

Another member says, "My obsessing could be about many things: working, not working, a co-worker, things that I wish someone hadn't done or had done, that I was afraid would happen, that I would rather be doing or not doing, etc." For many of us the obsessions were recurrent and progressive. We could stop for a while, but by our own unaided efforts, we could not prevent recurrence. "Dealing with my obsessing required help from a Power greater than me."

In Step Three of recovery, **"We made a decision to turn our will and our life over the care of God *as we understood God*."** Faced with this Step, many of us balked and felt uncomfortable that this was going to be too religious. Step Three involves making a commitment to letting a caring power outside of our "self-will" guide us. One way that we learn how to turn our will and our life over to the care of this Power greater than ourselves is by making a decision and commitment to working the remaining Twelve Steps of the program of Workaholics Anonymous. Letting our Higher Power help us requires giving up control, but we are still responsible for what we do. It means learning a new way of thinking. For those of us who pride ourselves on being self-sufficient, we discover we find a new power and peace that replaces the toxic compulsive thinking and doing.

Recovery is like coming home to our original selves that we forgot: playful, joyful, appreciative, and hopeful. Following the Steps and joining the W.A. fellowship brings us in touch with our inner wisdom and spirituality. As we learn to accept ourselves as we are, we experience a new attitude toward work and activity. We enjoy our work more and find ways to work more effectively. When work has its proper place, we find time to have fun and to nurture our health, relationships, and creativity. We welcome you to read our Book of Recovery and wish for you the serenity and enjoyment we have found.

Most W.A. meetings include reading from our list of tools to help develop a new way of thinking. At first it seemed like a foreign language, but as we begin to adopt these tools of action and thinking, we notice a welcome change.

We use these tools regularly and integrate them into our way of life. We find ourselves adopting them effortlessly when we ask our Higher Power to remove our shortcomings. We are grateful for these tools because they help us to live full and healthy lives; they are essential to our recovery.

# W.A. Tools of Recovery

### Listening
We set aside time each day for prayer and meditation. Before accepting any commitments, we ask our Higher Power and W.A. friends for guidance.

### Prioritizing
We decide which are the most important things to do first. Sometimes that may mean doing nothing. We strive to stay flexible to events, reorganizing our priorities as needed. We view interruptions and accidents as opportunities for growth.

### Substituting
We do not add a new activity without eliminating from our schedule one that demands equivalent time and energy.

### Underscheduling
We allow more time than we think we need for a task or trip, allowing a comfortable margin to accommodate the unexpected.

### Playing
We schedule time for play, refusing to let ourselves work non-stop. We do not make our play into a work project.

### Concentrating
We try to do one thing at a time.

### Pacing
We work at a comfortable pace and rest *before* we get tired. To remind ourselves, we check our level of energy before proceeding to our next activity. We do not get "wound up" in our work, so we don't have to unwind.

### Relaxing
We do not yield to pressure from others or attempt to pressure others. We remain alert to the people and situations that trigger feelings of pressure in us. We become aware of our own actions,

words, body sensations and feelings that tell us we are responding with pressure. When we feel energy building up, we stop; we reconnect with our Higher Power and others around us.

### Accepting
We accept the outcomes of our endeavors, whatever the results, whatever the timing. We know that impatience, rushing and insisting on perfect results only slow down our recovery. We are gentle with our efforts, knowing that our new way of living requires much practice.

### Asking
We admit our weaknesses and mistakes. We realize we don't have to do everything ourselves, and we ask our Higher Power and others for help.

### Meetings
We attend W.A. meetings to learn how the fellowship works and to share our experience, strength and hope with each other.

### Telephoning
We use the telephone to stay in contact with members of the fellowship between meetings. We communicate with our W.A. friends before and after a critical task.

### Balancing
We balance our involvement in work with our efforts to develop personal relationships, spiritual growth, creativity and playful attitudes.

### Serving
We readily extend help to other workaholics, knowing that assistance to others adds to the quality of our own recovery.

### Living in the Now
We realize we are where our Higher Power wants us to be—in the here and now. We try to live each moment with serenity, joy and gratitude.

# W.A. Principles of Recovery

### Abstinence
In Workaholics Anonymous, abstinence means to abstain from compulsive working, activity, worry, and work avoidance. For many workaholics, abstinence means far more than relief from

compulsive working on a physical level. It also means an attitude that comes as a result of surrendering to something greater than ourselves. Abstinence means not only freedom from compulsive working but also freedom from compulsive thinking and worrying. Each of us is free to determine our own way of being abstinent according to personal needs and preferences. Bottom lines define the point where we cross over from abstinence to work addiction. The tool of abstinence includes working with a sponsor to establish and maintain personal bottom lines, top lines, and guidelines for recovery as well as seeking support around bottom line behavior.

## Sponsorship

Sponsors are Workaholics Anonymous members who are committed to abstinence from compulsive working. They offer guidance through the recovery process on all three levels: physical, emotional and spiritual. Specifically, they can help us with tools such as work plans, phone calls, and working the Steps. A member may work with more than one sponsor and may change sponsors at will. Sometimes it is more practical to enter into a co-sponsoring arrangement. We become a sponsor or co-sponsor as a way of working The Twelfth Step: to carry the Workaholics Anonymous message and to put the principles of the program into practice. We ask to be sponsored or co-sponsored so we can benefit from the experience of someone who has achieved what we want. Ours is a program of attraction, so we find a sponsor who has what we want and ask how they achieved it.

## Writing

Often, writing clarifies our thoughts and helps us get to the root of the feelings that lie behind our compulsive working. It is an action that fosters self-reliance because we can write even when no one is available for us to talk with. Writing for ourselves may give us clarity over talking. This is partly because when we talk with other people we may find our choice of words and subjects are affected by our interaction with our audience. Writing records our expressions in a way that helps us understand what we are trying to say. Writings can be shared with others if we want to use them as a form of communication.

## Action Plan

We put on paper what we intend to do each day for our relationships, our activities, and ourselves. This helps us develop a healthier and more balanced lifestyle. It also helps us to overcome denial. Sharing our plan with another person gives us an opportunity to express feelings that are often at the root of our compulsive behavior.

## Humor
Seeing the funny side of our predicament can help free us from anxiety and worry.

## Time Out
We workaholics have found that having fun and relaxing are essential tools in our recovery from workaholism. By setting aside time for playfulness and for unstructured events without goals, we learn that there is more to life than our former identities around work and activity. Play and fun help heal us to live in the present moment, rather than driving ourselves for hoped-for fulfillment in some faraway future time.

## Nurturing
We nurture our bodies with healthy eating, exercise and rest. We nurture our minds by looking for positive aspects in every encounter. We nurture our spirits by surrounding ourselves with beauty, harmony, and tranquility. We recognize we are neither what we do nor what we feel. We foster our sense of self-worth and self-respect.

## Literature
Literature is a source of information, insight, experience, strength and hope. Reading on a daily basis impresses the truth on us and expands our horizons. This can be vital to our growth and reinforces our program of recovery. Program literature is an ever-available tool that gives insight into our problems, strength to deal with them and the knowledge that there is a process of recovery for us. We also study the literature of Alcoholics Anonymous and other Twelve Step programs to strengthen our understanding of compulsive disease. We can identify with many of the situations described by substituting the words "compulsive working" for alcohol.

## Anonymity
Anonymity means that whatever we share with another member is held in respect and confidence. It helps us place principles before personalities. It offers us freedom of expression and protection against gossip. The tradition of anonymity means that we do not publicly disclose in the media our full names in connection with Workaholics Anonymous.

## The Twelve Steps

Recovery from compulsive work and activity can be achieved by undertaking the Twelve Steps of Workaholics Anonymous. These Steps provide a source of hope as well as a structured way to achieve progress. Moving from one Step to another may take varying amounts of effort and time. We may revisit Steps and find new meanings in them. Ultimately, we find we practice the Steps by fully integrating them into our lives. We can create a Step group at our meetings and work the Steps together.

## Meditation

For many of us, being still and sitting quietly are difficult and painful at first. The practice of letting go of the constant chatter in our heads can lead to a gradually evolving peace of mind. This serenity is a soothing, healing contrast to the excitement, rush, and pleasurable intensity we have sought through our over-work, compulsive activity, and constant worry. Meditation lets us experience ourselves insulated from fears, insecurities, and resentments that drive work avoidance and the compulsivity of workaholism. Renewed, we are able to move back into our daily lives in a balanced way.

# The Promises of Workaholics Anonymous

If we are completely honest about ourselves and together we use the Twelve Steps of Workaholics Anonymous and the Tools of W.A. in our lives, we will soon begin to receive these gifts of sanity and balance:

1. We are not obsessed by work or plagued by work aversion.
2. Adrenaline seeking loses its hold on us. Excessive worry and anxiety become a thing of the past.
3. We have a daily plan of action that faces the reality of time, priorities, health, and relationships.
4. Fears that there won't be enough time, money or love leave us.
5. We learn to play and have fun together.
6. We repair broken relationships and form new ones.
7. Health and self-nurturance return.
8. Self-seeking and ego inflation do not drive our decisions.
9. We lose interest in selfish things and gain interest in and compassion for our partners, families, co-workers, and friends.

10.      We experience how well the tools of the program help us handle problems which used to confuse and defeat us.
11.      We ask for help and reach out to help others.
12.      We find that our Higher Power helps us in a way self-reliance never could.

Are these extravagant promises? We think not. They are already happening in the lives of many among us. For those of you who are new to our fellowship, there are no problems that you have experienced that are not common to us. We welcome you with the deepest respect. When we apply this program with honesty and compassion, a place of serenity grows in us one day at a time.

# How Recovery Happens

We compulsive workers have found that no amount of will power or self-determination can make us stick to a sensible program of work for any permanent or lasting length of time.

We have found that self-reliance failed us. Self-reliance is good as far as it goes, but it doesn't go far enough. Some of us once had self-confidence, but it didn't solve our work problem or any other problem fully.

We have felt a need and have been seeking an answer to our dilemma. We have realized that our work obsession is only the outward manifestation of our inner emotional turmoil and our essential spiritual disconnection.

We who are recovering from the destructive consequences of work addiction understand, as perhaps few others can, the fear, depression, anxiety, and loneliness of being a workaholic. We are learning that the praise we get from others, our desire to get 'lost' in our frantic behavior, and our sick sense of needing to avoid or accomplish goals, are all processes we use to escape the reality that we cannot completely control our life or our experience. We are learning that we can never get enough praise, money, or get enough accomplished to truly feel good about ourselves; that workaholism is a disease, and, like all other addictive diseases, it is progressive and fatal if not arrested.

We are also learning that recovery is possible. We learn to notice and identify our "bottom line" behavior. Unlike most chemical addictions, work addiction does not allow us to simply stop working and still survive. With Higher Power's assistance, by defining our personal "bottom line" behaviors, we can begin to notice when we are actively using work, and we can stop and pray, or call a fellow recovering addict for support. We have experienced the healing of the Workaholics Anonymous Program.

Our stories share what we were like before recovery, how we got into recovery, and what we are like now. We hope you decide you want what we have and are willing to join us at meetings, reading our literature, and practicing our Steps of recovery. We now know that we deal with an obsession—cunning, and powerful. Without help, it is destined to overwhelm us. But we have come to rely on a Power greater than ourselves.

We have found that half efforts slowed our progress.

Here are the Steps we took, which are suggested as a Program for Recovery...

# The Twelve Steps of Workaholics Anonymous

1. We admitted we were powerless over work—that our lives had become unmanageable.
2. Came to believe that a Power greater than ourselves could restore us to sanity.
3. Made a decision to turn our will and our lives over to the care of God *as we understood God*.
4. Made a searching and fearless moral inventory of ourselves.
5. Admitted to God, to ourselves, and to another human being the exact nature of our wrongs.
6. Became entirely ready to have God remove all these defects of character.
7. Humbly asked God to remove our shortcomings.
8. Made a list of all persons we had harmed, and became willing to make amends to them all.
9. Made direct amends to such people wherever possible, except when to do so would injure them or others.
10. Continued to take personal inventory and when we were wrong promptly admitted it.
11. Sought through prayer and meditation to improve our conscious contact with God *as we understood God*, praying only for knowledge of God's will for us and the power to carry that out.
12. Having had a spiritual awakening as the result of these steps, we tried to carry this message to workaholics, and to practice these principles in all our affairs.

# The Twelve Traditions of Workaholics Anonymous

1. Our common welfare should come first; personal recovery depends upon W.A. unity.

2. For our group purpose there is but one ultimate authority—a loving God as expressed in our group conscience. Our leaders are but trusted servants; they do not govern.

3. The only requirement for W.A. membership is a desire to stop working compulsively.

4. Each group should be autonomous except in matters affecting other groups or W.A. as a whole.

5. Each group has but one primary purpose—to carry its message to the workaholic who still suffers.

6. A Workaholics Anonymous group ought never endorse, finance or lend the W.A. name to any related facility or outside enterprise, lest problems of money, property and prestige divert us from our primary purpose.

7. Every W.A. group ought to be fully self-supporting, declining outside contributions.

8. Workaholics Anonymous should remain forever nonprofessional, but our service centers may employ special workers.

9. W.A., as such, ought never be organized; but we may create service boards or committees directly responsible to those they serve.

10. Workaholics Anonymous has no opinion on outside issues; hence the W.A. name ought never be drawn into public controversy.

11. Our public relations policy is based on attraction rather than promotion; we need always maintain personal anonymity at the level of press, radio, and films.

12. Anonymity is the spiritual foundation of all our traditions, ever reminding us to place principles before personalities.

# A.A. Source Materials

## The Twelve Steps of Alcoholics Anonymous

1. We admitted we were powerless over alcohol—that our lives had become unmanageable.
2. Came to believe that a Power greater than ourselves could restore us to sanity.
3. Made a decision to turn our will and our lives over to the care of God *as we understood Him*.
4. Made a searching and fearless moral inventory of ourselves.
5. Admitted to God, to ourselves, and to another human being the exact nature of our wrongs.
6. Were entirely ready to have God remove all these defects of character.
7. Humbly asked Him to remove our shortcomings.
8. Made a list of all persons we had harmed, and became willing to make amends to them all.
9. Made direct amends to such people wherever possible, except when to do so would injure them or others.
10. Continued to take personal inventory and when we were wrong promptly admitted it.
11. Sought through prayer and meditation to improve our conscious contact with God *as we understood Him*, praying only for knowledge of His will for us and the power to carry that out.
12. Having had a spiritual awakening as the result of these steps, we tried to carry this message to alcoholics, and to practice these principles in all our affairs.

*Copyright © Alcoholics Anonymous World Services, Inc. Reprinted with permission.*

## The Twelve Traditions of Alcoholics Anonymous

1. Our common welfare should come first; personal recovery depends upon A.A. unity.
2. For our group purpose there is but one ultimate authority—a loving God as He may express Himself in our group conscience. Our leaders are but trusted servants; they do not govern.
3. The only requirement for A.A. membership is a desire to stop drinking.
4. Each group should be autonomous except in matters affecting other groups or A.A. as a whole.
5. Each group has but one primary purpose—to carry its message to the alcoholic who still suffers.
6. An A.A. group ought never endorse, finance, or lend the A.A. name to any related facility or outside enterprise, lest problems of money, property, and prestige divert us from our primary purpose.
7. Every A.A. group ought to be fully self-supporting, declining outside contributions.
8. Alcoholics Anonymous should remain forever nonprofessional, but our service centers may employ special workers.
9. A.A., as such, ought never be organized; but we may create service boards or committees directly responsible to those they serve.
10. Alcoholics Anonymous has no opinion on outside issues; hence the A.A. name ought never be drawn into public controversy.

11. Our public relations policy is based on attraction rather than promotion; we need always maintain personal anonymity at the level of press, radio, and films.
12. Anonymity is the spiritual foundation of all our traditions, ever reminding us to place principles before personalities.

# OUR STORIES

## A Workaholic's Story

I've been a workaholic since 13. My childhood was the meat of a dysfunctional family sandwich. I was pressed on one side by a tyrannical, workaholic father whom I could rarely please. On the other was an apprehensive and distant mother always within arm's reach of potent prescription drugs. In the middle, aggressively competing with me for our parents' unfulfilled promises of conditional love was my sister: seven years older, braver, stronger, and smarter than me.

My father was a clergyman, civic leader, a force in state politics. Around him I was always fearful I would be (and often was) scolded or punished for some awkward, selfish, or mean-spirited thing I hadn't intended to do. My mother spoke four languages and digested books on all subjects like some people eat candy. Around her I experienced constant anxiety and rejection, concluding I simply wasn't worthy of love. Confusion and conflict dominated all family communication. Exuberance was criticized. Sadness was ridiculed. Tenderness was wrapped in mock gestures, delivered with sarcasm.

Ironically, my parents, houseguests, and teachers told me how fortunate I was to be raised in a model, loving home. What did I do with thoughts and feelings to the contrary? Like most kids in dysfunctional families, I denied them, stuffed them, or considered them proof of my selfishness and ingratitude. Indeed, I could not trust any positive emotions as real, only ones of guilt, shame, fear, hurt, and betrayal. In short, to survive my childhood, I accepted perpetual conflict and repressed emotions as normal and benign.

Around spontaneous, self-assured kids, I felt puny, ugly, and unpopular. I felt safest—most in control—when playing alone. I could then pretend I was one of my favorite fictional heroes: a strong, respected champion of justice, battling on behalf of the unloved and powerless. Thus childhood nurtured lethal seeds that later bloomed into workaholism: self-denial, self-control, and idealized self-images.

Then I hit puberty. Emotions swirled in a flood of hormones, forcing my mind to resort to more effective means to channel the raging waves. As my body grew stronger, I selected small arenas to play out hero fantasies. Pitching myself wholeheartedly into school and extra-curricular projects let me funnel my energies into creating respected self-images. The only price I had to pay was to spend every waking hour struggling towards some socially accepted goal.

By the time I was eighteen I had become a professional musician, seeded tennis player, boxing champion, state champion track athlete, straight-A student, and National Merit scholar. I was president of the statewide youth fellowship, and my high school's selection for Boys State. For two years I went steady with the school's most popular cheerleader, and a month before graduation was awarded a scholarship to Harvard.

Each day I stuffed into my hip pocket a worn, week-at-a-glance notebook. It was Bible and scorecard, directing every hour of devotion to my disease, insuring I wouldn't forget a commitment in my frenzied pace. Its margins were crammed with lists of tasks to accomplish between meetings and before going to sleep. As long as I was working, thinking about work, or lining up work in my notebook, I felt in control, important, powerful. When I recalled it—which wasn't often—the fearful, shameful, guilty self of my childhood seemed like someone from another planet.

Yet my parents' attitude toward me did not change. No accomplishment was enough to draw my father's praise or win my mother's warmth. My response? Already up to my knees in disease, I dug deeper, tried harder, and sought more accolades. I looked elsewhere for strokes of respect and approval: to teachers, coaches, teammates, and friends.

Workaholism totally engulfed my life. Proof? Awards, publicity, and self-images replaced love, affection, and self-acceptance. Even when I was out of the limelight, the relentless pace of work numbed my mind to haunting, un-faced feelings of lovelessness, powerlessness, resentment, and shame.

College devastated me. My sense of self-worth was completely dependent on high school triumphs. I viewed existence as a perpetual conflict where only superior people survived and were worthy. At Harvard, however, it seemed that every student was a better musician, scholar, or athlete than I. What's more, they all seemed to know exactly who they were and what they wanted to do with their lives—whereas I hadn't a clue. For me, workaholism had been so consuming that I'd been too busy (and, of course, too afraid) to discover who I really was or what career might actualize my true self.

For three undergraduate years I battled suicidal depression, interspersed with belligerent bouts of drunkenness and savage play on rugby fields. My college threatened to expel me for riotous behavior. Molding frustration and fear into macho fury made it easy to win the school's middleweight boxing title.

I now realize those three years I majored in English literature were a desperate attempt to retreat once more to the realm of fictional heroes. At the end of my junior year, foundering in warring emotions and seeing no other way out, I switched my major to psychology. Perhaps there I could safely discover who I was, why life had lost its direction and meaning.

I also became a Zen Buddhist and chose a career in criminal law. In Zen I could probe to reality's core. In court I could wield the power I'd fantasized about all my life. I could harness disparate skills and energies, wage real struggles to make justice more than a concept in books.

After a stint in the Air Force I finished law school, along the way becoming the only law student to argue and win a client's case before my state's supreme court. The latter won me fellowships for further legal studies. I relished the logic and rationality of the law. I was also in love with the most intelligent, talented, and beautiful woman I'd ever encountered: my wife.

For five years I litigated criminal cases for and against the government in Washington, D.C., got an advanced law degree, and mentored law students in court for five city law schools. Proud at not taking a vacation during that entire time, I pitched myself day and night into preparing for and conducting trials.

Relentless activity muffled latent self-doubt, while the stakes involved provided adrenalized, grandiose illusions that my work was a matter of life or death. I resumed playing rugby on weekends despite numerous concussions and broken bones.

Near the end of this litigation time, my six-year honeymoon jarred to a halt. My wife and I had fallen in love with each other's self-images and now found it difficult to sustain these fraying fictions. Yet we still feared letting each other see who we really were, displaying true emotions, or revealing how insecure we felt most of the time.

One month I was offered a book contract by a publishing firm and a teaching contract by a California school. Nearing burnout in the courtroom, I jumped at the chance to take what I later learned was a "geographic cure." My disease, of course, came with me and soon had me hurling myself into teaching, writing, and expanding the school's law-student clinic.

I toiled long hours in classroom and office, updating my law book until it became the nation's authority. Evenings and weekends (after long-distance runs and pumping iron) I'd occasionally swoop up my infant sons into a carrier and trudge off on mountain hikes. In my warped mind, paternal bonding could take place only through strenuous activity. Workaholism's lethal blend of anesthesia and adrenaline let seven priceless years of fatherhood slip by in a flash.

One day by sheer accident—or karmic design—I agreed to participate in a friend's addiction-recovery program. While I co-attended numerous meetings and workshops it gradually dawned on me that portrayals of addicts' lives, thoughts, and feelings also described *my* life. If I substituted "addictive activity" for "addictive drinking or using drugs," I was as much an addict as any I'd read of or met.

On 20 August 1983 (the day I consider the start of my recovery), I drafted a long letter to my friend's clinic, described my symptoms, and asked if there were any treatment programs for workaholics. Weeks later a response arrived from a therapist not certain my request had been serious. He offered what is now too familiar a phrase: "What, workaholism a disease?!" This spokes-man for a cutting-edge clinic for recovering addicts knew of no program for people like me.

For the next seven years I observed my mental habits in light of what was known of the addictive process. I shared experiences with dozens of alcoholics, addicts, and others who worked from compulsive mind-sets. To a few workaholic friends I sent a booklet of my findings, urging recognition of workaholism as a disease and detailing discoveries of my own addictive thoughts and acts. Nearly all were supportive; some said I must have been running for years in their shoes.

During this period I attended sundry meetings of Alcoholic Anonymous. But when I introduced myself as a "workaholic" or a "political alcoholic" I got little sympathy. As the former I was just another of those will-power people who'd been bashing alcoholics for centuries; as the latter I was a weirdo in search of a social disease. Still, A.A.'s Twelve Step program seemed relevant and immensely beneficial. On the gut level of shame, fear, escapism, and self-esteem, the stories I heard in A.A. were mine.

One perceptive recovering addict suggested I attend Overeaters Anonymous. Although not overweight, for me the experience was a major breakthrough. It was true, the exigencies of earning a living kept me from completely abstaining from work (as recovering alcoholics abstain from alcohol.). But could I learn to face work non-compulsively—as recovering overeaters must daily face food? Trying to synthesize wisdom from A.A. and O.A., I wrote a year's worth of daily meditations for recovering workaholics.

In 1990 I finally did find other recovering workaholics in the form of a W.A. meeting that had recently started in San Francisco. After contacting them, I decided I could no longer recover alone and started another city's first Workaholics Anonymous group. In two years, over a hundred people attended. Later that year, I volunteered for W.A.'s first World Service Organization. Getting to know scores of other recovering workaholics awakened me to the power and immensity of this insidious disease: its deep roots, its destruction of families and health, its religious and economic rationalizations, its encouragement by cultures around the globe.

I continue unearthing facets of workaholism in my life: how strong emotions spark tendencies to turn from feelings and engage in distracting projects instead; how feeling powerless beckons me to physically control (or mentally understand) whatever stands between me and my desires; how doubts of self-worth urge me to build and believe in self-images; how inaction prompts me to fidget and make plans; and how silence tempts me to fill my mind with music, movies, or news.

I'm resigned to the likelihood these mental propensities will never cease wailing their siren songs. But from all honest beings I encounter (including dogs, horses, and non-human beings), I learn how to meet what is real.

Though my parents are dead, I've accepted their steadfast refusal to see what their parenting caused. This includes their refusal to acknowledge who their son actually was and that their lives were ravaged by unrecognized fears. In a volatile marriage of thirty-plus years, my wife and I now discover, accept, and nurture each other's true selves, freely share them instead of dancing or sparring with ghosts and self-images.

My fictional life is finally over. I'm more real, more honest, more me. Most days I feel wonder and joy from just waking without yellow chalk silhouetting my form. On some days, fierce emotional weather blows in from far poles. But I welcome all genuine feelings, others and mine, and refuse to deny, distort, or flee from them.

As a practicing workaholic, I never imagined serenity dwelt in my core. Now I can feel it merely by reaching through layers of what is not me: not titles, not accomplishments, and not this story of past events. It seems like a daily miracle to me how serenity can prevail through battering, by chaos and free-falls, through mineshafts of I-don't-knows. And as sublime paradox and cosmic joke...I'm getting much more work done!

# Living Flowly

January 1988. I awoke one morning totally exhausted, the start of what I was later to learn was Chronic Fatigue Syndrome (the name CFIDS had not been invented yet). The doctor said it was flu and that it would vanish within a month.

It didn't. My normal rushed pace slowed to a crawl. For the first time in my life I, a perpetual motion machine, learned to rest. Grudgingly I cut back on my hectic round of activities, one by one. It was humbling not to be reliable, to say, "I can't," to surrender indispensability, to have to ask for help even in tiny things. As I lay in bed, my normally racing mind moved glacially.

Despite my frustration at not being able to fulfill my schedule, I felt a deeper peace of mind than I had ever known. I wanted to cling to this serenity forever. I also wanted my vitality to return—but I feared that if it did, I would plunge back into my nonstop pace. What I really wanted was energy without frenzy.

While resting, I recalled parental voices. "Hurry up!" "Can't you ever do anything right?" "Grab it before someone else does." No matter what I did growing up, it wasn't okay; it was either wrong or not enough. I absorbed my parents' attitudes of shame, guilt, and fear and beat myself up mentally on a daily basis.

The internal flogging made me driven and insatiable. The more I excelled, the higher I set unreasonable standards. My mind pushed my body to achieve the impossible as I tried to become the family heroine who would heal my retarded brother and psychotic sister, reconcile my battling, divorced parents, and rescue us all from poverty. I became a robot, out of touch with my body and being. I crawled out of bed when I awoke, no matter how little or badly I had slept, galvanized by the blaring, overloaded to-do list that ruled my existence. Then I raced to beat the clock by overdoing. Adrenaline and caffeine would keep me hyper until I'd collapse each night. Added to this driven-ness was my own racing, insatiably curious mind. I wanted to know and experience everything RIGHT NOW!

Years in Twelve Step programs had begun healing my addiction to achievement, worry, hurry, perfectionism, codependency, lack of focus, imbalance, and impatience. But I still had far to go. Because my family members had died before I could rescue them, I felt that I now had to live five lives—mine, my parents' and my two siblings'.

Even on Recovery Road, speeding is dangerous when powered by adrenaline and when racing without brakes. I thought my life was balanced because I had variety, but it was non-stop variety. I thought I worked sanely because I delegated, prioritized, set limits and rarely worked overtime. I thought I had made lots of progress because my activities and relationships were healthy. Unfortunately, the emphasis was on lots, not progress.

I thought I had healed the "rushaholic" by slowing from 150 mph to 90; the "careaholic" by no longer needing to be needed; the drudge by learning to do things just for pleasure; the self-hater by experiencing feelings instead of medicating myself with food and work; the compulsive who collapsed from non-stop activity binges. I now took breaks, working little and often, except that the "littles" came too often. My mechanical methods worked only superficially because I had transferred my addictive behavior to recovery. Too much service, too many hobbies, too many meetings.

From being a self-debtor who did not nurture myself, I now switched to beating myself up with, "You deserve this. And that. And that." My choices were good, but too much is still too much. Recovery opened endless opportunities, thus encouraging my "experience greed." No program taught me to be selective.

After I had driven myself mercilessly for 55 years, my body finally rebelled massively. Before this, my body had tried migraine, burnout, and breakdown to get through to me, but never this prolonged exhaustion even after ten hours of sleep! I knew this was the final wakeup call; if I ever were to recoup my strength, I'd surely overdo and then collapse with a fatal heart attack. I was terrified and stuck.

What a dilemma! I needed a program to teach me how to do less, yet adding it meant doing more. Wasn't that crazy? But fire is used to fight fire. Maybe the meeting could be used homeopathically the same way.

I didn't know whether a fellowship for workaholics even existed. Would it mean to start a whole new organization? Fortunately, a few months later I found W.A., but none of their meetings were near me. Having started Twelve Step meetings before, I knew how much time and energy they took, even in long-established programs.

I had always worked alone. No way I could do that now. I decided I would start W.A. in the area if my Higher Power were to send help. While waiting, I wrote a meeting format, acting "as if" and feeling this was right. Then I received literature from W.A. and the feeling intensified. I also got a "click," remembering I'd dreamt this sequence.

One day at the Twelve Step office where I worked a woman came in to buy literature. Noting she seemed anxious, I asked her whether she was all right. She asked whether I knew of a program for workaholics and said her husband needed help.

Finally! "I've been waiting for someone to start a W.A. meeting with me," I said.

"I'll tell my husband about you," she replied.

I waited several months for his call. Waiting is hard for me, but I knew that over-eagerness would distort the rhythm of the process.

When he phoned, we arranged to get together in my office to set up the recovery meeting. In September 1988, Thursday after Labor Day, we began the local W.A. meeting in a living room, which was on my way home from work. During some of these early meetings, I'd be so tired I'd just lie on the couch. To save my energy, my husband would drive me there.

For several months it was just one other person and myself, despite our best efforts to find others. That's when I learned to wait. My style had been to plunge into projects and they would take off. Not this time. It took a year of sporadic visitors until our meeting cohered into a committed group.

A month after our meeting began, my energy began slowly to return. Not the driven kind, but natural energy. I hadn't experienced that type since I was a child, so it felt unnatural. Evidently Higher Power understood that, because my natural energy was doled out slowly.

As it gradually increased, I stayed attuned to my body. I began to appreciate rest. Up to now, I'd resented rest as wasted time. Now I saw it as part of the cycle of activity and regained my natural pace and rhythm, just as I regained my natural hunger and appetite in Overeaters Anonymous.

My new awareness made my life a film running in slow motion. By catching myself in "do-aholic," adrenalized lapses, I watched with horror, sadness, and compassion as I followed a killing pace set by fear, guilt, greed, pride, low self-esteem and habit.

I became aware of how I would lose track of many of my thoughts, how I would act hurriedly and needlessly. In order to swell my self-importance, how I set overly high standards and did busy work. How I filled pauses by inserting activities. How I would read standing up, because sitting took too long. Or how I perched on the edge of a chair, my heels up ready to sprint.

How I created work stashes, filled calendar spaces without allowing time for transitions, and juggled three tasks at once. How I underestimated the time it took to do tasks, sometimes aware my guesses were fantasy. How I made mistakes because of rushing or not being prepared. How I sat in recovery meetings, filling in schedules to ensure that I would always be busy. How I repeatedly sacrificed my own needs and enabled others. How I raced to end a project so that I could plunge into yet another. How I let the telephone be a tyrant. How my conversation was completely task-oriented.

Then the film sped up to "normal" and my life blurred by. As observer, I tasted the adrenaline dancing in my blood and felt repelled, not exhilarated.

The moments of clarity lengthened. The to-do list and the clock loosened their grip. Impatience, impulsiveness, and living in "when I get caught up" were transformed into being deliberate, thorough, selective, and staying in the now. Some milestones:

1.  Learning the difference between driven and motivated
2.  Being content without feeling stagnant
3.  Able to postpone
4.  Saying NO without feeling deprived or guilty
5.  Giving only from my extra reserves of energy
6.  Enjoying emptiness
7.  Quieting the S.H.A.M.E. voice
    (Should Have Already Mastered Everything)
8.  Delaying the return of phone calls and the answering of mail
9.  Stopping before I ran out of enthusiasm by saying, "I've enjoyed as much of this as I can stand."
10. Valuing a comfortable pace
11. Making friends with time, rest, and sleep; knowing that I don't have time not to have time; that without sleep and rest, all is worthless.
12. Enjoying being with myself without distractions.

My early instincts for order, balance, timing, rhythm, gracefulness, and flexibility returned. Life became seamless instead of segmented into doing/being, work/play, and leisure/sleep/rest.

No longer racing from one achievement to another, I now acknowledge and celebrate my completions. Enjoyment, ease, and effortlessness have replaced quantity, speed, and struggle. Events happen through me, not to me. I call this way "living flowly," living without resistance, flowing with God's plan.

A good day used to be surpassing my to-do list by being Robot, Superwoman, and World Mother. Now it's living timelessly, moving at a rhythm that allows me to stay available to Higher Power. Being fully present. Registering and integrating impressions. Noticing small and simple pleasures such as shadows. Hearing and heeding my body. Speaking from my heart. Spotting patterns of ideas, objects, and events. Harvesting the messages from dreams and unusual experiences. Being mindful of my attention, energy, actions, and growth. Nurturing my new self-friendship.

When I live at the right pace, I fully experience a feeling. I pick up subtle messages from short-term memory. I see what is not there. I hear what goes unsaid. I consider the impact of my words and decisions. I incorporate change and surprise easily. Playfulness, joy, and humor all bubble up.

In these years of recovery, society sped up while I moved to the slow lane. As our W.A. meeting grew, I helped form World Service and wrote literature. Now I had almost the energy I had before, but without the push of adrenaline. It was a challenge to keep my sane pace and not use service to justify overdoing.

I owe my recovery from chronic fatigue syndrome to W.A., to willingness to change, and to my Higher Power. During the illness, if I tried to overexert, I got a firm thought that I must rest and that I had about five minutes' grace to stop, probably because Higher Power realized that years of overriding body signals had dulled my instincts. Those warnings gradually became more faint—similar to the volume of my sense of thirst. I thought I was imagining this, but later I heard others with CFS tell of sharing the same experience. They also said that their biggest problem was to resist the impulse to "seize the time" and overdo during energy surges. Because of W.A., I was able to avoid this.

My journey has been an example of divine order: locating W.A. and a partner in recovery to help me start a meeting at the right time; regaining my energy shortly after our meeting began; committed members arriving after we had some recovery; regaining my harmony with divine plan. I now act by timing, not time.

Joy is the energy of acceptance. When I stop using my will to force life to meet my desires and simply flow with life, the result is joy. By moving at God's pace, I am flowing with life. Join me.

# Time Prosperity is My Goal: Recovering from Work Anorexia

I am the adult child of a work addict and I was born in the early 1960's. My father was intensely work addicted (as well as afflicted with alcoholism and other addictions) and my mother, as a chief enabler to my father, was quite disengaged from herself. As my parents were in their forties by the time of my birth, their childhoods and early adult lives were profoundly affected by both the Great Depression and World War II. From an already poor family, my father had worked from the age of five years old only to see all his family's precious savings lost as banks worldwide failed in 1929, when he was just eleven. After this historic and unusual event, my father decided that the ability to perform hard work, without stopping, was the only hope onto which he could hold in uncertain or unstable times. Once he started running in a race with himself and the world, he never stopped, even many decades later. My mother's Victorian, moneyed, and fatherless upbringing had left her so emotionally shut down that when her husband to be, my father, first appeared in her life, I'm sure his intensity and addiction to constant action seemed like a wonderful, alive breath of fresh air to her.

I was born the youngest of five children and the third boy. I watched my parents and my siblings work hard, long hours simultaneously at many different self-employment styled businesses. All of my siblings and myself worked in these ventures for as long a period as my parents could pressure us into, usually well into our twenties or even thirties. My father was the entrepreneur breadwinner director of all action and my mother the housewife, eventually becoming his secretary and bookkeeper. Yet for all of my family's efforts, we repeatedly sold businesses at a loss. Only recently did I find a great description of this energy in the phrase "professional promiscuity." My father would start a relationship with a business, then withdraw his attention away from that one and start courting another business idea without continuing or finishing the first effort. Years later, my siblings and I discovered that many of the financial gains to which my parents had always credited hard work had actually come from money inherited by my mother and not acquired from any business gain. In fact, with all the financial losses we incurred, if my parents had just not gone into about half of the businesses at which we toiled we would have been far wealthier financially! But I came to learn that financial prosperity, while officially always the stated goal, was actually "the enemy" so to speak. That is to say, if we were to have gotten ahead financially, then there would have been a lot less justification for constant activity. So the money my mother inherited made it seem as though our work addict pace was getting us ahead. In actuality, it just hid the financial loss that I now believe always eventually accompanies the spiritual bankruptcy of work addiction.

From an early age my siblings and I were pressured by our father to engage in never-ending mental activity. We were told this was the only way to maintain enough hyper-vigilance to be safe from a dangerous world. "Always be on guard lest we be unguarded." "Don't take a break because that's when you'll fall behind." To stop thinking in order to acknowledge feelings, (in other words having any kind of internal spiritual experience) was considered weak and irresponsible. My father used to refer to people he didn't like, for instance those who were not constantly doing something (or men who had long hair!) as "lazy bums." The word lazy in my house was considered a terrible slight and my father used it frequently to shout at the television when he saw certain people appear on screen. If I were not constantly moving and "thinking ahead" as he put it, then he would accuse me of laziness, judging my effort to be a total waste and me to be incompetent. My father was happy to tell me just exactly what was a worthwhile effort and what was not, but just how I should determine that on my own, without him to do it for me, was never clearly defined. Even though he did encourage me to take the lead at times, when I did take charge, no matter what I did work-wise, he or my mother either criticized my effort for being wasteful and foolish, or, less often, they might go in the other direction completely and tell me my work was totally the best they had ever seen! It was all or nothing with little, ever, falling in between. What I learned from this treatment was that I was not capable of telling what was real in the world; was I stupid and lazy or was I a star genius? I didn't really feel qualified to be successful on my own without an "action critic" nearby. In many instances I can remember throwing myself into some kind of activity because I was afraid my parents would be arriving soon and I had better "get something (in other words anything and therefore ultimately nothing) done." For all of my father's talk of discipline he actually was constantly in a self-will run riot of ever-changing activity. He would talk of the need for a consistent effort at school or business or life but then he would display the exact opposite himself. By virtue of her silence about such insanity in my father, my mother's denial made it appear that she sanctioned his view of himself as an effective leader. In fact, it was my mother's and my older siblings' consistent work that kept things functioning, not my father's recurring work binges or erratic directives.

About the time I was twelve or thirteen, I started noticing other kids at school and adults as well who did not work as hard at their life as my parents had assured me I needed to do in order to succeed. My fellow students seemed unconcerned if they did not constantly try to learn everything they could every second. They played and took breaks without guilt and worry. And when the teacher assigned certain sections of a chapter to read, they would study pretty much those pages only. My father had taught me that if I studied all of the pages of all my schoolbooks, I would get ahead. I tried to do that but there were so many extra pages to read that I would get confused with all the additional information and do poorly on the test because I had tried to learn too much. Between school and my parents it was as though life were a sandcastle and there was always an approaching tide that kept washing away all of my efforts. So I didn't know what to think. Was life just a big work binge? Was the only way to prevent failure to make everything simultaneously a number one priority, staying vigilant and hurrying so I could keep all the sand in the castle? I began to question the dedication to "eternal work vigilance" that my father had never stopped preaching. I think this is when I became disillusioned with work and goal setting of any kind, believing action to be never ending as well as never truly fruitful. I saw other people succeed by taking action but I just felt frozen. Finally the intense shame I felt over what I perceived as my total inferiority to "real" goal pursuers caused the pendulum to swing the other way and my only solution became to try to work harder and harder at not committing to seek to achieve anything. To commit to or become excited by a goal just felt as though it was either creating false hope or signing up for self condemnation if I could not deliver by the deadline. I came not to trust any ongoing effort where the results were not immediately evident. Unlike the work addict who does and does and does just for the mood altering or approval that indiscriminate or repeated action brings, I became obsessed with only taking action that I could convince myself would pay off big and right away so as to prevent any delay, disappointment, waste, or regret. I was the quintessential perfectionist. Eventually all living became about just getting through each day and I avoided all thought of any plans beyond the current moment. I had lost any trust in my own desires or my own vision for myself at all, so what reason was there to create goals or endure sacrifices on the way to anything else? I believe it was in this giving up of my personal visions that I became a work anorexic.

After high school, I did have a go at college, but my experience of higher education was that these institutions felt entitled to ask a lot of work from me as it suited them and I didn't even have the benefit of knowing my own desires or goals inspiring me to face these challenges. So I quit college and drifted about, alternating many times between what I called "dead end blue collar jobs" and returning to work for my parents. In my personal time I turned to distracting myself from the intense pain of this "giving up on life" with endless television, fantasizing about women, and eventually compulsive eating, always pretending I was a successful action taker like some of the people I saw being interviewed on talk shows. Even setting goals felt too painful to risk. But without deciding on action and then taking it, I forfeited almost all of life's pleasures since such pleasures are only achieved or secured with repeated and conscious effort over a period of time longer than a drive thru meal order or a TV sitcom. When the pain of going nowhere in my life was unbearable I relied on the fantasy that I would be rescued from that hell by someone or something else- but I didn't know what. I lived in a day-to-day, random pattern acting as though I were in a waiting room and someday a happy life complete with achievements would be delivered. But I had better not move around too much in the meantime because I might miss the delivery person when they arrived at my door.

Finally, at the age of twenty-six, I crashed hard emotionally and couldn't work at all. I went to live, where else...back with my parents. I was facing other addictions and seeing a therapist and that was a good start. I did hold to a strict line of not working for my father who, of course, would have hired me in two seconds or less for his latest business. Instead I did odd jobs around the house for my mother, which was bearable. Sadly, my mother died very suddenly one day, from an aneurysm, after almost two years of my home based recovery effort. I knew if I stayed living alone with my dad I would explode. I moved out and went back to the entry-level blue-collar world I hated but I had the support of my early Twelve Step fellowships. I had not heard of Workaholics Anonymous yet but when I did, I thought to myself "Well I am certainly not a workaholic!" However, in early 1993, when a friend put the W.A. general pamphlet into my hand, I was impressed with the ideas inside. Just reading the tools started my healing and they still can give me a serenity break today. That W.A. pamphlet gave me hope I had never felt about work. The idea that some things are better left undone—that was completely revolutionary when compared with the way I was taught to think. I could feel my anorexic fear about all goal setting always turning into a runaway train of action begin to melt away with my first reading of the literature. But I still didn't go to the one W.A. group I had heard was recently started in town because I knew I couldn't be a work addict. After all, I hated my jobs and would have loved nothing more than quitting them right away.

Then, on July 1st of that year, I got a speeding ticket for doing 51 mph in a 35 mph zone on my way to a haircut appointment across town. It was my day off and I had plenty of time to leave early enough... but I never could seem to leave early enough for anything. I would always deny how long it actually took me to get anywhere. Then as the time window to act came and went I would suddenly come alive in an adrenalizing frenzy to be on time. Only this time, as with so many, my "rolling under the gate before it shut" took the form of speeding in my car, and police tend to frown on this. Or smile. The ticket cost me about $115, I think, but in an unusual move, I paid it the same day I received it and took it as a message from God to get myself to W.A., and so I did.

Since initially attending W.A., my recovery has been in fits and starts and I still have a ways to go. I can say that I am now definitely better able to survive, without so much reaction, the unexpected change in events, or someone failing my expectations. I have struggled with getting and keeping a sponsor (or a therapist for that matter) in *any* of the several programs for which I qualify. W.A. meetings have been very small and scarce where I live in the Southeastern United States (although now I use the telephone to connect with W.A. members from other areas) and other unmanageabilities have pulled me in many directions. And those of us who are "multiple winners" can appreciate how multiple addiction recovery makes simply getting out of bed on some days an act of overscheduling! Part of my stuck-ness has also been that all of my employers, without exception, were active work addicts. Working for and with active work addicts almost every day for many, many years coupled with underearning, meaning there is never enough money to take much or any time off, can make the work of recovery seem like...well—*just more dang work!* Towards that end, God sent me a wonderful doctor of homeopathy, but being distrustful of his help, I pushed the idea away for over two years. Then A.A. literature helped me to "lower my standards and raise my behavior" as they say. Page 133 of Alcoholics Anonymous says, "Try to remember that though God has wrought miracles among us, we should never belittle a good doctor or psychiatrist. Their services are often indispensable in treating a newcomer and in following his case afterward." While at a meeting I read this paragraph and I realized I had been fending off a prompting to go to this doctor who, in his case, is really a holistic version of a psychiatrist. I have been his patient for several years, now, and it has really helped my recovery tremendously. Things are not perfect, but they are so much better than I could have done without his help. Of course, my goal is to work with a W.A. sponsor and go through all of the Steps formally. But I wanted to acknowledge that "Bad breath is better than no breath!" and until relatively recently, this doctor was the closest thing to a sponsor I could accept, without quitting the relationship. I have never felt pressured by him to achieve anything- except perhaps patience with my own process!

Defining powerlessness for work anorexia has been a slow process and sometimes I feel like I am still working to define it today. I have called myself a quit-aholic or a dishonest prioritizer! But there is also a surrender to personal or professional long term plans or dreams that is usually absent in the life of an anorexic.

Using a "Prioritizing Prayer" to ask for help seems to really work to help me get off the dime if I am frozen. Getting back to personal plans, what helps me to feel inspired enough to take action, even when fear has me stuck, is to get as clear as I can about what I really want for my life (as an anorexic I was always clear on what I *didn't* want in my life!). I make what I want known by writing it out at a minimum but also speaking about it with friends/sponsors on an ongoing basis is a good idea for me. I used to think admitting what I really wanted was the same as demanding that God make my dreams come true—and that I would then turn into a runaway work addict like my father. But I do not pray for God to give me what I want. If God is my employer, I need only pray for God's will for me, and the power to carry that out. I do believe desire is a God-given energy. For me, admitting what my desires are is a form of humility and clarity of self that is necessary to guide my goal setting. I also use a definition of happiness I found recently. The quote was "Happiness is overcoming obstacles on the way to a goal of your own choosing." Before I attended W.A., my disease would not allow me to risk any effort towards personal goals. But now, with the passing of a few seasons in fellowship, I see that God gave me willingness to begin such efforts some time ago.

My parents are gone now, and although my habit of earning from work-addicted employers is less problematic, my Work-Anon issues are indeed worth revisiting from time to time. If I get stuck in avoidance or perfection seeking and I lose sight of goals until I grind down to a halt, that pattern can create a vacuum that draws a work-addicted person of some kind into my life. Yet it really is my own work anorexia that paves the way for that pattern. So today I am careful to be aware of my part in any relationships with active work addicts.

In summary, here is a list of benefits to me, so far, from the fellowship of W.A. I am better at facing the music now in many of life's arenas without the near constant pattern of self-sabotage that once plagued me. My relationship with the work I do for earning is much better. I have some money from an investment that I am using to start my own business. I would like to get married (probably should date first!) and I believe in taking my life one day at a time. I can have fun now during my workday and if I can't—I get out of that space or relationship. I used to be in denial about priorities too. I knew about them but I used to push them away as though my awareness of them was optional. Prayer and meditation, which I call daily quiet time, is now a reality for me after years of being totally uncomfortable being alone with just my own thoughts and feelings and no distractions allowed. And while there is much healing I would like to have achieved for myself by now, I can usually come to accept that I am O.K. just as I am this moment, whatever that may look like. I try to remember to include playful attitudes, so that if my day feels too serious, I sometimes step back from it all. I know that "enlightenment means lightening up!" When my recovery efforts have gotten sporadic, service to others has helped me return to W.A. time and again. Staying connected to other W.A. members also makes it easier for me to remember that work is not an end in itself but my means to God's ends.

I still have days where I leave too little time for errands or I overschedule the travel time to an appointment and arrive late. My goal is to leave consistently early enough so that I will not be tempted to hurry. That way, I actually have some waiting time when I arrive at my destination, an outcome I used to think of as a "total waste." If I do indulge in overscheduling or refuse to reprioritize when circumstances warrant, I can count on feeling "time poor," driven, and desperate. In contrast, when I make "Time Prosperity" my goal, I surrender (with the help of ongoing Step work) all that my Higher Power indicates I need not do today. Then serenity is mine and I feel time prosperous, relaxed, and much saner with what I *do* choose to do today.

For these things and more, I have W.A. to thank. So thank you W.A. Thank you!

# Choices: Hitting a Bottom And Connecting to the Queen of Everything

### How it was

I grew up in a small, multi-addicted family in countries of extreme poverty. I was the adult child, and I grew up fast. Legally emancipated at fourteen, I was accustomed to using work to achieve self-reliance and freedom. After moving to an English-speaking country and learning English, I was lucky to encounter some kind people from whom I asked for help with a couple of things, including my addictions. When Twelve Step programs were suggested to me at seventeen years of age, I joined enthusiastically, and I immediately worked the program.

I have been fortunate to not relapse, and I have 22 years of clean, sober, and abstinent living. The first five years were a journey of self-discovery. Some random examples include: I had interests and talents in dancing and sports, I loved animals, I

enjoyed travel, I was a lesbian, and I was a night owl. In terms of
W.A.-related matters, I learned how much my parents' personal
values affected their professional lives, and that I had adopted
their values about education, freedom, and social equality. Both
teachers, they had immense passion about their careers, and
embodied their values fully at home and at work, despite their
addictions. I learned that there was a career combination in which
I could fulfill my own dreams of helping people in their personal
and professional lives.

In order to achieve this goal, I worked fulltime to fund my
studies, completed a Dual Ph.D., and I set up two businesses (a
practice of clinical psychotherapy and a human resources
consultancy). I enjoyed the work itself. I also liked my clients in
both businesses, and we were able to accomplish their goals
together. I enjoyed the fruits of my labor: I could afford nice
vacations and a nice home, and I shared my wealth with friends
and gave to charity. I also had rewarding relationships, danced,
and exercised regularly. I worked and played hard. I was
passionate about life, and I had a good time at and outside work.
This was the case for years.

**What happened**

Then, somehow, the balance tipped. Passion turned to
compulsion. Perhaps the guilt of being an immigrant caught up
with me during the 2002 US recession; perhaps I hit a level of
seniority in my work where gender differences increased and
competing was harder; perhaps memories of extreme poverty in
Africa resurfaced; perhaps a dormant disease of workaholism
awakened. The way I worked changed markedly within months.
Sprinkled in my usual enjoyment were episodes of worry and
compulsion, both at work and on weekends. I then took on a
sense of seriousness and pressure with projects—even household
ones! I started to obsess about work in my free time, and soon
enough I couldn't leave projects until they were finished (which
meant I sometimes went to bed at dawn). This new
compulsion/addiction impacted the amount and quality of time
with my loved ones and my interests (such as art, dancing,
running, foster-parenting kittens, etc.). I didn't stop any of these
hobbies entirely, but they sure slowed down. My hours spent
working might have increased a little, but it was the way I worked
that really changed.

I have a great network of friends, and I asked some of
them if they noticed anything different over a period of months.
Most said no, but a close friend agreed that going to a W.A.
meeting would be a good idea. I must say that, as a high bottom, I
did not lose what many others did, such as health, relationships,
time, or jobs. Instead, I am a workaholic who jumped off a fast

descending elevator, and I am very grateful I took notice and action quickly. I had already lost work-life balance, peace of mind, perspective, and conscious contact with HP.

**How it is now**

 I am new to W.A., and I attacked the W.A. program with some perfectionism and compulsion for the first month, but I have settled into a healthy pace now. I balance my work and personal time by asking my Higher Power to remove my money worries and work obsessions. You'd think this would come naturally to me, since I have been turning my life and my will over to The Queen of Everything (my HP) for so many years—but it is a daily, conscious effort. Practically speaking, I have also set boundaries on maximum hours worked a week, weekends, lunch breaks, etc. Additionally, I find that carving out gaps in my work and personal schedules for spontaneity yields nice surprises—how can little miracles and fun things happen to me if I am always rushing around?

 Another thing that works for me is to make amends immediately to folks around me at work when I get compulsive or impatient, as per the Tenth Step. I have let a couple of close corporate colleagues know about W.A., and they support me when I fall off the turnip truck. Sometimes, they laughingly ask me to read my daily meditations, and I can't help but notice how closely they listen to the meditations when I read them out loud.

 I believe that it is Q of E's will for me to continue my lines of work, and to maintain my work-life balance. I believe that, just like my parents and grandparents, I was destined to be of service in the world. I believe many of us are, particularly we addicts. I find that, just like my other addictions, my journey of recovery from workaholism enriches my existence and increases my ability to serve others. God knows the planet needs more socially responsible world citizens who give back as much, or more, than they take.

 I might be suffering from a huge case of projection, but it does seem to me that workaholism is a common, under-diagnosed, socially reinforced disease.

# The Myth of a Workaholic Geographic Cure

 While I know, intellectually, that this is wrong, I have had a workaholic equivalent of the "geographic cure" in the back of my head for years. I am self-employed and have worked excessively trying to make my business successful. The story I tell myself is that, if my workaholism ever gets so bad I can't take it anymore, I can give up my self-employment dream and get a "real" job and my troubles will go away. If I had an office job working for someone else, the story goes, I would be able to leave work at the office and lead a normal life, as long as I pick a low-stress occupation. I recently proved to myself what I already knew: that my workaholism goes with me wherever I go. I had been working at a part-time temporary assignment as a secretary. This is work I have done off and on for years and one I consider fairly low-stress and not challenging to me. On top of this, I was a temp, not even a real employee. And yet, during a busy week, I found myself awake at 3:00 a.m., going over in my head a list of things I had to do at the office the next day and strategizing about how I could get everything done. This experience shook me because it proved once and for all that I would never be able to escape my disease by changing jobs. The truth is, I am an adrenaline addict and I will find my drug wherever I go. My self-employment has given me an opportunity to work unchecked and to work myself into high states of stress. But I know that, even if I worked doing something completely mindless, I would bring my perfectionism, my need for approval, my desire to be the best, and my physical need for adrenaline with me. While some work situations lend themselves to stress more than others, I have to face the reality that I can find stress anywhere. Now that my mental escape hatch is closed, I am more committed than ever to working my program. A change of scenery won't help me; only the spiritual solution I can find through W.A. will save me from my addiction.

# Cutting Loose from the Workplace

"So what are you going to do with all of your free time?" This is the most common question I encountered after announcing my retirement plans.

My initial reaction was to respond by listing all of the activities I planned to do in my typical workaholic mode. However, after reflecting on it, my response evolved into: "What am I going to do? —Anything I want to."

After 41 years of government service, I am looking forward to having the flexibility of being able to choose what I would like to do each day, whether it be playing with my three year-old grandson, taking long walks with my wife, visiting my daughter and son-in-law, or working out at the gym or enrolling in classes.

My retirement on Dec. 31st, 2002 has come after a long journey. I was eligible eight years ago but was too wrapped up in my job to let go. I loved the work and the people. I still do but have come to realize that too much of my time revolved around the workplace.

I am 63 and although I have been blessed with good health, I don't want to jeopardize future good times with my wife and family that could come with declining health.

I spent those eight years plunging into new exciting projects promoting energy efficiency in the construction of homes and the selection of lighting products. It was rewarding but it consumed valuable time from my family.

A few months ago, I was visiting my daughter and grandson, whom I am lucky enough to have live in the same city. My grandson asked if I was going to stay after lunch so we could play. I had to tell him "no" because I had to get back to work. As I left, I asked myself how could I give up these priceless moments with him.

Trips to the Pacific Coast by my wife and I also had to be cut short because of work obligations. Now, we're looking forward to extended visits to the seashore.

I really don't know what I'm going to do in retirement. My highest priority is spending more time with my family and retaining and improving my mental and physical health. W.A. has introduced me to many healthy attitudes toward loved ones and work so that I was finally able to make the decision to retire in November 2002.

Although I had some trepidation before turning in my retirement papers, I experienced terrific relief right afterwards. Now, each day, as I clean out my office, I feel more and more relaxed. Even the photos, letters, and articles that I am removing are not a sad experience but relocations of wonderful past experiences. However, I realize that it's time to look up from the treadmill I've been on and experience the rest of the world besides work.

I was hiking one morning recently with my wife when she volunteered to carry my knapsack for a while. It didn't feel heavy, so I continued to carry it for two more miles. Then I asked her to carry it. Although it hadn't felt heavy on my back, as soon as I took it off, I experienced great relief.

I think that I am going to feel the same after leaving my job. Retirees have already told me that I won't believe the relief of pressure until after I leave. In fact, some have advised me to do nothing for three months to decompress from the work environment.

One final admonition that I am taking from my W.A. advisors is to realize that I will have to remain vigilant to my workaholic tendencies, even in retirement. In other words, just because I have left the workplace, doesn't mean that I have left my work characteristics behind.

I'm looking forward to this interesting transition in my life.

# My Friend the Clock

Growing up in a home with two workaholics, I was patterned early on to ignore my biological needs in enslavement to the anesthesia of compulsive doing and worrying. My father worked 16 to 20 hours a day as a research chemist. What time he was home was spent raging or silent or compulsively reading or watching TV. My mother sheathed herself in a world of compulsive writing and reading day and night, and secretly suffered from an eating disorder. Twenty cups of coffee a day and four packs of cigarettes each, daily, augmented their fixations. Verbal abuse was shared for anything less than perfect behavior. The only planned meal was dinner, and my parents were incapable of sleeping regular hours and did not teach us consistent self-care including regular food, exercise, or sleep. Our home was a temple to the impulsive doing of the moment. Long hours playing in the yard offered some salve to the afflictions within the house. Public school was my island of interactivity and normality into which I threw myself with the fervor of a true young workaholic.

I was a young perfectionist and mostly received perfect marks. My fifth grade teacher marked me a "2" (on a scale of 1 to 5, 1 being best) for self-control (I would fly in to a crying fit whenever things didn't go my way or kids called me names), and she noticed that there was a connection between how much sleep I had gotten the night before and my emotional state. She began to have check-ins with me each morning to see how much sleep I had gotten. What she and I never consciously discovered then was that sleep deprivation was a great way to start adrenaline cycling.

By high school my disease had perfected an intersection of eating disorder, sleep and time debting, and work addiction to maximize adrenaline cycling. I would get 2-3 hours of sleep, begin school with a 6:30 am "Zero period" Academic Competition Class, then grind through seven more classes (while also leading a 50-person service club and a 300-person academic performance group). In retrospect, I see how sleep deprivation would set me up for a day of being off balance and pre-disposed for emotional drama (really, just a way to get a "fix" of adrenaline from my body's own pharmacy from highly charged emotional releases). By lunch I would be feeling particularly angry or sad, eat a sugary cookie only for lunch, and then travel the peaks and valleys of that sugar high through the afternoon. Food withholding will force the body into an adrenaline reaction because of the body's need to maintain at least a minimal blood sugar; skipping meals is an emergency for the body's desire for homeostasis. Sugar bingeing will also generate that "buzz." I used both to maintain the adrenaline. My first meal of the day was usually a fast food burrito around 5 or 6pm. I would then stay up until 2am again, avoiding or plunging into my homework. One of the tricks of maintaining an adrenaline high is to rightly time the balance of food withholding, sugar bingeing, sleep deprivation, and emotional stress. Of course this was all unconscious at the time.

Being late was an adrenaline feast for my disease. Because I was "high" I was behind and out of my body a lot of the time. I had crammed too much into my schedule. Because of the tunnel of perception I was living in, the character defect of perfectionism, and the emotional roller coaster from the adrenaline cycling, I perceived being late as a crisis. I would swear, curse, and speed. I would have internal or external emotional dramas. I had a million stories of victimization and justification for each incident. Of course, all along it was really a way to get more adrenaline. To say I was out of control and my life was unmanageable was an understatement. I was like "Pigpen" in the comic strip Snoopy, in a dust cloud of drama, self-abuse, and internal "speed"—I was mainlining my own body as a drug source.

The process also feeds on itself. I was so out of control I was late on everything. Every time I was late, my perfectionism, self-involved anxiety, sugar addiction, and sleep deprivation kept me fully stocked. My body could not sustain the ravages of the adrenaline cycling. By age 16, this resulted in a desperate suicide attempt, intense feelings of self-hate, and isolation. My parents forced me to see a psychotherapist, a kind well-intentioned professional who was uneducated about the disease and who tried to work with me to reduce my commitments, but with a "pull yourself up by your bootstraps," self-will cognitive approach that was of no long-term help. (Also, by sixteen, I was getting sick a lot. I missed a third of the days of school due to illness, and because my parents would let me stay home to get caught up on the schoolwork I was behind on, but only causing me to get further behind by missing classes). By eighteen, from adrenaline racing, I had caused a car wreck and been run over on my way (late) to a scholarship interview. This is not to mention the other five car accidents in high school. I went to school every summer also. By graduation, I received over thirty awards, including several national awards and scholarships.

I moved to a different state for a rigorous college education. Although I had completely left my family (addiction of origin) context by then, the addiction had successfully mastered me and I was faithful to its practices. In college, I was the editor of the school paper, director of the educational winter term, and ran over twenty student organizations while helping develop new college programs and doing intensive political organizing (and going to classes). I was adrenaline cycling constantly. By this point, I was having not only the emotional effects (daily suicidal ideation, alienating others with my intense drama, perfectionism, and black and white thinking) but also the physical deterioration from the disease. I was frequently sick. I took a year off to take it easy and to try to feel better, only to enroll in classes and teach twelve courses in my sister's town. This was demonstrative of an increasing trend: binge/avoid work addiction, where I'd work full tilt and then have a physical or emotional collapse. I also had the pattern of the "3-P's— perfectionism, paralysis, and procrastination. (Something I understood well enough to give a presentation on to my advanced study skills class I was teaching at a university when I was eighteen. At the time, I advised my students to break the project down into hour-long tasks, at least the first one, and get started.) Self-will eventually failed me in this regard. I could get adrenaline from overworking and from avoiding work (intense mental self-abuse and recrimination leading to explosive emotional drama-anything for an adrenaline fix!).

My workaholism was fueled by a strange twist; the better I did at school or in life, the more intense the verbal and emotional abuse from my family:

- Response to a report card with 6 As and A+s and one A minus: "What is this A minus doing here?"
- Response to my graduating Phi Beta Kappa from a top college: a twenty minute yelling scene, including how I was "worthless," "didn't believe in anything," and "had wasted years of my parents lives that I could never give back to them."

But negative attention was better than no attention at all, and I continued on my march to stuff the gaping hole in my spiritual life and internal well being (and self-esteem) with work.

By the time I graduated college, I knew I needed healing. I began a body-centered therapy process, and the disease continued. I was beginning to understand myself better, but I was having no relief from the progressive nature of the disease.

As a graduate, I innovated curriculum for gifted kids until the hundreds of books from the research libraries, and long nights of preparation for what was only 15 hours of paid work per week grew out of control. I stopped teaching and started working in a health food restaurant. Then I moved out to a rural community where I could live at my workplace (a great comfort for a workaholic to have a work stash always ready to hand), learning databases and publishing. Then I moved back to the city, to working with nonprofits, then construction, publishing again, then house cleaning, county government, then software development, often having two or three jobs at once. As if that weren't enough, I would unconsciously increase the chaos (and adrenaline) by moving frequently. I kept living in the illusion that if I could just find the right job, right home, right relationship, etc., I would be happier.

Medical science has confirmed that adrenaline eats at the digestive system, cardiac tissue, immune system, and soft tissues and joints. Adrenaline and stress turn off the body's usual self-nurturing, tissue building, and assimilation and repair mode in favor of mobilizing for "fight or flight"—it is an evolutionary response that was never designed for constant use. Constantly used, the adrenaline response and its effects destroy the body and lead to death.

By the time I was hitting my 30th birthday, I was confronted with progressive deterioration and chronic pain in my tissues and joints, I got a medical test and my body had aged to that of a 45 year old. My digestive system no longer functioned correctly. I had to close my construction business because I could not walk without pain. (Not to mention my business partners left me because I would take on enormous projects on impossible timelines without enough funding or staffing to complete them, and they had had enough—also, they were increasingly uncomfortable with my emotional dramas.) Adrenal exhaustion and chronic pain afflicted me. I was once again very close to killing myself. I knew that therapy, naturopathy, and self-help books on burnout and perfectionism all by themselves were not bringing me relief.

I hit bottom, swallowed my pride (I did not like the "God" talk), and became willing to work the Twelve Steps to save my life. I went to open A.A. meetings and eventually discovered that Workaholics Anonymous existed. Higher Power gave me a nudge and I asked someone to sponsor me who it turned out had also used the Twelve Steps to find relief from their converting a hobby into a business and overworking, as well as being a decade-plus A.A. and O.A. member. This sponsor helped me tremendously, including guiding me to develop a Recovery plan, including bottom lines, guidelines, and top lines. She helped me learn that for a recovering perfectionist, I had to keep things simple and focus on gentleness. With the help of my Higher Power, we developed a definition of abstinence that was "not working more than an average of 45 hours per week." Guidelines include: not working more than 9 hours per day, having two days in a row off per week, and getting off the computer by midnight. My office is no longer in my bedroom or living room (and soon- not even in my house!). In order to avoid adrenaline cycling, it is vital for me to allow Higher Power (H.P.) to restore me to sanity on a daily basis, through regular nourishment (including recently celebrating H.P.'s gift of five years of abstinence from sugar and sweetener with a guideline of three solid meals per day), regular sleep and rest, exercise, time for fun and creativity, and time for relationships. Guidelines for me include focusing on self-care (a top line of "sleeping at least 6 hours of night" has become a guideline of "keeping a daily time log on sleep and work," "sleeping at least 7 hours a night" and a top line of "sleeping at least 8 hours a night."). I also attend an average of four to five Twelve Step meetings per week, do Step work on a regular basis, call my sponsor Monday through Friday, make and receive program calls, and enjoy a daily prayer and meditation practice. My sponsor has given me assignments to enjoy "purposeless fun," and I currently enjoy several hobbies that I have permission to "be bad at." The greater translation of this, instead of a lifetime of obligation, fear, and illusion of control, is H.P.'s awakening vision for me of a life of spaciousness, joy, and faith. Slowly, after decades of diseased contraction, I am beginning to step into the freedom to explore and learn about what I enjoy. And to learn from the process and my deep internal experience instead of forcing solutions by constructing my life to look a certain way on the outside while being miserable inside of it.

I have to stay off adrenaline in order to maintain conscious contact with my Higher Power. And Higher Power helps me stay away from adrenaline cycling. Putting spirituality time first in my day helps me with "a daily reprieve contingent on the maintenance of my spiritual condition." That is the most important thing to keeping me sane and alive.

Step work has helped me tremendously to "clear away the wreckage" and learn (in Step Four through Five, Step Six through Seven) about the character assets underneath many of my negative coping mechanisms (a.k.a. character defects). For example, caring and self-love are underneath the guarded negative coping mechanisms of illusion of control and playing God, both motivated by fear (love that's in a container that's too small). Enthusiasm and delight are available beneath obsessive interest. W.A. is helping to unknot my spirit's natural impulse toward health. For a guilt-ridden workaholic who was sure I had years of groveling and apologizing ahead of me (life is mandatory suffering and I'm the center of the universe defects) in Steps Eight and Nine, it was surprising to discover that I myself was at the top of my Eighth Step amends list (positive self-care is pleasurable and I am a beloved part of the universe assets). And that taking trips to the beach, getting to go slowly with developing interests, enjoying massages and great medical care, savoring the sunset, and receiving help from others were the "punishments" of recovery. As well as eating wonderful fresh food, deeply resting through full nights of sleep, gently exercising my body, and leaning into the deep truth that I am OK whatever I "do for a living." Living the W.A. Program of Recovery, one day at a time, has been the Ninth Step living amends to myself.

Step Eleven has helped me deepen in my spiritual conscious contact. I am grateful to the other W.A.'s who have helped me find other words for inner translations for "God." Higher Power. Deeper Power, Great Spirit, Spirit of Creation, Breath of Life, Spirit of Life, Entire Universe, Deep Self, Inner Knowing, Inner Wisdom, Great Blessing, and my current favorite: Divine Love.

Step Twelve has brought me the blessing of learning to live in balance while showing up for healthy service work. I have been deeply nourished and my recovery greatly deepened by sponsoring and by doing service work at all levels (in some cases, after praying for clear divine guidance about an opportunity for over two years before saying "yes"). I am stepping into learning about living from inner spaciousness and divine delight, about feeling into each day's rhythm. Conscious contact leads me to a deeper synchronicity that is more satisfying and grounded than "racing to beat the clock." Deepening in Step Twelve and balanced service brings me out of obligation and into clarity, moving me out of compulsion and into joy and grace.

# Recovering All Of Me

My name is M----- and I'm a workaholic. I started working a Workaholics Anonymous (W.A.) recovery program in September 1988 when the first W.A. meeting started in my area. Over the years, I have learned that my addiction to compulsive working and activity happens for two basic reasons: to get a high and to avoid something in my life. My Higher Power, whom I call God, and the W.A. program have given me recovery in both areas. For this great gift I am grateful. This is my story.

I remember awakening from a nap sometime between three and four years of age and realizing that my growing up just didn't feel right. All the "boyish" things I was being taught (i.e. how to think, feel, act, do) left out the very strong feminine side of my self-identity. So, I began to slowly express my "girlish" side and quickly learned that that was not OK. If fact, not only was I laughed at, I was led to believe that "boys just don't act that way" and that it was shameful to feel that way. I took all this in and along the way concluded that even though I was somehow flawed, I could nevertheless redeem myself by exceptional performance.

I have now come to understand that this way of proving myself to be worthy set in motion a life long pattern of compulsively using work and activity to avoid any and all difficult and painful feelings. In particular, I have engaged in this addiction to avoid the pain and fear associated with being "different" and embracing all of who I am: a transgender person. But more about this part of my recovery later.

Throughout my school years, I learned to practice my addiction very well. I always strived to finish my schoolwork before anyone else so I could just feel inside that I was as good as the other kids in my class. In high school I completed three majors (math, science and foreign language). But even that was not enough to satisfy my inner needs to gain acceptance and to be considered as one of the "in group." I completed college in three and a half years. After finishing a Masters degree in one year, I didn't even go to my own graduation, as I already had a job and was working extra hours. This intense focus on accomplishment gave me the illusion of power and control even while I still had this nagging feeling inside that whatever I did and however well I did it, it would never be enough.

I married a wonderful woman while finishing college and beginning to work on my Masters degree. Early in the marriage relationship, I discovered that I was not very good at intimacy--- sharing what I was thinking, feeling, who I was, etc. You see, I was terrified that my wife would find out about that feminine part of me that I was trying desperately to hide and leave behind. So, over time, my work addiction progressed to the point that I had great difficulty "turning it off" at night when I needed to sleep. I even took my addiction into the night's sleep by thinking that I needed to "sleep fast" so that I could get up early in the morning to get to work. As I approached my bottom, I would awake at two or three in the morning and just go into work. I had rashes over my body from the stress. My wife and children were afraid of me and would hide out in another part of the house when I finally did come home. This is because I wanted everything to be perfect at home because I was not able to attain perfection at work that day, and I would be hyper-critical of everyone at home and of the condition of the household. Even the dog would hide out. My marriage was on the verge of break-up for serious lack of loving attention.

I hit bottom when my wife started attending her own Twelve Step program. She slowly stopped enabling me like bringing the kids and dinner down to my office, and making excuses when I didn't show up for important events because I was working. It started to feel like I was playing a left-handed tennis player. The ball was not spinning right for me anymore. Conflict between us increased substantially. Eventually, she suggested that I look into meeting with another person who was interested in starting W.A. in the area. It took me six months to call this other person. In September 1988, she and I met for the first time, and recovery started for me.

I can see now that over years of recovery---years of working the Steps several times---I became increasingly focused on really understanding just how powerless I was about working compulsively. By attending meetings, working the Steps and sharing what I was discovering with a sponsor, I slowly began to see that I was unable to stop my addictive behaviors on my own power, and how much damage I had done to myself and to everyone around me because of them. I also saw that the depth and extent of my destructive behaviors and the resultant damage was clearly beyond my ability to repair. Out of that carnage, I was also able to first catch a glimmer of a Higher Power that could restore me to sanity and serenity. Each time I completed Step Two, my understanding of my Higher Power sharpened. Eventually, I prepared a collage of my Higher Power. I hung up the collage in our home, where I could see it every day. The more I looked at it the more I learned about my Higher Power. The process of my surrender to my Higher Power began and then deepened each time I completed a Step Three.

As I completed several iterations of Steps Four and Five, I was also learning how to take contrary action when I observed that I was moving into a workaholic state. I learned to stop and breathe deeply and allow my body to relax. I learned to get up from my desk and walk around for a few minutes. I learned to go into the men's room and say the Serenity Prayer several times. I learned to call another W.A. member. At first, I was able to take these contrary actions only after having acted out my addiction. Later I was able to take the necessary contrary action while I was acting out. Eventually, I was able to shift to more functional behavior when I saw that my actions and thoughts were about to lead me into a workaholic state. Then one day I realized for the first time that these contrary actions were a more desirable alternative to the "high" I got from compulsive working and activity. The day that insight happened was truly an "Aha!" moment—purely a gift from my Higher Power, and I was deeply grateful.

Several cycles of completing Steps Six through Nine took me through a process of slowly peeling back, layer by layer, the defenses I had built up over a lifetime to that part of myself that I did not want to face. During this period, I also began working a Co-Dependents Anonymous program to extend my understanding of how my family of origin contributed to my addiction, and how I relied upon the feelings of others to determine how I was to feel from moment to moment. The descent into that place of fear and shame that surrounded what I did not want to face and that I had so long avoided was very difficult. I got outside professional help and I turned to my Higher Power in my quest for understanding, acceptance, and eventual liberation.

One night in the front room of my home when everyone was asleep, I got on my knees and asked God to either take my life or to show me a way out of that dark place. Over the next several months I somehow found doorways to connect with the local transgender community. Then on my natal birthday, September 11, 1999, I walked into the world for the first time as my feminine self at a transgender support group meeting. On that date, I experienced a rebirth of sorts. On that date, I began the process of embracing all of me, without shame and fear, and expressing in an open and honest way to the world what I had avoided almost all of my life.

During this period of liberation, working Steps Ten through Twelve increasingly became a celebration of living a more balanced life: a life increasingly filled with love, honesty, compassion, calmness, and peace; a life of increasing connection to those I loved. The desire to work compulsively has not gone away, but its power has moderated considerably. From time to time I still fall into the old patterns, but I am quick to recognize them and quick to realize that I no longer need to act them out. There is no longer a need for me to hide my feminine side. The path of recovery has indeed become sweet.

I have been truly blessed by my Higher Power, the Workaholics Anonymous program of recovery, the W.A. members who have been part of my life over the years, sponsors, and loving friends and family members who are growing to love me in all my imperfection. I don't have to run and hide anymore. Today I am learning what it means to stop my avoidance behaviors and to live in the moment. I am becoming more complete every day, as my relationship with my Higher Power grows deeper. Yes, my name is M-----, and I'm a grateful and blessed Workaholic.

# Keep Coming Back—It Happens

I was fortunate to grow up in a loving family. I was well cared for—but there were also big expectations, in terms of my values and lifestyle and the type of person I would become. My parents had a certain career choice and status level in mind for me, and while it wasn't what I desired, the overall idea of being "successful" was something that seemed mandatory. On some level, I always wanted their approval—as most children do.

I coped with this ongoing conflict between what my parents wanted and who I really was with drugs and alcohol all through high school, college and beyond, although I have been abstinent for many years. I now understand that I coped with workaholism as well; for example, I would get high during school, but also study hard.

When I was nineteen, my workaholic father died suddenly (of a heart attack at age forty-six). We had been arguing at the time, and this trauma crystallized my inner conflict: for many years I carried around the feeling that if I just worked harder and was an even better person, perhaps nothing else terrible would happen, like losing my other parent. At the time I had just moved into my first apartment. I was literally at the doorstep of my independence and separation from home. When my dad died, rather than spend the summer grieving, I went to summer school and got straight A's.

Jumping ahead a few years, I established a career in the health care field, working in various settings until eleven years ago when I began my own business around an innovative program I had pioneered. I wrote a book, and was invited to speak across the US and in other countries; I went to conferences as an expert; I was 'famous'. I enjoyed the adrenaline rush, the ego boost, and the thrill of it all, but I was constantly pushing myself way beyond my limits and struggled often with deep depression. Periodically I would become suicidal. I'd tell my family I might not be around much longer. They'd beg me to modify my workload and work style (working at home, isolated). I clearly remember looking them in the eye and saying, "No, the work is the most important thing." And actually believing that it was more important than my family or my own health! I did give some thought to how I could change things, but was not willing to give up being on the "cutting edge" of my field, staying on top of who was doing what and trying to keep others from entering my niche; traveling extensively to show up at all the events of national and international health care organizations; and since I was self-employed, having to do everything from my own marketing to buying the paper clips myself.

I did everything with great zeal and zest, but also obsessively and perfectionistically. Nothing was ever quite good enough, and I kept trying harder. To deal with the depression I went into therapy, and took antidepressants for many years. Like many others, these medications did not work well for me. I would have to go on and off of them and try different ones. They would cause uncomfortable side effects and would also lose their effectiveness. My therapist tried to get me to cut down or change my work by recognizing and accepting my limitations, but I would continue to repeat the same pattern. I really didn't know how to say no, or how to let go. Looking back I'm not sure whether I didn't see the relationship between workaholism and the chronic depletion and depression, or if I just didn't make it a priority to do something about it.

About five years ago, I found out about W.A. The tools sounded good, but impossible. I kept at it, and eventually worked with a sponsor for a time, which was helpful. I continued in therapy, exploring my family dynamics. Close to three years ago my therapist recommended that I take a sabbatical for six months to rest and seek a new perspective. It took me about six months to plan it and then so long to give myself permission and fuss around getting ready for it that I ended up with about a month and a half off. But it was a major breakthrough to go from all I had been doing to doing nothing for any time at all.

At first the silence and stillness were so disorienting. I was racked with anxiety. Who was I without my professional identity and activities? What was I supposed to be doing with my time?? I was at a total loss. Then somebody told me about a local Buddhist meditation center, and I began to listen, learn, and practice. This was the perfect thing at the time. Meditation teaches you to observe the habits of the mind, and to be kind to yourself. I saw how my thoughts were filled with self-judgment and criticism, and I eventually supplanted those with permission and self-acceptance. I discovered that one didn't have to be busy and productive to be a worthy person; one could "simply be." I learned that slowing down and re-building a life with recreational activities and social relationships apart from work was an even more important accomplishment than what I'd strived for in my career—and that I could approach it with just as much passion and determination.

At this time, I also began exploring yoga. I literally felt detoxification happen on a cellular level as I breathed and stretched. The meditation continued to be emotionally healing, intellectually fascinating, and spiritually new for me. All of this overlapped nicely with W.A., which also emphasized staying present, listening to oneself, and finding a spiritual path.

After the sabbatical I went back to work. It took a while to find the right amount and mix of projects and trips, and to integrate work with the new activities I'd developed in the rest of my life. While the negative side of self-employment can be the lack of built-in boundaries against over-doing, the positive side can be flexibility and the autonomy to do something about over-doing once you get a handle on it.

For these past three years, I've worked part-time and monitored myself pretty closely. There's been a slow but steady and significant transformation from being irritable and depleted to having prolonged peace, calm, and well-being. I think it's been a synergistic combination of reducing work stress, doing meditation and yoga, working through life issues in therapy (which I've ended close to a year ago now), taking fish oil capsules (which seem to impact my mood more than medication ever did), and attending W.A. meetings—all of which have given me new ways to take care of myself. The wisdom, consistency, and support of my peers in W.A. has helped me to incorporate the "tools" into my life, such as underscheduling, prioritizing, substituting, balancing, and nurturing. I work less, take fewer trips and do fewer projects at one time; I allow time to recuperate between tasks and trips, and space them apart more consciously. I no longer try to be everywhere in my field, and I no longer have quite as much of an emotional investment in being at the forefront of it. It took me a long time to come to terms with other people getting into my niche, but once I finally surrendered to that, I've been surprised to find that new opportunities have opened up to me.

In these past three years, I haven't experienced depression or been on any medication, and I have a confident sense that I never will again. I've built a new lifestyle and coping skills, new habits. I feel so much healthier and happier. I've now surpassed the age at which my father died, and am so grateful to have "turned my own ship around" before heading for a similar fate.

I've always been fortunate to have a good marriage, but now it's even better. I'm about to celebrate my twelfth anniversary, and instead of my husband spending so much of his time picking me up from the puddles of my depression, we both have more time and energy for a high-quality relationship. I am a better partner, and I hold up my end of the responsibilities. I no longer put my husband's needs behind my work demands—I am there for him, as he has incredibly been there for me time and again.

Looking back it almost seems too good to be true, but this is how it all happened. Now there is a new chapter. As I've continued to feel so good, I have more energy, interest and enthusiasm for my work again, so I have to be careful that the pendulum doesn't swing back the other way. I'm working more than I was, and feeling excited about new challenges in my field. Now I see what people mean when they say that recovery is a continuous process: it doesn't end. I'll have an ongoing need for W.A. and have to stay vigilant. But now I recognize my old habits when they kick up and I am not willing to become so fatigued and miserable again. I believe I've begun to establish new patterns that form a mental, physical, and emotional road map inside of me. If I pay attention, I know when to stop and what direction will keep me healthy.

In conclusion, then, as we say at the end of our W.A. meeting: "Keep coming back—It happens!" (We don't say, "It works"!) There is hope. Keep at it, and supplement W.A. with whatever else you discover that works for you. Thank you for listening and for your own contribution to this organization that has truly changed my life.

# Before, During and After

I was not born a workaholic. I do not believe there is a genetic predisposition toward workaholism. I was born into a middle class family where the father worked and the mother stayed home to care for me. There was enough time and enough money and enough emotional stability to bring up a normal child.

When I was six months old my family uprooted and moved across the country to my mother's home. My father took up a new career and my mother stayed home to care for me and do volunteer political work. Life must have been a little unsettled, especially for my father, but they had a community of friends to support them and my mother's family for help and all in all life must have seemed positive for them.

By the early fifties however, things were falling apart. The government was cracking down on communists and my mother was on the verge of going underground without my father or me. The FBI was harassing them and their friends and coworkers. People were being arrested and imprisoned and deported. People were being blacklisted and some were leaving the country to find work. At home, people were losing their jobs after the FBI pressured their employers. In my opinion, my parents must have been under a lot of pressure and feeling quite frightened. As I remember, none of this pressure and fear was communicated to me directly. I do not remember being told what was going on. All I remember was witnessing my parents being frightened and their instructing me in the procedures necessary to protect them and myself from exposure and persecution.

I lived with this unexplained and unacknowledged fear in my house for many years. I was expected to understand the situation and act appropriately without ever specifically discussing it. For example, when my parents were in their seventies, many years later, they expected me to understand their reluctance to subscribe to a magazine they enjoyed because they did not want their names to appear on its subscription list. It was up to me to figure out what appropriate behavior was in each situation and act accordingly. It was also up to me to figure out how to "fix" things for my parents—to make it safe for them and thus for me. This, I believe, was the beginning of my workaholism.

I found that by "behaving normally" I could affect my family situation in beneficial ways. As long as I held my tongue and "acted normal" I could make things seem normal and safe. If I looked busy and productive I would not add to my parents' burdens and the household could function more smoothly. I developed a repertoire of "normally busy" activities. It was not necessary to be productive, merely to appear normally busy and thus not in need of supervision or assistance.

This coping "tool," using "normal busyness" to bring about the appearance of emotional stability, became a resource for me in other times of stress. I developed a kind of tool kit of strategies for managing in a tumultuous household. I developed the habit of keeping secrets; of alertly observing, remembering, and inferring the meaning of situations as they occurred; and of not sharing what I observed or inferred. I became hypervigilant, constantly scanning my environment for information and anticipating possible threats or problems. I began to lie to present the appearance of order and appropriateness even when I plainly knew otherwise. I developed a secret life in which all of my motives were clear and all of my actions clearly consistent with my motives. I came to believe in the reality of my secret life no matter how much it conflicted with external reality. I lived in a dream world insulated by my various survival strategies. In short, I learned how to use work to protect myself from feelings and experiences that I wished to avoid and that I was powerless to prevent.

The impulse to protect myself from painful feelings and experiences is normal and healthy and wise. What is not normal or healthy or wise is the choice of strategies for protecting myself.

The strategies I developed carried a high price. I found myself generalizing from the specific instances where protection of some kind was called for to a policy of protecting myself all the time. At this point I became a workaholic.

As a beginning workaholic I needed to be at work all the time. I needed to place myself in a work situation, surrounded by my tools and confronted visually with the materials of my work. I was not an imaginative workaholic. In school I needed to be in the library surrounded with my papers; as a truck driver I needed to be on the road; at work I needed to be in the warehouse with a full inventory or else on the street, in the market, or on the phone. I needed the combination of fatigue and adrenaline that comes from prolonged overwork. I needed the satisfying oblivion that comes from an exclusive focus on work-related tasks. I enjoyed the privileges of prolonged, visible overwork. I was angry, insensitive, rude, preoccupied, and erratic. I lived on high-powered coffee and rode the emotional roller coaster that comes with caffeine abuse. I isolated myself and became proud of my isolation, experiencing it as the consequence of my ability and willingness to outwork my coworkers. I wore my fatigue as a badge of honor. I took my work home with me, treating friends and family the same way I treated coworkers; taking work with me on vacations or not taking vacations at all; disdaining birthday and Christmas presents because there was nothing I needed or wanted besides work. I grew angry and depressed on Sunday afternoons.

As far as I was concerned, all of my problems stemmed from the chronic disorganization at work and the failure of my friends and family to correctly understand and value my work agenda. My values and my behavior were not the issue. After all, I reasoned, I was able to squeeze them and their requirements into my busy schedule. I attended mandatory family occasions and met the necessary obligations for presents and cards. I was available if my friends wished to contact me.

Eventually, I got what I wanted. My wife retreated into polite silence. She kept my young son from "bothering" me when I was home. My parents and friends became distant and I began to achieve some success at organizing my work so that it took up all of my waking time and energy. I got up early every day and was busy all day until I went home and collapsed into bed. My anger and frustration conveniently insulated me from any awareness of how I was feeling. The absence of any real intimacy between my wife and me and the habit of relying on our six-year old son to "fix" the quarrels we regularly fell into were not part of my awareness. The fact that I was spending seventy or eighty unproductive hours at work every week was not really an issue either. I was busy all the time I was awake—and that was all that mattered. We had a house to live in and the bills were paid; I had met my obligations to support my family and that was the end of it as far as I was concerned.

This kind of frozen, loveless, frenzy continued for several years. I lived in isolation, fear, resentment, fatigue, and anger in a house of strangers who wondered what had become of me. Out of my sight, the people closest to me, the people I loved the most and depended on the most, began to drift away from me because I was too busy to notice. I remember the day it came to an end. My wife and I were standing by the front door of our house and she very calmly said to me that if "we" didn't get some help real soon she was leaving.

We started seeing a counselor and very quickly the counselor suggested that I might be a workaholic and I simply said yes. I didn't even have to think about it. It was just obvious. The counselor suggested Workaholics Anonymous and I went. That was it.

It was hard to squeeze in time for the meetings. I rushed from work straight to the meetings and didn't usually have time for dinner. The meetings started at 7:30 pm and I started working at about 4:00 am so by the time I got to the meetings I was exhausted and angry at having to rush to this new obligation at the end of my day. For the first few meetings I sat on a couch and dozed and tried to listen to the speakers while I wondered what kind of a cult I had wandered into. Characteristically, I gathered up all the literature on display and read it all as fast as I could. I had the program figured out after only a couple of meetings. The only reason I kept on going to those meetings was that I had promised the counselor. I didn't like them and I didn't like the people and I didn't experience any great revelation. I was a workaholic, and my family was falling apart and here I was at this meeting full of people just like me.

Gradually, I began to appreciate the presence of other people who shared my addiction to work and I began to appreciate their willingness to talk about their experiences with work addiction honestly and candidly. I began to work the Steps and use the Tools and to see my life begin to change. I was so impatient and so unfamiliar with the process of recovery that I exaggerated the importance of every little change and imagined that every small improvement in my life was the final and most significant change. I had no clue about how much my life could and would change. I joined a group that was studying the Steps intensively and really began to take a close look at my life.

As I began to work the Steps and commit to attending meetings I found myself developing a relationship with a Higher Power I called "the Cosmic Forces of the Universe" and later called "the Cosmic Gremlins" or "the Gods of Laughter." I began to pray and to learn how to turn my life over to the Gods of Laughter. As the extent of my powerlessness became apparent to me I became willing to take a close look at exactly how my character defects, my lack of honesty, and my impatience had affected my relationships with coworkers, customers and vendors. I became willing to make amends to them.

I began to make amends and to experience firsthand some of the results of the pain I had caused by my workaholic behavior. Left to my own resources I never would have been willing to confront these situations and to witness the anger, the hurt, the recriminations, and the frustration that my workaholism had brought about. Approaching them with the awareness that I was powerless over these situations as well as the rest of my life and that the Gods of Laughter had a plan for me made it possible for me to make my amends with gratitude and humility instead of fear and shame.

My relationships with my family—my parents, my wife, and my son—gradually began to change. I began to become willing to approach them with a sense of trust in the will of the Gods of Laughter. My impatience with them diminished and I began to respond more truthfully to them. In retrospect, I can see that this new willingness to be present and witness the feelings and behavior of my loved ones was a gift from the Gods of Laughter. At the time, however, I thought it was the result of my having begun to manage my time better. I had, in fact, begun to manage my time better and I was working fewer hours but it was a long time before I was genuinely grateful to the Gods of Laughter for this gift. My workaholism led me to believe that it was me and my will and my cleverness that had allowed me to become such a skillful manager of my time.

It has taken me many years and I am nowhere near done, but I recognize the Promises of the Program for what they are. They are being fulfilled every day among those who work the Program. Not all at once. Not once and for all. Over and over, a little bit at a time, one day at a time. I still live on the earth with everybody else and my life has all of the challenges that living on the planet brings with it, but I know I am subject to the will of the Gods of Laughter and am grateful and humble. I am more willing than ever before to live truly in the present and to acknowledge things as they are. I am more willing to live at peace inside my own skin and do just the work that is given to me each day. For this I am grateful.

## The Gods of Laughter

It has been my experience that recovery from workaholism is not possible without a robust relationship with a Higher Power. Maintaining a continual awareness of a power greater than me has proven essential to my recovery from the grandiosity that goes with addiction. This awareness has also led to the humility that is a cornerstone of recovery.

As I began to work my way into an awareness of the presence of a Higher Power in my life, via the acknowledgement of the frequent occurrence of uncanny coincidences, for example, I had to admit that something like a Higher Power did show up in my life from time to time. I began to admit to parking karma and traveling weather karma, for example. But the more I began to reflect on the order of my experience, the more I began to notice that not all of the instances of Higher Power intervention in my life looked exactly beneficial to me from my point of view. Sometimes things did not work out the way I had in mind or even for my advantage. Sometimes, it seemed to me that my own personal Higher Power seemed determined to make me the goat of my schemes. At the same time, paradoxically, I was learning to acknowledge, accept, and even trust my Higher Power.

Looking back, I realize that I was beginning to be able to distinguish between those things that I was supposed to do and those things I was not supposed to do because my Higher Power was going to do them instead of me. Every time I found a new one it made me laugh. "There I am again, playing god," I would say. Not being very smart I had to start with some pretty basic things like daytime and nighttime and how many hours there were in a day. Being a workaholic, it was a new experience for me to accept limits on the infinite expandability and compressibility of time.

There were really two issues: I had to learn that having a Higher Power did not mean that I was the hero of the story and that everything would always work out the way I wanted. I also had to change my perspective on what I was supposed to be doing, from setting my own agenda to seeking the will of my Higher Power. As I began to recognize the presence of my Higher Power's will in my life, I began to laugh. Not that I would always do my Higher Power's will and not that things would work out for me even if I did, but it was clear that sanity for me lay in the direction of seeking my Higher Power's will and then doing my best to carry it out.

As an addict I was committed to controlling the flow of the events of my life in order to protect myself from experiences I intended to avoid. All of my actions were directed toward managing the affairs of that unruly obstacle that was my life. I was the manager of my life not its inhabitant. I occupied a place outside of the world from which I strove fruitlessly to order everything to my satisfaction. Acknowledging a Higher Power was the beginning of a process of rejoining the planet, rejoining my own life. It meant recognizing that I was part of the world; in the work situation, it meant I was another member of the work place crew and not an indispensable heroically legendary figure beyond time and place. It meant seeking my place as one more member of the natural world, no more but no less.

Seeking my place in the natural world, however, has proven to be a rather subtler project than I first imagined. The natural world, the concrete site of my everyday work, turned out to consist of a continuously evolving set of variously relevant contingencies not all of which I recognized or understood. Mastering them, setting them in order and then determining my place among them once and for all, proved an illusion I was predisposed to prefer. The temptation to consider my place in the natural world settled, I eventually realized, was merely an invitation to begin all over again. It turned out that the seeking was what I was looking for. I began to strive for a perpetual state of seeking. As I began to spend more time seeking and less time pretending to find I began to notice a peculiar kind of harmony. When I became willing to acknowledge the continuously evolving flow of my experience, to accept the contingency of my place in the natural world, of my Higher Power's will for me, I felt a kind of harmony. I began to laugh. Laughter became a kind of acknowledgment of the presence in my life of a power greater than me, of a plan for my life—the Gods of Laughter.

## Tales of the Cosmos: Encounters with the Cosmic Gremlins

A relationship with a Higher Power has given me my life back. Only a fool even greater than me would not value this relationship. Nevertheless. Ah, the fabled nevertheless. The nevertheless that leads to sanity, that deflates pomposity, that prevents grandiosity. There is no good reason to take the whole thing so seriously. My experience suggests that my relationship with my Higher Power is important but not serious. In fact, one of the gifts of my relationship with my Higher Power has been the recovery of whimsy, lifesaving frivolity, and inconsequential playfulness.

I am a servant of the Cosmic Forces of the Universe (CFUs). This was big news to me. It's not that the CFUs were particularly interested in me or my affairs or even in my awareness of them. The Universe was perfectly capable of going on its own way without any input from me. The CFUs did not especially need my help in managing things and they didn't care whether I knew anything about them or not. Not only that—the CFUs weren't especially interested in me, either. They were not about keeping a Cosmic eye on me or my plans or my destiny. They weren't hostile to me; they just didn't really concern themselves on that level.

Nevertheless—there is that word again—there was a point in my recovery when I was quite concerned about the whole Higher Power issue and whether an atheist like me could legitimately have a Higher Power. So, one night I went to an Overeaters Anonymous meeting in a log cabin in West Hollywood and listened to a bunch of skinny, beautiful young women talk about how hard it is to work in the film industry as makeup artists, costumers, or other craft workers and maintain any form of sobriety. I clearly didn't have anything in common with them and all their talk about Higher Powers. So I was entirely unprepared when, after walking out of the log cabin and into the middle of the street in the cloudy darkness of the night, the Cosmos made itself manifest to me (all right, I might as well say the clouds parted and a mighty voice spoke to me) and made it clear that whether I liked it or not, the CFUs were the CFUs and it was their Universe and not mine and that was that. They weren't mad about it; in fact, they were more than willing to extend a kind of Cosmic welcome to the Universe to me but they weren't about to invite me over for coffee and cookies. It was more in the way of a "since you asked..." kind of experience. So, after I was finished staring at the empty dark sky in astonished awe and carried myself over to the sidewalk and finished shaking and all the goose bumps went away, I decided that I had a Higher Power.

## The Cosmic Gremlins

Just because there are Cosmic Forces in the Universe and the Gods of Laughter have something in mind for me and I know it, doesn't mean everything is smooth sailing. It's all well and good to seek the will of my Higher Power and attempt to carry that out. Finding out my Higher Power's will and actually carrying it out turn out to be entirely different matters. My experience is that I fall into my Higher Power's will by accident and only retrospectively realize that I have inadvertently managed to carry it out. On the other hand, sometimes I feel completely certain of my Higher Power's will and realize later that I was wrong. Sometimes I work at carrying out my Higher Power's will and get distracted or misdirected or find that it's just too hard or that I'm just too tired. Other times everything goes so smoothly that I can't figure out how come it doesn't go this way all the time. Then I blame myself for my sloppy recovery and judge that if only I worked harder then I would find my Higher Power's will more often and carry it out more successfully. Afterward, something reminds me that I am as powerless over my recovery as I am over my disease and that my sloppy recovery is just what it is—no more, no less.

I am willing to be rid of my disease. I am really, truly willing to be rid of my disease once and for all. Sometimes. Other times I am the willing, enthusiastic addict rushing about and overworking mindlessly. The power greater than me that is responsible for this mess I call the Cosmic Gremlins. I don't know why my recovery goes so well for a while and then goes bad. I don't know why things go so badly and then work out anyway. As I begin to detach from the results of my efforts and focus, instead, on the effort of seeking my Higher Power's will I become aware of the constant interference of the Cosmic Gremlins in my life. It is the Cosmic Gremlins who confuse my awareness of my Higher Power's will with the plotlines of television and movie dramas. It is the Gremlins who hide things in plain sight. I have realized that in large measure I was put on the planet for no other purpose than to amuse the Cosmic Gremlins. These Olympian delinquents are perfectly capable of quarreling among themselves and then causing me to enact the results.

If it were simply a matter of being smart, of working hard, recovery would be a relatively straightforward project and I could look forward to a cure for my disease. The Cosmic Gremlins suggest otherwise. There is no working around them. There is no appeasing or propitiating them. There is only seeking the will of my Higher Power, struggling to carry that out and acknowledging the results and accepting them with gratitude. The ebb and flow of my experience, the ceaseless succession of sensations that are my embodied existence on the planet, are not other than me. In my addiction, I distinguish myself from my experience and judge it. I inspect it to see if it is good enough as if it is some work project or commodity I can offer to sell or barter. The Gremlins remind me, every day in the midst of every routine motion and chore, that it is they and not me who determine the outcome of my efforts. What is mine is my embodied presence on the planet. It is my dwelling, my home, and when I cherish it and do not betray it I find my recovery.

# The Power of Underscheduling

I used to think I was a very honest person. In W.A., I finally saw how dishonest I was with myself and others. In particular, I was frequently dishonest about how much time it would take to do something, about how long it would take me to get somewhere, and about my limitations and skills. Of course I could get it done! As soon as you need it!

When I came in to W.A., I started keeping track of how much time I spent on various projects at work. Whenever I started a new task or project, I would write down the current time with the project name. In this way I learned a lot about how I spend my time at work.

When I had been in W.A. a few months, my boss gave me a new project, to fact-check a long report. She asked me when I could get it done. Normally I would have guessed, and then started the crazy cycle of working extra hours, stress, and shortchanging other projects to get it done. Instead, I asked if I could get back to her. I decided to start the work and see how much I got done in two hours. I got through a certain number of pages. I then looked at how many pages were in the document, and figured out how many hours I would likely have to spend on the document.

At first I thought I could spend five days a week, all day on this one project. But then I realized I had other responsibilities. In fact, I couldn't take this project on at all if I didn't have something to give up. I turned back to my task log. I had two projects that were ending that week. I could use the time I normally spent on those old projects for this new project. I figured out how many weeks it would take me to finish the new project, based on my average hours per week on the old projects. Then I doubled it, just to be safe and "underschedule."

I told my boss when I could get it done. She told me that was unacceptable, that it had to be done sooner. Again, I was tempted to say, "OK, sure." Instead, I explained how I had figured out the amount of time it would take. If I needed to get it done sooner, we had to take something else off my plate. I suggested that we delay another project assigned to me, or give part of this new project to someone else. None of these suggestions were acceptable to her. She said "Can't you just streamline it?" Again, I was tempted to say "sure." But this time I said, "What does that mean? Do you want me to check only some of the facts? Only do part of the document? How could I streamline it?"

The reason I could discuss this with her that way is because I had honesty on my side. She couldn't argue with the facts, which were that I had evidence of how long the project would take, and a record of how much time I spent on other projects. For this project to get done sooner, something had to go.

My boss finally said she would get back to me on this. The next day she called and said that it was OK for me to get it done when I said I could. She wasn't willing to take any other projects away from me in order to get this done sooner.

What a miracle it was to have a project where I didn't have to lie about my progress, or work free over-time to get it done, or skip parts of the work hoping no one would notice! As it turned out, I got the project done early. My boss was happy. And I had some experience with serenity. Now I know when I am feeling rushed or stressed about a project, I probably just need to get honest with myself and my boss about how long it will take.

# The Benefits of Prioritizing

A few months into my W.A. recovery, I felt a pain in my hand when I clicked the mouse on my computer. I clicked again, and felt the pain again. Before W.A., I would have just kept on clicking until I couldn't use my hand anymore. Maybe I would have taken some aspirin.

I had a number of acquaintances who had repetitive strain injuries, such as carpal tunnel syndrome, which had resulted in serious impairment of their ability to do necessary daily activities like dial a telephone. Their injuries had begun with a small pain, but they had continued to work. I already had another disability as a result of my previous compulsive working. I knew I needed to prioritize taking care of this problem. I needed to put off the immediate gratification of completing just one more task.

I called my boss and explained that I needed to find out about alternate mouse technologies, because I did not want this injury to progress. I had to tell a client that my work for them might be delayed. I spent the rest of the day investigating my options. I tried a number of solutions over the next week until I finally found one that worked for me. I also found that I could not work as fast with this new device.

I re-negotiated my deadlines with some clients and with my boss. I had to pray frequently throughout each day, asking my Higher Power to help me continue to use this new device. I felt the members of my W.A. were the only people who truly understood what I was going through.

I had to let go of my idea that the faster I worked, the more my Higher Power and others would value me. For me, working more slowly meant I had to turn my entire will and life over to my Higher Power. What if I get fired? What if we lose clients? What if I can never find another job because I can't work as fast as I used to? Whenever these fears came up, I reaffirmed that I was not willing to risk a permanent disability just so I could work more or faster. I had to trust that my Higher Power would give me the tools to deal with whatever happened.

More than two years later, I still use this alternative device. I was not fired, and we did not lose clients.

I believe that without W.A., I likely would have continued to work "through the pain" until I was disabled. Instead, every day I am grateful to have the full use of my hand.

# The Pleasure of Play

Play is a four-letter word. As an adult I often experience the feeling of play as uncomfortable, it implies a child-like attitude anathema to appropriate adult behavior, especially if one yearns for a life of success. As a workaholic whose disease displayed symptoms as a young teenager, I became angry and self-righteous at the frolicking behavior of my peers who enjoyed laughter and a good party.

These are but a few symptoms I have shared with my W.A. friends at our meeting. Others in the meeting experienced similar feelings that led to burnout and isolation. So we decided to have a meeting set aside every several weeks to explore the solution of play in our lives, as an antidote to our disease.

When I hit bottom eight years ago, I worked a forty-hour plus week with my weeknights filled with spiritual work in and outside of church. The next year, a friend offered to accompany him and others to a weekend at the beach. The ocean, three hours from my front door, invited me into discovering something new about myself. The pleasure of running up and down the shoreline, being chased by waves, throwing myself into water. I constructed sand castles and accepted the stares and comments of children as they observed my handmade creations, something I hadn't aspired to in over thirty years. Lying in the sun with the sound of waves crashing upon the shore put me in a succession of naps throughout the afternoon, the cadence of the waves simmered through my body well into the night and as I awoke the following morning. Speaking of mornings, I rose prior to the sun's ascending in the east above the ocean. Standing on the beach, I witnessed the dolphins voyage along the coastline. With their presence ten yards offshore, I accepted their playful energy into my heart.

I carried this experience back to my home where workaholism runs rampant among government workers and technological gurus. I attended sporting events with an attitude of enjoyment. I enrolled at a local recreation center and played in the pool, turning somersaults underwater and participating in a water aerobics class dancing with hits from the sixties. Approaching these activities, I got out of my head and into my body. Feeling the heart's lightness as my response to the world rather than the intellect's "why." Yes, I experience slips in this endeavor when I find my days and weeks overloaded. However I accept this aspect of my recovery, like other aspects, one day at a time.

Play is a four-letter word and a behavior where God wants us to experience her pleasure.

# Enough

W.A. got started in our metro area and was soon quite robust: there were four active recovery meetings each week, one as large as twenty members, and three more in nearby cities. Perhaps the local Intergroup had already started as well. At the time I was fresh into recovery and part of a small Adult Children of Alcoholics (ACA) group; another member had attended a recent ACA conference, and she shared the tapes. One was on workaholism. It seemed I could immediately identify with what the speaker and participants were saying—and also I heard mention of those local W.A. meetings in our area.

Like that conference tape on workaholism, our early W.A. meetings seemed mostly about "The Problem": in our community, little workaholic recovery experience had yet been built up, perhaps unlike the first W.A. meeting founded years earlier in New Rochelle, New York. So naturally New Rochelle would get lots and lots of phone calls with lots and lots of our questions.

Just what the problem might be—our disorder around work and activity—seemed murky at best to most of us. Was it working compulsively and way too much? Was it overdosing on excessive corrosive activity in general? Was it constant worrying and fear about work performance and careers and wage earning? Was it compulsive inactivity, underemployment, or a roller coaster of frantic activity and unexplainable unemployment? (Further into recovery, some of us either found an answer or simply lost interest in the search.)

Another big confusion: was active service in W.A. part of recovery, or just another continuation of our compulsivity? We seemed to share a sense of uncertainty, work-related exhaustion and grimness, fear, bewilderment, and more. (Someone mentioned having all the early-recovery grace of a dog on the freeway.) Many of us reported keeping our noses earnestly near the grindstone of self-improvement. Certainly we were not a fun-loving bunch.

Some of us thought we could learn a great deal about this from certain recovered cardiac patients. One member's horrible story was of starting a critical business negotiation, experiencing a heart attack right in the middle of the meeting, then staying to finish the lengthy negotiation and only then finally driving himself to the emergency room. For some other W.A. members there was even greater tragedy—one was murdered (whether job-related was unclear), another committed suicide, and still another did die of a work-related heart attack.

Our workaholism seemed to keep most of us away from any real closeness with another human being. Many of us shared how we would rush heedlessly along, impatient with anything that slowed us down. There seemed to be almost a compulsion to go on to the end, to get it over with **now**. Other sharings would relate how time after time some of us had made hopeless attempts to find social confidence in the workplace. Some of us practically demanded to be valued and appreciated and even doted upon in the workplace. When this didn't take place, we often felt a deep sense of not belonging. Our over-dependence and neediness sometimes turned people from us. For some of us this led to excuses for under-performing, or reasons to leave, or behavior that got us fired.

One W.A member in particular at the time seemed to stand out. He was in coupleship with another recovering person. His story about his workaholism was full of pain. He had suffered a near-fatal stroke, yet much later now he looked and sounded calm and content. When he took me on as a W.A. sponsee, he already had ten years in Al-Anon, and that level of recovery and serenity was very attractive. In his home is where we heard my W.A. Fourth Step.

This connection with my W.A. sponsor brought unexpected hope and gratitude, and somehow more of a sense of purpose. It was suggested that it was not a question of how much we worked, or when, or why, but of how our working affected our lives—what happened when we worked compulsively. In another program there had been some good advice: "Go to meetings. Don't [do the addictive activity] between meetings. Get into service. Do a Fourth Step. And you'll probably never have to [    ] again." The support of my W.A. sponsor, freely given, offered similar hope around my work disorder. Also, because of his influence, I was surprised soon to find myself making two spontaneous sincere amends at work.

Sometime around this period I found myself writing out my W.A. story as I understood it at the time. There was lots of vomiting up the past and the bewilderment of the present, but little actual recovery or strength to share or give away—and seemingly little realistic hope for the future. In our local Intergroup there had been animated talk about creating a W.A. "Big Book," and I was quite stimulated at the splendid prospect of having my own admirable personal history among the very first stories.

That Intergroup effort faded out. Still I found myself writing my work history, and it became quite a revelation: always seeking prestigious companies to associate with, maybe to build up my own low self-confidence; always drawn to ultra-rapidly-growing enterprises, on the bleeding edge of their competitive field, probably for the excitement and adrenaline rush and splendid chaos; stumbling into situations requiring a fixer and a prescriber of remedies. Once hired, then over-doing and over-exerting, to display a mistake-undetectable, praise-evoking work product. Coolly certain of my indispensability, or else anxiously concerned I might not be. Never being a quitter, not stopping, not giving up. Time management classes, stress-management seminars. Protecting my work to keep it beyond criticism.

Also in my story I saw that in all my work history I'd accepted every single one of the many jobs ever offered me. This was not a pleasant awareness. Somehow this might mean in reality I was adrift and directionless in my work life, not purposeful and in command, as I wanted to believe; that I was heavily into people pleasing, grandiosity, and approval seeking. My vanity was exposed. Not take-it-or-leave-it or independent, the prideful balloon floating above it all. One particularly ugly phrase stood out: "A close, watchful intolerance of other people's incompetence."

I got to see how my other addiction had masked my workaholism, how I had sustained the courage and bluster and craziness of my compulsive over-working via the medication of that first addiction. How running ten miles a day and graphing my results and insisting on lowering my times all made drudge and work out of what many others found as release and recreation. How during after-work socializing and with a few relaxants in me, those guarded co-workers who would keep their distance during the workday suddenly found me amusing, engaging, spontaneous, and charming.

And then how unsupported withdrawal had left me vulnerable to a severe suicidal depression. I had been in the rigid habit of not seeking other's help or not accepting help offered, and so I had no clue that the first non-workaholic weeks and months were likely to be periods of great emotional vulnerability. I fled a high-level position, feeling wretchedly inadequate and impotent in all ways; I found myself in bed for weeks and weeks, trying to sleep round the clock, while my partner maintained a suicide watch and joined Al-Anon. A psychiatrist's insistence pushed me into 12-Step meetings. In my own experience, convalescence from the illness of active workaholism would take a long time.

In early recovery I found myself feeling so worthless and inadequate that I sought out and took tiny volunteer positions only. I reasoned that if I wasn't getting paid, I couldn't be judged worthless or get fired for not earning my keep.

Repeatedly during my first few years in recovery I tried forcing myself back into careers and industries where I'd been before my bottom. One prospective job was described as "A rocket ride—and you're hanging on to the outside of the rocket by your fingernails." That sounded just fine with me—apparently, falling back into denial was quite easy and effortless. But the jobs didn't last. One contract ended and wasn't renewed. Three other outfits fired me. Severance pay was nice, but the feeling of shame wasn't. It seemed more and more that working for others or with others was impossible ever again somehow and for some mysterious reason. Feeling sorry for myself and ashamed, still I tried three other careers briefly, in entry-level jobs, and none were a fit, so I tried starting a couple of businesses on my own, but these failed too.

Yet in some ways I was feeling better, or at least different: no late-night work; no bringing the briefcase and work papers into the bedroom; giving myself leeway and saying I'd arrive somewhere between 10:00 and 10:30 but not 10:17 sharp; still having "Working Dreams," but not as frightening; attending spiritual retreats; not always in the freeway fast lane; saying no; meditating, mental health days, pausing, napping.

The former anxiety attacks, near-fainting spells, and terrifying panic attacks had ceased; I'd cut back to decaf coffee, learned to walk slower, learned occasionally to look at people directly and listen when then talked to me. But still I could get pulled into a seemingly critical project or deadline, then resent all interruption, especially from family.

Several years into recovery, I was active in three Twelve Step fellowships, active in service in each, and feeling good about myself when centered just on these fellowships. (The Twelve Step principle of regular service rotation can be a spiritual safety net for a recovering workaholic.) More and more, it seemed, I was coming to share in how we get our true feelings sorted out, by the simple means of expressing them aloud in meetings.

But the contrast became more and more jarring between joy of service and fellowship versus job failures and getting fired and rejected in interviews and with near-zero income and near-zero prospects. The need to make amends to the IRS became paralyzing while mandatory. Particularly humiliating and despairing was my first day in the two-hour-long line for Unemployment Benefits. How had I gotten to this point! At least I had remembered just in time not to wear my best business suit that day. (Some people in meetings tell how they'd much prefer being in a life-threatening situation than an ego-threatening situation.)

Then at a Step Study there was yet another reading of a passage heard over and over. This time a member who knew me well repeated it. She had experienced a work bottom similar to mine, yet now she was thriving in her chosen field, enthused about her work, making adequate money, dignified and engaging and at peace in her recovery after many years of floundering. The reading was:

> "This all meant, of course, that we were still far off balance. When a job still looked like a mere means of getting money rather than an opportunity for service, when the acquisition of money for financial independence looked more important than a right dependence upon God, we were still the victims of unreasonable fears. And these were fears which would make a serene and useful existence, at any financial level, quite impossible."
>
> (Excerpted from the Chapter on Step Twelve in Alcoholics Anonymous Twelve Steps and Twelve Traditions, 121)

Well, this time that reading somehow struck home. It must have been important that my friend was doing the reading, and especially because now she had made it to the other side, out from under, happy joyous and free. This maybe is the point at which I came to accept my workaholism and its many implications. That active workaholism no longer meant excitement and self-satisfaction and winning at life, it meant sickness and sorrow. The initial exposure to W.A. years earlier had brought the awareness, and in the several following years came the acceptance. Some people say that powerlessness gets us here, while tolerance and patience and humility can keep us here.

Other recovery literature addresses progress in recovery, the spiritual awakening that can occur for us: "Our lives unaccountably transformed.... What we have received is a free gift, and yet usually, at least in some small part, we have made ourselves ready to receive it." That seems to sum up the rest of my story these past ten years.

After some more time I found myself in my current service (paying) position, which is with a small non-profit bookstore. But in between I started a business, Recovery Job Support. I delivered newspapers around the metro area for a weekly recovery publication. And a friend knew of a need where he worked, at a residential home for newly recovering Latino alcoholics—"Just to help us out, you know, maybe for just a few weeks"—a clerical position, minimum wage plus some meals. This two-week taxi job continued for three years.

Also I took a position at that community recovery center where our Adult Children of Alcoholics (A.C.A.) group had met, and where W.A. Intergroup now met. The place had another special significance for me: early in my recovery and as a sour atheist I'd attended weekly guided meditations there, led by a couple in recovery, and eventually found myself connected with my spirit guide and a Higher Power.

Of course two jobs meant a lesser degree of financial instability and maybe even the prospect of financial recovery, but then the many hours of work did hint lightly at a slippery slope for my workaholism. Thankfully the jobs kept me around lots of other recovering people. One person I leaned on as my recovery-home job sponsor had 30 years of continuous sobriety when we met. He'd been in and out of prisons and treatment nine times, before the 10th try took. He was calm and caring. Every time he saw me he'd brighten and smile and affectionately call me his "Esteemed Colleague." It was healthy just to be around him and his calm wisdom. His many and persistent tries at a contented recovery were an inspiration.

And then one day at home was a small ad in a little neighborhood newspaper. Seeking a person with marketing and retail experience, working with volunteers, to manage a new non-profit bookshop. "Proceeds support our local public libraries." I was re-reading the ad, feeling excited and hopeful, when my partner appeared. "Listen to this!" I yelped as I recited the ad. She considers me a tease and a pleasant buffoon, and she thought I was making it all up, so I handed her the ad.

Close by. A ten-minute commute. Active in our local community. A kind of a service position, really. Full-time position. Low pay and no medical or other benefits to speak of, but my steadily employed professional partner had full benefits for both of us. And...BOOKS! I loved books. And as it turned out, it was a store I'd been frequenting delightedly for the past two years: it had been a lunch-break destination for me during two other local jobs I'd tried and flunked. As we stared at the ad, I recalled during one earlier bout of debilitating unemployment what a career counselor had said: "Each person is the exact right key for a particular lock somewhere. The task is to find that lock."

I dashed off a letter, sharing my enthusiasm for the store and the position, matching my background to their requirements, concerned I'd be seen as way over-qualified or a flake or job-hopper, or too old or something. They interviewed me, they re-interviewed me, they hired me, later they told me they had received a hundred resumes, and now this Fall marks my tenth anniversary with the store.

So this current position really does seem like a gift, in a way. And it does seem the program literature is true and not just hokey and Pollyannaish—we do make ourselves ready in some small ways to receive these gifts.

This present service job with pay does have its temptations toward workaholism. There's always way more to do and do perfectly than available time and energy. Sub-par store selling for a month or longer can get me questioning my adequacy.

The fifty part-time staffers are all volunteers and can contribute or desist as they choose to, and so great power and vast ego-inflating resources are not readily at my disposal. Lots of heavy boxes of books await my heroic exertion, or I can deal with them just a few volumes at a time. There's a benign Board of Directors, but they too are part-time volunteers with lives away from the store, so there's negligible audience for approval seeking, no unreasonable or unappreciatively harsh authority figures to resent, and no career ladder to climb. There are no shareholders to enrich, no stupendous annual goals and aggressive expansion plans to fulfill.

And I've learned to be a "quitter" and live with myself afterward; it's said in program that being a "quitter" can take courage and make very good sense if we're quitting something that is not good for us. For me all of this is a valuable daily reminder of powerlessness, and it's a fun, relaxed enterprise.

Some staffers and some customers are in recovery themselves, so there's on-the-job occasion for in-the-moment sharing of gratitudes as well as the painful difficulties (a parental death, a mentally ill adult child, the puzzle of money for retirement). Another sense of service comes from the fact that for many customers and many staffers the bookshop is a haven during the over-stressing workday.

As I look at what I've written to this point, it feels like this is becoming too long. There's just not enough time to shorten it! Enough.

And so, participation in program and gradual recovery have extended over lots of years. More and more it feels true we act ourselves into right living rather than think ourselves into right acting. It really does work, the Promises can come true, there is to be found a contented freedom and release from compulsive working and excessive activity.

# How to Make Decisions: A Tug of War with a Surprise Third Step Ending

Making *any* decision had always been difficult for me, even when I was a child. But making the *major* decision to retire was as hard for workaholic me as sobering up is for an alcoholic. Then I learned it's never too late to seek God's caring will.

When my company announced an incentive to retire early, my first reaction shocked me: "I'd love to!" I immediately scolded myself, discounting my feelings and reasoning "Nonsense. You're only 52. What would people think? Your father worked till 69, found part-time work at 74, and worked till he died. Don't throw away your high-paying job just because you've come to hate it." (I was exhausted from overwork and had been hunting a new position for months.)

The incentive required retirement before July 1989 to obtain medical benefits; after July, new rules mandated working till 55 for such benefits. Reason conscientiously insisted, "Hang on for three more years, or the whole world will think you're lazy." Feelings timidly objected: "Don't feel guilty. Please talk it over with someone objective who likes you, before missing this opportunity."

So I told my doctor and was surprised when he said, "Go for it! You've fought insomnia, burnout, and countless stress-related illnesses for years." But Reason righteously preached, "You can't afford it."

Weeks later my attorney said, "Sounds good. You have enough savings. And you need time to empty your late mother's home, where she lived for 52 years. Your idea to rent it and do part-time freelance editing is excellent."

Why didn't I feel reassured? The inner decision-making tug of war wakened me every night, Reason fighting with Feelings: "You have an obligation to continue. Who else could please those perfectionist customers as well? How would you stand the loneliness—no office to escape to?" But Feelings persisted: "Two experts think you work too hard and need a change."

Discouraged, I consulted my career counselor. She helped me prepare a "retirement budget." She also had me list retirement's advantages and disadvantages. I wrote as many pros as cons. Only I could decide, but she obviously believed that downshifting was OK. She knew people who were happily living a simpler lifestyle after mid-career change. Her common sense made retiring seem respectable. And she pointed out I could always find another job. But I still hesitated. Time was running short.

Desperate, I thought about visiting my work addiction therapist. But I already knew what she would patiently repeat: "Go with how you feel." Each night, Reason battered Feelings. I was so weary. I missed Mother, who had died of cancer only a few months before. I wished I could talk to her. Wondering if grief was fueling my indecision, I visited a grief support group, where I discovered an inspiring book on transitions that actually recommended "lying fallow" as opposed to producing constantly—a whole new idea to me.

I also regularly attended several Twelve Step meetings modeled on Alcoholics Anonymous. I slowly realized that my workaholism had me stuck on Step Three—"Made a decision to turn our will and our lives over to the care of God as we understood Him." How simple. Here was the answer about how to decide what to do.

After six months of indecision, I prayed: "God, I'm turning my life over to You." My fears left. The tug of war ended. I had my first peaceful sleep in months. Next day I signed the retirement papers, meeting the deadline with enough time to give a month's notice. Was my boss ever surprised! Even before I left the job, life began blossoming, with unexpected people helping me understand God's will for me and feel His caring.

For example, on Mother's Day weekend, Feelings kept nudging me to quit my housework and visit the garden store, which I would normally avoid on a crowded holiday. In case it might be God's will, I drove there. The parking lot traffic jam made me cross. A police officer motioned me to park near an unfamiliar door. I almost walked into M., loaded down with tomato plants, coming out that door. (Before establishing his own firm, he was my company's public relations director.) When he heard about my upcoming retirement, he said "Great! Work part-time for me." We shook hands on it. The roof gutter began dripping water on our heads, so he left, and I bought my impatiens. Later, the career counselor laughed heartily: "That was no coincidence. The water was God baptizing your future freelancing career."

At work, several coworkers confided that they envied me. There was no sign of the anticipated ridicule. A heartwarming eighty people came to my farewell party, where I gave away "going out of business" cards printed with the serenity prayer.

Once I began paying attention to God's will and trusting in His care, help came from unlikely sources. Soon after retiring, for example, I was thrilled to win a supermarket gift certificate equal to nearly half my monthly pension check, perhaps today's version of manna from heaven.

Each time I tried to inventory the objects in Mother's home, I began crying after only an hour and had to stop. Then, while sitting at her little old desk, I discovered her membership book in the women's club at the university where my father had taught. Feelings whispered, "Call their thrift shop." I recognized God's nudge in the whisper, phoned, and learned that the professors' wives had raised $11,000 the year before by selling used household goods. They could use anything I gave them. I quit crying at Mother's house, because I was now helping raise scholarship funds. Both parents would have been delighted. That autumn, the thrift shop filled two vans with useful things from Mother's home. It felt good to plan for the future, no longer weeping over breaking up a home full of memories.

Even my first customer was a gift from God. I had decided to rent the house before I began freelancing. But one wintry day while I was hunting kitchen vinyl floor covering, the sales clerk begged me to do some special editing. Her former husband was in prison and had discovered a talent for writing while taking courses behind bars. They had been praying for guidance. Was he good enough to pursue writing as a career? She paid me to critique his writing samples, do library research he needed, and prepare a report to help him decide whether to pursue his dream.

I began attending a professional freelancers' support group. A speaker from a publisher who visited the group eventually began using my freelance services. A., another woman in the group, gave me an excellent customer when she moved away. When I got around to contacting M., he no longer had work suited to my skills, but I already had other customers. His early encouragement had served its purpose, and the turndown did not devastate my faith.

My worry about loneliness after retirement was unfounded, too. I had survived more than 60 unfulfilling dating relationships, most sabotaged by my workaholism, and had bitterly resigned myself to spinsterhood after a former boyfriend had broken my heart. God used my friend E. to urge me to join the group for divorced and separated people at a church. The group welcomed me, where the support, reading, sharing, and exercises in letting go helped me understand, accept, talk about, and overcome the grief I had unsuccessfully hidden and ignored for a decade. I symbolically poured out my festering, angry heartache by dumping a treasured sand-art bowl from my ex-boyfriend. The tiny colored grains spilled into a box where I recycled soil for potting plants. Then I went to bed and had a good cry, which left me limp, sleepy, and feeling peaceful. When I woke, I was healed. That healing serenity showed up vividly on "before" and "after" psychological questionnaire graphs from the group. My trust of people skyrocketed from 10 percent to 65 percent. This course and the Twelve Step groups taught me new, healthier ways of relating to people.

Trust built my confidence and self-esteem. Now that I felt like a whole person, I began dating, enjoying it for the first time, and getting to know a variety of men. Then my Higher Power brought J. into my life. For our first date, we chose to walk around a pretty lake in a lovely park. We walked many hours in many more parks during the sunshiny autumn, talking and sharing deep-felt dreams.

J. and I were married a year later. It still seems like an impossible dream come true that someone 54 and retired would get married for the first time, becoming an instant stepmother, mother-in-law, and grandma. But then I'm getting used to God's plans being much better than mine. One day at a time, I continue listening to my feelings to discover God's will through His still small voice. Only now I listen more confidently. Even Reason admits that it's the best way to make decisions.

My first draft of this story ended here. However, the story does not end with "happily ever after." There is an unusual sequel, and the ending has changed drastically. Less than a year into the marriage, J. left me. Another tug of war began in my soul. I started questioning God's will as soon as J. told me that he was moving out. However, something happened on moving day that not only warmed my heart, but also re-centered my faith. Shortly after we met he had tried to give me a beautiful silver cross, but I felt I did not know him well enough to accept such an expensive gift at the time. I reminded him of that the day before he moved out, and he sadly told me he had lost the cross, but that he would have loved for me to have it. I was deeply disappointed.

Late in the afternoon the next day, about an hour before he drove away, we were in the basement with the movers and a friend of mine, all exhausted. To simplify the packing yet to be done, I offered to see that a charity receive any unwanted leftovers, and I asked J. to check the remaining debris, broken boxes, and miscellaneous trash in one area of the basement. He wandered over, bent down to pick up a dirty old broken plastic dishpan—and turned toward me in surprise. He lifted out of it a small cloth jeweler's pouch. He opened the blue pouch and handed me the missing cross.

My heart filled with warmth and serenity. I realized instinctively that my decision to marry him had not been wrong after all. I was so grateful for this unexpected sign from God that His will was indeed at work, even in this painful parting, and that I was in His care—despite the ending of my marriage. This beautiful incident is too full of symbolic meaning and hope to be mere coincidence. The painful tug of war in my soul ended because Step Three and my Higher Power are intact and remain so to this day.

# It's About the Body

Around the age of five I started saying that I wanted to be a doctor when I grew up. Considering that no one in my family ever had finished high school, the year was 1950, the schools in my small town were among the poorest in the country and I was a girl, my plan seemed pretty far fetched—but not entirely.

My mother used to tell the story that I was so strong-willed as a child that she decided when I was two years old to "let me raise myself." For a long time I liked feeling that I was running the show, and it really scared me.

When I started school I excelled, but sensed that being ahead of the class came at a price. I remember standing in front of the class in second grade staring at my feet, trying not to catch the eyes of the other children as I ate the cookies the teacher gave me, and sometimes another student or two, each week for getting all the spelling words right. I spent much of my childhood alone.

Despite the isolation, or perhaps because of it, I felt compelled to achieve. Besides giving me an identity as "the brain," making straight A's helped me feel acceptable. The awards and accolades also drew attention away from what was going on in the family—the addictions, affairs, unwanted pregnancies, the subtle or not-so-subtle abuse. A lot seemed to be riding on my success.

In high school I fueled myself with extra food—the more sugary or salty or greasy the better. I didn't do well at sports, so I rarely played. When I gained weight, which at times I did, I dieted as compulsively as I ate. I drank can after can of diet cola. Extra-curricular activities were chosen for what would look good on my college application. I finished first in my high school class and was accepted to college.

The higher I climbed, the higher the stakes became. I felt as though I was bluffing my way along, and didn't really belong in any of the places I was striving so hard to get. I continued to turn to substances for "fortification." I used caffeine and sugar to keep me going in order to study—27 cups of coffee one night. I must not have been able to get any amphetamines that particular night or I wouldn't have needed all that coffee. I graduated college with honors.

I went on to medical school and did get an M.D. degree. My father had once had aspirations of his own of becoming a doctor. For a long time I resented his having "foisted" his dream onto me. I now consider that I adopted his dream as my own. There was a point, however, when the dream became a nightmare.

Parts of my medical training were traumatic, not just the grueling hours, but the sights of people sick and injured, sometimes in violent ways. I mostly felt numb to the effects of what I witnessed. For a very long time I was able to ignore the sensations of tiredness or revulsion, and ignore my own physical and emotional pain. In a sense I needed to be "out of my body." To slow down and feel was too painful or too frightening or both. Years later, when I got into recovery, I found out that I didn't exactly know how to tell I was thirsty. I had focused my concern on other people's bodies and needs, but had very little awareness of my own.

When I was growing up, nobody in my family had seemed to know what to do with strong feelings, especially grief when someone died. My mentors in medical school didn't seem to know either. A sense of failure was the common response to loss. Feelings of vulnerability, confusion, neediness, sadness, and even anger could be sidestepped, at least temporarily, if I/we stayed in constant work mode. Being compulsive has its rewards in my profession.

My personal brand of workaholism manifested not only as compulsive activity but also as mental obsession—relentless, faultfinding, nit-picking, worry, and negativity directed at myself. Oddly these thoughts seemed to serve as a form of protection—perhaps from failure or rejection or abandonment. The obsessions gave me an illusion of control. If I were to blame for events and outcomes, I must still be in charge.

In the face of strong emotions, mine or anyone else's, I went "into my head," into the future (planning), or into the past (regretting, replaying past events). There was an almost constant awareness that if I made a significant mistake someone could die. Guilt and regret felt familiar and safer than profound sadness or even joy or happiness, which, of course, could be taken away. It astounds me that I preferred to hang out in my head as much as I did, despite what went on there! The truth is, I am powerless over obsessive thoughts.

I hid behind my white coat. There was a person there, but I had a hard time finding her. I could be warm and approachable at times, but friends knew that I disappeared for months on end. Closeness felt suffocating. In order to avoid conflict, I avoided people whenever I could. My schedule barely left room to breathe, but contemplating change made me uneasy. To "let up" felt like failure. I could justify a vacation if it was connected with a medical conference. Leaving work at the end of a day was difficult. I would stand at my desk moving papers from one stack to another, unable to get anything accomplished, but unable to call it a day. There was always more to do.

I sometimes felt burdened by having a physical body. It was one more thing to take care of. When I got sick, I went in to work anyway. Slowing down seemed risky or even overwhelming—as though I'd die or cease to exist if I stopped. It was almost as though I was risking annihilation. Since my identity was my work, in a manner of speaking, this was a valid fear.

Although I was in the habit of ignoring my body, I could feel anxiety and the sensation of my heart slamming around in my chest every time I raced to the emergency room in response to a call. I raced other places as well--pretty much everywhere I went. I performed tasks hurriedly, and often resentfully. Despite all the activity, and how revved up I felt inside, I also felt sort of deadened and numb. Many of my actions were reflexive and unconscious.

For me, workaholism brings together grandiosity and low self-esteem--particularly the latter. I believed that my patients deserved someone smarter and better than I, but I also wanted to be in charge of everything myself. Because of my insecurity, I tried very hard to never make anybody angry or upset—a difficult task when surrounded by people who are scared and in pain. Despite all the effort I made, no amount of knowledge or obsessive attention to detail, and no amount of people pleasing allowed me to manage my life or the forces of nature. Everything around me seemed to be, and was, out of my control. I felt alone. I didn't know to ask for help. My constant doing lead me to a state of disillusionment and despair. I was miserable. No matter what I accomplished it was never enough. Despite the fact that I had chosen my profession, I felt resentful and put upon.

My physical health suffered. I got stomach pains and headaches. I developed signs of an ulcer. I vomited blood.

I felt bombarded by all types of requests, including social invitations. My relationships suffered. The man I lived with during my training, and eventually married, had similar attitudes toward work as mine. He encouraged me in my career, but the child we had together did not understand our chaotic schedules and long absences. My job, even more than my husband's, required shifts at the hospital that kept me away more than 36 hours at a stretch. Despite my own absences, I became resentful of my husband's unavailability and reacted by withdrawing from him. As a consequence I felt even more abandoned. Whatever time and energy I had left over from work, I gave as best I could to my son. I was so exhausted from trying to be "on top of everything," it is a miracle I could relate at all.

I recall a day I left my son home alone for many hours when he was really too young to tend to himself. I believed that he would be OK, but leaving him to go to work wasn't rational. It was a compulsion. I didn't think: What's important here? I just went. Work for me was an addiction—something I did compulsively and couldn't stop doing without help.

In my early thirties I had gone into therapy hoping to learn how to have more successful relationships. I remember one day sitting in my psychiatrist's waiting room, still rushing inside from fighting heavy traffic to get from my office to his. Just as he came to call me in for my appointment, I noticed my nose was bleeding and the center of my upturned palm was filling with blood. That morning I had repeated a familiar ritual—inhaling line after line of cocaine, ignoring the burning sensation inside my nose. I had finished my supply just as the sky was starting to lighten. I had been at it all night.

For many days in a row during my morning commute, I had the recurrent thought of swerving my car full speed into the concrete embankment along the side of the road. I couldn't imagine a life other than the one I had worked so hard to create since the age of five. The way I managed to find time for myself was to steal it. Using cocaine gave me the illusion of more time.

Eventually, during my all-nighters, I began to have heart palpitations. One night when I tried to count my pulse and couldn't, because I couldn't count that fast, I admitted to myself, that the cocaine could (and possibly would) kill me. I said aloud to whomever or whatever was listening: "Dear God, if you get me through this night, I'll never touch this stuff again."

Thankfully, when I got to this stage of desperation, I had people in my life who were already in recovery. They gave me literature to read and offered to go with me to meetings. It was after I got clean from the substance addictions that I realized I was also using work as a drug, to medicate or mask feelings, to alter my mood, to escape aspects of reality I didn't know how to face any other way. The fact was that the way I was treating myself was still abusive and insane.

Nowadays I believe that my compulsive behaviors had a purpose. They helped me survive. They protected a core part of me that did risk annihilation in childhood. At times I felt overwhelmed, but had nowhere to turn. I learned to use substances and compulsive behaviors as a way to bind my anxiety and to try to replace what was missing.

Once I started getting help for my food and drug addictions and began to wake up to how I was feeling, I could no longer work the hours I was working with the same frenetic drive. I needed to make a change, but was ambivalent. I had a distorted view of my role both at home and at work--something just short of omniscience and omnipotence. Carrying what felt like the weight of the world on my shoulders was exhausting. I didn't fully understand the concept of surrender, or "turning it over." Even in recovery I was still trying to get straight A's.

Being genuinely present with my husband or son (or parents!) required skills I didn't possess. Practicing medicine felt easier. Despite my shortcomings, I was respected by my colleagues. My patients and their families loved me and I loved them, but I had grown to hate my job and dreaded going to work.

Did I have such a fragile ego that it needed shoring up eighteen or twenty or twenty-four hours a day? I knew that I needed to make a change, but I was stuck. I wanted a clear sign about what to do. Anything, up to and including a burning bush, would be ok by me.

One of my best friends, who is a member of W.A. and A.A., had told me about a time she got help making a career decision by meditating on her choices. I had tried meditating in the past, back when I was still working addictively. I felt as though I would jump out of my skin. The restlessness and jumpiness gradually shifted a little over time. One night I went to an Eleventh Step meditation meeting in my area, determined to get an answer to my question about whether or not to leave my job, and leave medicine. During the meditation, when I felt somewhat relaxed, I asked: "Should I stay in medicine?"

Truthfully, as I asked the question, I thought I knew the answer already. I assumed that whoever or whatever answers such questions was going to direct me to stay put because medicine was obviously the most "useful" and worthwhile option I had at the time. (My version of the ruler of the universe back then had a very strong work ethic.) The answer to my question came in auditory form. I literally heard the words: "God is great. God is good. You are lovable. You are loved." The voice was not the usual voice in my head. It wasn't a black and white, "you should do this" kind of answer. The voice sounded kind.

Sometimes when I tell the meditation story, I omit the sentences with the word God. For me, the word has associations to fanaticism from which I want to separate myself. Over time I have pieced together a concept of Higher Power. I feel a connection with something larger and smarter and stronger and more dependable and compassionate and forgiving than myself. The connection with this something helps quell my anxiety, allowing me to live more freely and enjoy my life.

For a very long time I tried like hell to be perfect. Nowadays I'd rather be honest and real. I feel more secure and far less overwhelmed when feelings arise. When I have someone or something to turn to, I feel less burdened and less alone. In order to stay sober, to refrain from harmful compulsions, I have had to reach out to both give and receive help. In the process I get to be an ordinary human with ordinary wants and needs. I get to have a life.

I fuel myself differently these days. I get sustenance and pleasure from art and music, dancing, walking the hills near my house and especially from my relationships. I have friendships beyond my wildest dreams. I have a job that I like that has social relevance.

At night when I wake up I can meditate to calm myself. It's relaxing to just breathe. I take pleasure in my body and being in true human connection. Slowing down and leaving things out has made more space for me to feel and notice what's going on inside me and around me. Being more conscious in the present moment makes me feel more alive.

I think of recovery as having given me my life back. Sometimes I feel exuberant and childlike. Strangers on the street comment on my smile. Whereas I once felt assaulted and bombarded by people, I now seek company and revel in the connection. In a sense one of my first conscious experiences of spiritual connection, being "one among many," came from reading a newspaper article about Workaholics Anonymous and realizing that I qualified for the program. I was not alone. I definitely belonged.

Practicing the principle of anonymity has been good for me. I offer my skills and experience in the form of service, but instead of hoping to impress or please or appease someone, I participate because of how pleasant it feels to be useful. My identity is no longer synonymous with my profession. At times when I feel sad or afraid, I am still glad to be alive. I am grateful. A lot of the time I know that I am acceptable. I am lovable. I am loved.

I have been able to reduce my work schedule and even take a sabbatical. I won't pretend that once I began to deal with my workaholism that everything was rosy. The year that I took my sabbatical, I felt raw and exposed. Some nights I woke up terrified. I was experiencing feelings that I had kept at bay for years. Luckily by then I had built a support system. A friend frequently reminds me, "Life is not for sissies." Neither is recovery. In contradistinction to the hero slaying the dragon single-handedly, recovery takes community. I might be able to pretend that I succeeded in my career by single-minded determination and force of will, but I know that I don't recover from negative obsessions and destructive compulsions alone.

Since coming into recovery, I have experienced a physical and spiritual awakening. Perhaps they are the same thing. My sponsor said recently, "It's all about the body." I think I know what she means. I feel my connection to myself and to a Higher Power as a physical experience in my body, for instance as a sense of excitement and pleasure when I wake up in the morning. I feel my emotional connections to other people as physical sensations as well. Listening to someone tell the absolute truth can cause a tingle or bring tears to my eyes. The contrast from earlier times is remarkable since for so much of my life I was alienated from my body.

Several years into recovery I started taking classes in mindfulness meditation and yoga. One day a meditation teacher mentioned that she no longer resisted washing dishes, that as she washed them, especially the bowls, she imagined bathing the belly of the baby Buddha. Some days I try her method. When I start to tell myself, "I don't have time for this," I remember that I can "let go" and come back to my breath.

This morning, standing in the golden autumn sunlight at my kitchen sink, I slowly washed several bowls and utensils, glad to be conscious, glad to be able to perceive my hands in the water and my feet on the floor, grateful for the Twelve Steps of Workaholics Anonymous, and grateful to have nowhere that I have to rush to all day.

The condensed version of my story is: I used compulsive overworking as a drug. I couldn't stop despite negative consequences in every aspect of my life. No human power (not mine or that of any other individual acting alone) could have relieved my compulsion. I found relief in community, in connection to myself and other workaholics, and a connection with a transcendent power that I experience in the fellowship and in relationship to other members of the group.

# Keeping Busy for Life

My father was a general practitioner, a doctor who practiced the traditional way—total availability to his patients. He received calls at home, had a telephone at the side of his bed and a hook for it on the dining room table. There were no answering services or on-call schedules in those days. He and I didn't interact much. When he came home in the evenings he read Astounding Stories magazines in his car until Mom called him to eat. In the evenings he read Saturday Evening Post stories to her as she knitted or darned socks. On the weekends he worked in the yard, where I sometimes helped, trimming vines and hedges and burning the trimmings, mixing cement and building stone walls and barbecues, laying walks of old brick, or other yard projects. Sometimes he'd be in his woodshop turning table legs on an old lathe or sharpening tools on a foot-operated grinding wheel. I learned from watching him, and he answered my questions but didn't offer much conversation. I was busy with friends, too, all of who lived within bicycling distance in our small town.

My mother ran the home and the family. She was always busy with home chores or community involvement. If I wanted to talk to her, she told me to find something to do. If I appeared unoccupied, she or my (older) sisters would say, "Don't just stand there. DO something!" If I complained about something, Mom told me to find something to do and I'd feel better. In those days we didn't know how to notice our feelings, much less describe them.

And so I learned early to follow the rules and keep busy. These learnings have lasted the rest of my life.

In college I joined singing groups and had a job waiting on tables in the campus coffee shop and later in a girls' dorm. I was on the rally committee and had a Model A flivver with no front fenders, which I painted red. I completed four years of college in three years by choosing to take the tough lab courses in the summer instead of vacationing. Later, in medical school, I enjoyed being a subject of class experiments.

In medical school I learned more about doing without feelings. I learned, "Don't get emotionally involved with your patients," which at some level I interpreted as, "Don't have feelings." Also, I learned to see the patient's disorder (the part of the patient I was concerned with) objectively (as an object, a problem to be solved) and to treat them scientifically (like experiments). I accepted the illusion of objectivity. And of course, many times every day doctors do "experiment" with the many options for "treatment."

My wife and I were married a week after I completed medical school and one week before my internship started. For me the internship was the next step in my professional career. For my bride, who fixed meals, saved and rewarmed them, who absorbed my anger over difficulties and who heard my anxieties when the stakes were high, it was a suddenly and totally new life. During that year I had an episode of gastrointestinal bleeding for which no physical cause ever was found and no non-physical cause ever was considered. In retrospect, I believe it was due to stress.

The military draft stopped soon after World War II ended, except for the "doctor draft," and after my internship I went into the Navy. After a year at sea and a year ashore I was released from the Navy. During three more years of medical and surgical residencies, I was found to have an inflammation of one eye for which no cause ever was found. The eye doctor had me use cortisone eye drops, and although the inflammation got better, a cataract formed in that eye and had to be surgically removed. Then glaucoma developed in the same eye, resulting in two operations and years of additional eye drops plus frequent visits to the eye doctor to hold the eye pressure down.

After the residencies were completed, I entered a two-man practice with an established physician. The office was between inner city Oakland and its near suburbs. I took calls from the city telephone exchange at night and covered the practice when the other doctor was away, including delivering babies at any hour. My wife says I was sitting on the edge of my chair whenever I was at home for a meal, anticipating the ring of the telephone. During these years I developed weakness in one vocal cord and one leg at the same time. The throat specialist referred me to a neurologist, who thought it might be M.S. (Multiple Sclerosis), or maybe "a virus." I also saw an orthopedist, who thought it was polio, although I had had all the appropriate immunizations. Both symptoms gradually disappeared. No cause ever was found. No non-physical cause ever was considered. I believe it was "stress."

The prospect of a partnership fell apart, and I left that practice to work in the medical division of the Napa State Hospital. I ran a medical clinic for the hospital community and took a share of night call on the medical wards. When acquaintances in town asked me to run for the school board, I assumed I could do that, too, and found myself campaigning on my own, neither asking for nor receiving either financial or volunteer support. I came in second, thankfully no higher, for, on reflection, I was not gifted for politics and had run to please others.

After four years the state hospital bureaucracy got to me and I looked for a private group. My next twenty-five years were spent in the Family Practice Department of a large multi-specialty clinic. Early in those years I had an episode of numbness on one side of my face. The neurologist called it neuropathy of no specific cause. I believe that it could have been related to stress.

One professor had warned us, "Medicine is a jealous mistress." My experience suggested that Medicine is a Siren calling to physicians to devote their total time and energies to their profession. I often thought it was ideally suited for single people. I realize now that I had lost the distinction between my life and my profession. I was a human doing, not a human being.

At the Clinic I dived into a busy practice. I dictated my notes carefully and learned to keep my feelings out of them, for legal protection. I followed my rule of "doing my share." I volunteered for Clinic committee work over breakfast, county medical society committee work on my afternoons off and giving talks to corporate employees for the American Cancer Society during the lunch break, which back then was two hours long.

The patients I saw each day were really interesting people with many stories of the excitement and pathos of life to tell. I lived off the feelings of those patients. I loved retelling the gist of these stories to my family at home and didn't notice they weren't listening. Years later they were able to tell me they would rather have heard what was going on in my inner world and what I was feeling. I couldn't have told them. I didn't know.

I found that I didn't have time both to give adequate time to my patients and to dictate a complete note without delaying the next patient's visit, and so I made brief written notes and completed the dictation after office hours. In order to be home for dinner I would sometimes go back to the office after dinner to finish dictating. My family saw me mostly coming or going, and even when I was home I was busy moving about the house doing small chores. I didn't notice that our children rarely invited their friends inside our home. Only many years later, after I had begun my own recovery and my children now thought it was safe to talk to me, did they tell me that in their teens they had wanted to leave home.

I didn't know then that I had an addiction to work and was choosing the comfort of the office over the challenge of participating in conversations or games or other pastimes with my family—a choice for which I would pay dearly as the years rolled on.

One son was an avid skier, and the family went skiing on occasional winter and spring weekends. One Sunday afternoon, after two full days of skiing, I squeezed in one last run before going home. Part way down I noticed my fatigue, pulled off and stopped, still a little wobbly. I fell sideways, my skis sticking in the spring snow ("Sierra Cement"), and tore a knee ligament that required an operation and a full leg cast. Once out of the hospital, I used forearm crutches and kept on working every day.

For years our summer vacations were taken at the Boy Scout camp where our boys went, which had a family camp for wives and younger siblings. I was the camp doctor during our week in the mountains, and the environment was so refreshing it never occurred to me that I was working. My wife went along with this a few years beyond the time our boys were graduated and off to college and finally brought to my notice that I didn't need to be doing this any more. Since being awakened, I have enjoyed real vacations!

When portable dictating machines became available, I got one in order to use every available second to do dictation while walking down the hall between patients. This made my voice warble and so I used the portable recorder seated at my desk. After months of using this heavy early model I developed painful tendonitis in the right shoulder. I quit doing committee work on my day off so I could do the leftover dictation then and got a lighter dictating machine.

Due to administrative pressure to see more patients, I chose to shorten my lunch period to one hour. There was still time to eat a hearty meal at the clinic's lunchroom, although I could no longer give the Cancer Society talks. When I couldn't finish all the dictation before supper, I went in early the next morning and finished up before office hours started, sometimes shaving as I drove to work. As my practice got busier, I stopped going to the lunch room at all, shortened the lunch break to half an hour and took a bag lunch so I could stay at my desk and read my mail, answer telephone calls and catch up on dictation while I ate. I no longer participated in Clinic committees because they interfered with my morning catch-up time.

Sometimes my dictation would back up to the weekend, and I would go in on my Saturday morning off or stay as long as necessary into Saturday afternoon to get the dictation completely finished. If something was planned for the family, or, during the summer, if I had a charter sail on the bay scheduled for Saturday with friends, I'd go in at 3:00 a.m. Sunday morning to finish dictating before breakfast. Eventually, the dictation was almost never finished. Monday morning was no longer a fresh start, because there was work hanging over from last week. During appointments I could not interrupt patients to suit the clock, nor did I stop instructions until they were understood, and usually I was behind schedule. Often I was tired in the afternoons. I was found to have a mild case of sleep apnea and yet assumed there was not enough time for a nap.

In the last years of my practice, my son was having difficulty expressing his feelings with his future bride. He sought help and was advised to read, *Co-Dependence, Misunderstood, Mistreated*, by Anne Wilson Schaef. He asked me to read it, and I did. She seemed to be writing about my family. I read more of Schaef's books, learned about Living In Process, and became aware of Twelve Step programs, most importantly Al-Anon and Workaholics Anonymous. I took a whole new look at my relationships with my family, my practice, and myself. I became aware that I was addicted to relationships and to work, for starters. I began a long process of becoming aware of my own feelings, and this felt good. I began to notice how I felt during office interactions.

It occurred to me, but never as a serious consideration, that I could see fewer patients. However, I had a relationship addiction to the clinic. It was a supportive practice environment of high quality, and I chose to go along with the requests of the board to see more patients rather than risk being called a slacker. Also, I was getting close to retirement and chose to keep my earnings as high as possible during my last years so as to earn the highest possible pension—not having gotten appropriate advice for building a retirement fund until late in my practice years.

I began to ask myself, "How do I feel" and "What do I need?" and to follow my intuition when with patients. I gave patients time to cry and on occasion was led to give them hugs, with their permission. My receptionist learned to allow extra time for some people, and I let her know I liked that. I was feeling good, more like a physician!

One weekend, while vacationing with relatives, I slipped entering a hot tub and tore my right shoulder muscles. This required surgery, and for six weeks after the operation my right arm was bound to a bolster on my chest. This was the longest time I had ever stopped working and stopped being busy, and I got my first good look at the way I was slowly killing myself, one illness or injury at a time. I let what I saw sink in, and the thought came that it was time to retire. Although I was 62 and had planned to salt away earnings until age 65, I decided to chance it. My wife was pleased. My department head was surprised and already had a new physician coming who was able to take over my practice. I was able to say goodbye to some of my patients and wrote a letter to all of them. I finished all my remaining dictation and cleaned out my office. The final humbling act, turning in my key, was optional. I struggled with the loss of control that would follow if I did. Finally I really knew it was time to let go of this symbol of special status, authority, and power and turned it in.

The next Monday morning the same cloud of expectation of unfinished paperwork was still hanging over me, and I could hardly believe there was no more paperwork to do! It was another two days before I could greet the morning with real assurance of my new freedom. It was several months before the tension from suppressing my resentment of the constant pressure gradually faded away. I still have a quick response to the first ring of the telephone, only now I have the option to let it ring.

The addiction to work followed me into retirement. The activity is different—more physical and less demanding. I still tend to keep doing whatever I'm doing without remembering to take mealtimes and breaks. If someone asks me to help set up chairs or carry heavy boxes, I feel comfortable, relaxed, in a familiar place, being invited to "do something." Now, though, I no longer need to get busy to remove myself from uncomfortable social situations. Practicing the Twelve Steps has shown me options that have made my life vastly more free and fun. My relationships with my wife and children are being renewed and refreshed. And I accept as a bonus gift of this recovery that the sleep apnea disappeared, I have been able to stop the treatment for glaucoma, and the nerve weaknesses of the early practice years have never returned.

A computer is now a part of my life, and for a time the busyness multiplied. I learned that as long as I run the computer and don't let it run me, it's a wonderful help in many ways. Gradually I have developed limits and set boundaries with the help of practicing the Twelve Steps, making the time to attend W.A. meetings and being in regular touch with a sponsor who doesn't let me ignore or minimize my feelings.

When I feel tired, now I can stop and rest or take a nap. I know there is enough time for what really needs to be done. If an opportunity arises that would keep me from interacting with people or would distract me from the things I need to do for myself, such as rest or read, I can choose to say "no" graciously, without an explanation, and still feel all right about myself.... I make full stops at stop signs.... I go up stairs one at a time....

# A Race with the Clock

"I could work circles around you." I allowed these critical words of my mother's to mold me into a "driven" workaholic. There never has been a moment to be wasted, and I just didn't work fast enough! After living with these attitudes for 59 years, I am exhausted, burned out, over weight, sick and unable to relax in my own home.

Time was my key issue. My favorite workaholic behavior was to get so totally involved in a project, so completely focused on accomplishment, that all the other elements of life were shut out. I didn't use the bathroom. I didn't drink any liquids, my butt would be so numb I'd have trouble standing, and I didn't have a clue as to what time it was. I simply didn't want to be responsible about time. The "charge" of accomplishment was so great that I didn't "care" what time it was. There was a lack of reality with time. I looked at the clock; it was 2:10. I went away and did two hours of work; when I checked the time again I expected the clock to say 2:20; instead it was 4:10. I felt shocked! How could it be that late? I had to rush to my next appointment.... I felt flummoxed by time. But when my sponsor wanted me to write down how long each task took, I found that I really wanted to be vague about time. I liked denial.

In W.A. I learned that this is a victim's stance. One of our group members gave me a tape of a song about dwelling on accomplishment and how you must love the precious person you are, just because you exist! She even typed out the lyrics! I was so touched by the love that exists in W.A. This woman is my daughter's age. She actually spent her time on me. In the Summer 2004 issue of the W.A. newsletter, an article on underscheduling discusses how recording how much time is spent on various projects gave the writer the power to stand up to her boss's insistence that a new task be done quickly. W.A. is teaching me how to live.

When I was a kid the worst thing you could do was waste my father's time. There was so much shame attached to bothering my parents. My fear of wasting time was so great that for our 25th wedding anniversary I filled a whole suitcase with projects and flew it to Hawaii. My husband said, "You can't waste a second, can you?" I had the attitude, "Jesus is coming! Look busy!" There is a saying in our W.A. group that if you say the *A.A. Big Book*'s Third Step Prayer every day you will stop controlling. I was at a gathering where Twelve Step items were being sold and I found a tin canister shaped like an antique mantle clock and labeled "God Can." Now I say the Third Step prayer, write my action plan, and turn over my day by putting it all in the God Can.

"The excitement, rush and pleasurable intensity" (W.A. Tool, Meditation) is the exact description of my former rushing in order to be on time. I have been so lost in space that I didn't leave on time and so had to rush once again. When I was a kid my parents left the house rushing, yelling and screaming, blaming each other or one of us kids for being late. I continued this behavior when my daughter was little. Always ignoring the clock, and then rushing her, "Hurry up, we'll be late!" I never left enough time to get ready to leave, so when she wanted to stop and look at a rock, just like any other little kid, I didn't have time to let her. She grew up, so then I didn't have anyone else to blame and I was still late!

After all those years of rushing, when I finally made it into the car, I often felt the urge to cry. This meant my adrenaline had dropped because I had used up too much energy rushing. "I'll be late for my own funeral...the hearse will have a flat tire," was a joke I used to make. I had a button that said "I'm not late—I'm early for the next time!" And then there was the post-it, "Always late but worth the wait." I knew it was wrong to be late but I (ego) was too busy to stop my task early enough to be prompt. W.A. opened my eyes to this "rushing," "panic" behavior. "The Problem" section of the W.A. Brochure called "Recovery from Workaholism" says "It is both a substance addiction (adrenaline) and a process addiction (over-doing)." If there is not enough time to finish a job, I get to panic, giving myself an adrenaline rush. It's no joke now, I'm sick, and part of my illness is after 59 years of rushing my adrenaline glands are worn out. I'm so happy to have learned the "substance/process" principle. Awareness is the key to change.

One thing for sure, since I surround myself with task (otherwise known as clutter): there is always something to do. I'm amazed when people say they are bored. I'm overwhelmed all the time. I think I should do everything myself (superwoman), and I have such an immature sense of time. I could always use a couple more hours in the day than twenty-four. Once in the Sunday comics the parents were having a garage sale; they changed the word "garage" to "mirage." I like that better, it's so much less shaming than clutter. At our meeting every week we read the principles and the tools. I found prioritizing, pacing, and underscheduling such a great help.

I despise things I think are a waste of time. Standing in line at the grocery or post office is sheer torture. We had a speaker once who said he grocery shopped at midnight because there were no lines and plenty of parking. I totally related. But then he said, "Grocery shopping at midnight is nuts." Another good reason to go to meetings: we learn from everyone. Commuting is another "waste of time." I find myself eating meals in the car. (In our W.A. meeting there is no multitasking allowed. People really complained about this rule.) I listen to tapes in the car too. And as I careen down from the Caldecott Tunnel, I brush my teeth with my trusty electric toothbrush. Not only is this a very dangerous activity for driving, THERE IS SPIT ALL OVER MY WINDSHIELD! Other W.A. members have told me they keep a toothbrush in the car too.

If you go to meetings, you learn you are not alone. After nearly 20 years in another Twelve Step Program, I don't speed. Once a woman said that speeding is very egocentric since it means I don't have to follow the rules. I turned this character defect (speeding) over in Step Seven, and now when I hear the voice of God say, "Look at your speedometer," I pay attention and slow down. I subscribe to the fabulous W.A. newsletter, *Living in Balance*, which comes four times a year chock full of W.A. member experiences. In the work world we are encouraged to call the above behavior "Multi-tasking," but in the Summer 2004 issue it's called "Time-stuffing." This is in a proposed article for our Step Book called "Adrenalizing." I do want to mention here that many, but not all, my credits from one Twelve Step program were transferable to W.A. As always, humility is key to learning new behaviors.

I never had time to cultivate friendships—I just had too much to do. After coming to W.A. I learned about ISOLATION and how it is one of the ways we can avoid intimacy. (Isolation is the dark room where I develop my negatives.) This is where a sponsor is so useful. I've had two W.A. sponsors. The first one let me call her only once a week and we just had a general chat. The second sponsor and I e-mailed each other our action plans. When I write my action plan, the "For Ourselves" I took to mean something for my body, like hand cream. In "For Our Relationships," I state what I will do with my husband or daughter that day to create intimacy. I commit to being with one a week. In "For Our Activities," I always try to commit to a fifteen-minute play activity. I need play in my life because I am responsible for making my life fun. A newcomer at our meeting said, "In Europe they know how to live and in the U.S. they know how to work." That's one of those expect God at K-mart things; we just never know where our next lesson is coming from. A cancer doctor once said, "Play is mandatory." In my meditation I tell myself, "It is safe to play today."

Of course I overschedule. I don't leave myself time to eat lunch or (heaven forbid) time enough to drive if there is traffic congestion. My calendar is so busy I don't have time to finish projects or clean up. Recently I was facing the "big chunk of truth" concerning weight loss. I need time to shop, wash, chop, cook and chew vegetables. I need time for exercise, time for meetings and support, and time to plan and write down my food and call it in. W.A. has opened my eyes to the fact that if I want to lose weight, I will have to give up some of my "precious time."

Prayer and meditation are so important to me. I already mentioned that I say that Third Step prayer every day. I also say a prayer, "Oh Clothe Me in Your Beauty" (*Overeaters Anonymous Lifeline Sampler*, p.59). There is a line that says, "Make me patient, gentle, and wise." I have embellished this to "Make me patient, gentle, and wise with myself, so I can be patient, gentle, and wise with others." Then I add, "You are so smart, you are such a good girl, you work hard enough, you work fast enough, you get enough done. God loves you even if you are just sucking air. I love you even if you are just sucking air." These affirmations repeated every day have helped me overcome the old childhood criticisms. I am more patient, gentle and wise with myself than ever before. I also feel a sense of "ease and comfort" in my "just being." The next line is, "Help me see beyond what seems to be." The first time I say this line I say, "See beyond what seems to be with people." This has given me so much insight into my relationships. The second time I say, "See beyond what seems to be with time." This has kept me from being late sometimes and has provided me with insights like "Leave time for traveling" or "Include time for lunch." *Signed, Recovering in W.A., Superwoman*

# A Vision of Recovery from Workaholism

When I am able to live my life without the frenzy of excessive work I am recovering from workaholism. When I am able to live without substituting the obligations of work for the inevitable joys and pains of life I am recovering from workaholism. When I am able to take responsibility for my behavior without attributing it to the demands of work or other obligations I am recovering from workaholism. When I am able to face difficult situations without resentment or fear I am recovering from workaholism. When I can remember the past without recrimination and guilt I am recovering from workaholism.

When joy replaces fear and faith replaces desperation I am recovering from workaholism. When I am at peace in my own skin and fully alive in the present I am recovering from workaholism. When pride in my own achievements replaces boundless competition I am recovering from workaholism. When humble membership in community replaces loneliness I am recovering from workaholism. When faith in the abiding presence of a power greater than me replaces the arrogant independence of self-will I am recovering from workaholism.

When I rejoin the human race as one among many, living each day according to the will of my Higher Power, I am recovering from workaholism.

# OUR PROBLEM

## The Physical Consequences of Workaholism and the Nature of Recovery—A Doctor's Opinion

*We of Workaholics Anonymous believe that workaholism is a disease. We believe it to be both a physical addiction to adrenaline and stress hormones and a process addiction to compulsive activity. Our experience has shown that the disease of workaholism is progressive and potentially fatal. Workaholics experience chronic high levels of stress hormones known to have major effects on vital body functions and known to interfere with the body's normal repairing mechanisms. In the following account, an M.D., herself in recovery from addiction, outlines some of the physical consequences of the disease.*

One commonly accepted definition of addiction is continued use of a substance or activity despite negative consequences. The medical complications of certain addictions are well known; for example, chronic alcoholism can lead to cirrhosis of the liver and damage to the nervous system. Nicotine addiction is associated with the development of heart disease, lung cancer, and emphysema.

But what are the medical complications of work addiction?

The physical effects of work addiction are not published in medical literature as such, but we can infer from the extensive literature concerning the effects of stress on the body, and from our own personal experiences, that we are dealing with a serious, life-threatening illness.

Reviewing the list of symptoms and illnesses known to be associated with chronic stress can be helpful. Some physical ailments that you have experienced may not have seemed related to your attitudes and behaviors toward work, but may well be related.

When an alcoholic drinks excessively and has a motor vehicle accident, the accident is tallied as such, as an alcohol-related accident or death. What about the workaholic who, after an eighty-hour workweek, falls asleep at the wheel and runs the car off the road? Law enforcement officers would never make a connection of the behavior with the accident. Often family members and workaholics themselves don't make the connection between physical symptoms and work behaviors until the disease has progressed significantly or until they get into recovery. Many workaholics suffer serious bodily harm before waking to the fact that we have a life threatening illness and require help to arrest its progression.

In addition, psychological harm to individuals and families results from the social isolation brought about by the disease. Depression, divorce, chemical dependency, anxiety disorders, and obsessive-compulsive disorders are all negative consequences that further qualify workaholism as an addiction.

The stereotypical version of the workaholic depicted in popular culture is of a man sitting up in his hospital bed after a heart attack, talking (or yelling) into the phone to an employee at work, with the EKG electrodes still attached to his chest.

Many people could have predicted the results of the research concerning the association of the so-called type A personality and heart disease even if it hadn't been widely publicized. Type A's are described in the medical literature as competitive, impatient, hostile, aggressive, and driven by a sense of time urgency.

Of course, not everyone with a Type A personality develops heart disease. Factors such as heredity, diet, exercise, and smoking history are important contributors to the etiology of cardiac problems. Recent research on the Type A personality has identified that the characteristic most clearly related to the development of cardiac disease is free floating hostility.

Not every workaholic has all the characteristics of Type A personality. Some of us do not come across as hostile or even aggressive. We may exert considerable control over our feelings and appear calm in emergencies. However, common sense and medical science agree that if certain feelings, such as anger or fear, are not discharged, they get stored in the body. These suppressed feelings sometimes find expression in illness and accidents.

Many of the physical consequences of workaholism can be traced back to the body's "fight or flight response." When an animal perceives a threat to its safety, a protective mechanism gets activated which leads to the release of stress hormones (one of which is adrenaline), and to a series of changes in the nervous system. The reaction prepares the animal to flee or to fight for its life. Once the mechanism is activated, the body responds with an elevation of heart rate and blood pressure, increased blood flow to muscles and decreased blood flow to the digestive organs.

Adrenaline and other stress hormones produce the "rush" that is associated with the fight or flight response.

Besides the direct ill effects of prolonged exposure to stress hormones, there are co-morbidities related to overuse/abuse of other substances. Many of us became multiply addicted. We used other addictive substances to counteract the feelings of depletion and/or anxiety associated with workaholism. Some of us used alcohol to "come down" after work. Many of us used caffeine and sugar to fuel our workaholic behavior in order to be able to sustain the level of output required to keep up our work habit. As a result of other addictions, some of us developed other medical problems such as obesity, Type 2 diabetes, lung disease, and liver dysfunction.

Over time, long hours coupled with character traits such as perfectionism and obsessive worry caused added stress. Many of the body's organ systems can be affected by chronic stress. The following is a partial list of the symptoms commonly associated with stress, listed by organ system:

> Cardiovascular—hypertension, heart disease
> Neurological—migraine headaches and stress headaches
> Psychiatric—depression, anxiety disorder, chemical dependency
> Musculoskeletal---back and other injuries, repetitive stress syndrome
> Gastrointestinal—colitis, ulcer
> Respiratory—shortness of breath, stress-induced asthma
> Immunological—decreased immunity, susceptibility to infection, and perhaps cancer,
> Reproductive—sexual dysfunction/impotence, menstrual irregularity, premature labor
> Dental-tooth loss due to teeth grinding
> Dermatology- Psoriasis

Notably, research also suggests a connection between suppressing emotional expression and the development of cancer (of various types).

The diseases and symptoms listed above are "commonly associated" with chronic stress. Identifying as a workaholic does not mean that you will acquire any of these conditions. However, you may be at increased risk for the development of one or more of these conditions. We are not ignoring the importance of such variables as heredity, environmental toxins, diet, and other "lifestyle" factors.

In addition to being a contributing factor in the development of certain symptoms and illness, workaholism can have a major impact on physical health in the area of health maintenance. Many of us have been so busy working that we failed to take care of routine health practices for years at a time. Work came first; we put other things off. In recovery we are learning to make time for self-care.

When is the last time you had a physical check up or routine screening for cancer and other serious illness? Are you current on your immunizations? Do you keep up with routine dental care? Having a lot of work to do is a common excuse for delaying seeing a health practitioner for a new symptom or complaint. Following up on necessary medical care and making time for exercise and positive health habits can be a way of making "living amends" to ourselves.

Knowing that suppressed emotions can lead to physical problems helps remind us of the importance of working the Steps and using the Tools of the program. Letting go of pent-up resentment has physical benefits as well as emotional and spiritual benefits. Working Step Eleven (practicing meditation) can help reverse or prevent some of the serious health consequences of workaholism.

Meditation has been shown to improve survival in certain disease states. Meditation cannot only prolong life; it can enhance life as well. The founders of A.A. were on to something. They gave us the benefit of their wisdom in the form of the Eleventh Step. Meetings and contact with fellow members and sponsors provide an opportunity to express emotions. Doing a Fifth Step or listening to one helps us feel less alone. Doing an inventory in the Fourth Step or in regular Tenth Steps allows us to admit (and then release) resentments thereby providing an effective way of processing some of the anger and hostility that can literally kill us or make us sick. We do the Steps for spiritual, social and emotional reasons and we reap physical benefits as well.

Prayer (also part of the Eleventh Step) has been shown to be efficacious in shortening the length of stay of patients in Intensive Care Units. These patients didn't know they were being prayed for, but nevertheless reaped the benefits.

People who do not understand the concept of powerlessness sometimes ask why a person would continue to indulge in an activity that is potentially fatal to themselves and harmful to others or fail to do things for themselves that are obviously beneficial.

Many of us trace the roots of our addiction to childhood. Current psychological theories and physiological evidence strongly support our intuition in this regard. Certain types of childhood trauma threaten not only physical survival, but threaten the very essence of the child's being—the spirit or core identity—with annihilation.

Some of us experienced such profoundly disturbing events that ordinary defenses were inadequate to deal with them. Some of us had caretakers who were inadequate to the task of helping us to learn to cope with strong feelings because they carried their own unhealed traumas inside.

When a child experiences trauma that overwhelms "ordinary" defense mechanisms (like dissociation), they develop extraordinary defenses. These defenses will protect the essence (spirit) of the individual at the expense of everything, up to and including life itself. Strong emotions later in life evoke the trauma defense. Because closeness brings up strong emotions, intimacy itself can feel threatening. A trauma survivor will go to great lengths to avoid intimacy, including acting in ways that jeopardize his or her health. Once trauma defenses are in place, they persist indefinitely unless there is some type of intervention. A single individual is no match for these defensive maneuvers, in the same way that, alone, we are no match for the disease of addiction.

When a person is experiencing a flood of stress hormones, situations that are not actually "life and death" seem to be. We wonder why other people are not as excited about some detail as we are. Everything feels like an emergency. Ironically, the converse is also true. Actual dangers are sometimes treated as trivial. For self-defeating, "protective" reasons, we remain in denial.

Let us take another look at the scene of the man in the hospital bed after his heart attack. We can imagine what feelings he might be trying to avoid. Overwhelming feelings of fear, sadness, anger, terror, and outrage ("You mean I really am mortal?!") arise in such situations. Without a recovery program, compulsive work is a tempting option for exerting some control when one's life feels unmanageable.

People who cannot tolerate the experience of strong emotions persist in old behaviors until there is enough support available to allow them to change. The *A.A. Big Book*, in reference to alcoholism, states, "Without help it was too much for us." Illness is frightening. Change of any type can be terrifying. Studies on childhood attachment and emotional development have given rise to theories about why feelings are so terrifying for many people.

Recovery begins as we find a "home" meeting, get a sponsor, and begin to establish a relationship with a Higher Power of our own understanding. We know we are no longer alone. We are perhaps forming the kinds of attachments that many people miss out on earlier in life.

We are forming the kinds of alliances that will be a match for the pull toward destructive compulsions and other "defects" or defenses. With help, we can develop inner resources and no longer have to avoid life and rely on old outmoded behaviors that set us apart from our fellows. We can come down to earth, walk among peers as free and equal, released from the bondage of fear and the compulsion to do and do, and work and work, and achieve. We can just BE.

Human connection can prevent the progression of physical disease; it allows infants to thrive and keeps elderly people alive longer. With the help of the program and a sense of a Higher Power, we can benefit from all that life has to offer, including the benefits of intimacy and connection. We can experience happiness and peace.

# Work Aversion

Work Aversion, Work Avoidance, Slowaholism, Action Anorexia, Procrastination, Work Anorexia. The terms are many but the destructive patterns of those who have this disease, by whatever name, are very similar. As with any illness, identifying the problem is the prerequisite to implementing a solution. This problem, like many other forms of "reduced living" such as underearning and/or spending anorexia, sex and relationship avoidance, or food anorexia, can be quite difficult to see as it hides in subtle shades and shadows.

It has been said that we work anorexics would rather perfectly avoid life than imperfectly live it. Addicts of many kinds can identify with that approach to living. However, what separates the Work Avoidance addict from other kinds of work addicts is a severe and recurring pattern around the refusal to deliberately act at all. The only counterbalance, at times, is to throw ourselves into action towards a certain direction or goal with the fervent hope of a perfect outcome. However, we usually putter along, spending a lot of our days on non-priority living, sometimes using food, television, or rescuing others to occupy our time. We engage in these diversions from the pain born out of a wholesale avoidance of the true priorities in our lives. By deliberately facing problems, allowing others to help with solutions, and admitting our dreams and aspirations and then acting to achieve them, recovery can begin.

The delay and distract pattern is characterized in the expression that "Work Anorexics are overachievers at underachieving." We who have this illness work very hard; indeed, we work very hard to avoid having to commit to any specific action or plan. Unlike other work addicts, we can be very conscious of our actions. Where we go unconscious is in the goal-making or planning department. As such, we especially avoid awareness of the results of our actions that aren't the ideal we sought. Of course, perfect results would suit us perfectly, or so we think. Deep down, though, we know worshipping such standards is only trouble in the long run. We have avoided adjusting these perfectionist standards. To do so means that we would risk realizing our greatest fear: we are only human and, as such, we cannot completely control outcomes. Our pain-filled pasts have already convinced us that outcomes or results are always painful and just recur. Sadly, therefore, our game plan has become to prevent as many results from occurring as possible. We reason that if we take less action, then we'll get fewer results and therefore experience less pain. And it's true we can't lose a race we haven't entered. Or is it? There are many desirable experiences in life that are only reached at the expense of experiencing at least some losses along the way. And that is where we have become stuck. Somehow work anorexics have come to be inspired by damage control as a long-term plan, as a standard way of facing all of life's situations. We have become obsessed with preventing any disappointment, only taking action we believe will result in perfect "loss free" outcomes. But there are no truly perfect outcomes, only imperfect ones. Furthermore, the trouble with using damage control as a centerpiece is that life becomes so safe and uninspiring that eventually we cannot let in the light of hope or new solutions either. Ignoring these facts results in a very painful downward spiritual spiral, and we can be blocked from any real progress or forward momentum.

The pain of such a block drives us into working more and more to commit to less and less as we progressively back away from life's challenges and choices. It has been said "the greatest risk is not to risk at all," and that is exactly what this disease ultimately brings us to do: not to risk, at any expense. Therefore we have justified our over-procrastinated life with sky-high standards, which we have become terrified to release or reconsider.

As time goes on, some of us desperately want to take action in certain areas of our lives, but we are frozen. We may find the only way to justify the hope that a particular effort will turn out to be worthwhile is to lie to ourselves, promising ourselves a perfect outcome. Then we commit to involvement, sometimes heavily, and the pendulum swings the other way for a time. At some point, though, we come out of our fantasy and are forced to see the imperfections about this new endeavor. At that point our voices tell us that we are "losers, once again" and the best way to live is to cut our losses by stopping. So we do.

Most work anorexics have trouble in getting and/or holding jobs for any appreciable length of time. If we do have jobs we may find that we work for or with an active work addict. In such cases it would be easy to blame this person for our troubles by saying that if they didn't wear us out with ever increasing demands we wouldn't try to slow things down so much. However, many of us discover, upon examination, that we have a childhood that includes a work addict in the form of a parent, guardian, or sibling. Our work avoidance may be a reaction to such family models and the abuse we once received. In fact, we are probably attracted to working with work addicts in order to heal our old wounds or because it feels familiar and normal. But the pain of teaming up with other work addicts makes things very confusing, so much so that many practicing work anorexics find ways to stop working with others altogether. We become self-employed or are enabled financially by family, friends, or disability payments. At some point, we see that we are rarely if ever satisfied with the results of our actions. Such hopelessness is too painful to bear alone. We realize we need to risk letting others in.

In W.A. we find help for taking actions of all kinds and for letting go of results, however imperfect they may be. We even learn to celebrate unexpected outcomes as part of life. We may need outside help. A therapist, caring church member, or doctor can help us to face the new emotional and physical workload involved in recovering from the spiritual abuse and rigid perfectionism that is often behind anorexia in any form. With the encouragement of W.A. friends, sponsor-guided Step work, and the experience of no longer being alone with the problem, we finally have courage to take positive steps on our own behalf. These actions are not compulsive, intense bursts followed by quitting; rather, in recovery, we learn to take slow, small, solid steps to build a forward momentum of healing.

At some point, however, we may be tempted to quit our connection with W.A. The quitting may be part of our illness. Many of us approach recovery as we do work and so our disease may tell us to avoid or quit recovery altogether. If that is the case, we don't worry about someone judging us for leaving; instead, we pray to Higher Power for the willingness to return. We have no requirement for perfect attendance. The only requirement for membership is a desire to stop working (or avoiding work) compulsively. Work anorexics in relapse need not feel ashamed to return to the W.A. program. Many in the fellowship have experienced such flip-flops.

Recovery is a kind of work—as much as or more so than most paying jobs! And it is a job that will, in time, pay us back many spiritual dividends not found anywhere else. Therefore we are encouraged to risk disappointment by taking the action of sharing our secret practices of perfection-worship with one or more recovering acquaintances. Such alliances, combined with a healing spiritual framework for self-discovery such as the Twelve Steps of W.A., provide essential relief from this kind of painful living. Sometimes we are not skillful in choosing safe people with whom to share our recovery journey. Rather than condemn ourselves for failing again, if we find this is the imperfect result of our actions, we persevere with new dignity of purpose, remembering that imperfect outcomes are not to be feared, only recognized and accepted. We know we have reached a new place in our lives when we come to embrace the "paradox of acceptance." The way to serenity, ironically, is found not by achieving perfection, as we had always thought, but rather through the acquired discipline of taking regular intervals (several times each day) to connect with a power greater than ourselves and to accept—and even embrace—the imperfections that any particular moment may bring to us.

Finally, we wish you peace in your recovery work towards this new serenity and we firmly believe that undertaking recovery from work avoidance is a risk well worth taking.

# Getting High—Adrenalizing

Adrenalizing: Creating pressure, suspense, and chaos by overscheduling and underpreparation. Forgetting priorities and pacing; operating with a scattered, cluttered, racing mind. Too little forethought, savoring, and assimilation.

1. Starting trips and projects without enough information or preparation.
2. Not asking when you're lost or puzzled.
3. Not reading instructions before using something.
4. Worry.
5. Difficult people (angry, unstable, controlling, critical, scattered, demanding, rushaholics, people who talk too fast), codependent relationships.
6. Adrenaline junkies.
7. Provoking people—you provoke them because you're bored.
8. No social life.

9. Car maintenance/imminent breakdown, not refilling gas tank until almost empty.
10. Speeding.
11. Illness.
12. Ignoring body signals.
13. Junk food-especially sweets. Overeating.
14. Not enough rest, exercise, or play.
15. Not getting regular physical checkups.
16. Overspending; living without a spending plan.
17. Not balancing checkbook and not checking due dates for payments or forms.
18. Too many credit cards.
19. Unrealistic deadlines.
20. Time-stuffing (adding to agendas, cramming one more item into a spare minute).
21. Simultaneously running water, heating food, starting car—requiring one to be in sync. Multitasking.
22. Leaving a message for someone to call you back on one line and then making a complex call on another line.
23. Too-hard classes.
24. Unrealistic to-do lists; overly tight scheduling.
25. Not allowing for the unexpected.
26. Too many interruptions.
27. Non-stop work, no bathroom break.
28. Hurry.
29. Lateness.
30. No extra keys; inadequate security for your property.
31. Data overload.
32. Too much world news.
33. Too many magazine subscriptions.
34. Too many library books out at one time and putting in even more reserves.
35. Too many classes, lectures, organizations, commitments.
36. Not keeping your clothes and property in repair.
37. Clutter. Break, drop, spill, misplace, trip over.
38. Not putting items away.
39. Being disorganized about time, paper, people, ideas, objects, space.
40. Practicing addictions. Not following your program.

# Progress not Perfection— and not Procrastination

Many of us in Workaholics Anonymous struggle with perfectionism and procrastination. In our disease, untreated, we have painful, perfectionistic, and procrastinating behaviors:

- We cannot accept our own imperfections or those of others.
- We put excessive demands on others and ourselves.
- Our judgments are severe; we judge things either good or bad, not complex and gray. Our critic is an incessant voice that we believe as the truth. It fuels our poor self-esteem. Because our minds are so critical, we respond with devastation to critical feedback. Our drive to high performance is essential to antidote our constant diet of critical self-messages.
- We suffer from intense shame if we do not have all the answers or our work is regarded as lacking. We sometimes practice shame avoidance by blaming others.
- We can be totally caught up in ourselves, obsessed with getting everyone's approval, and being the center of all processes. We believe another's behavior reflects on us.
- We cannot stop a project to take care of ourselves with regular meals, sleep, and exercise.
- We have trouble shifting gears; getting started can be as hard as stopping.
- We loose track of our most important priorities, getting lost in the details.
- We are plagued with the consequences of dishonesty. We wish to cover up our imperfections.
- We avoid work: if we do not start or finish projects, they will never have to meet our perfect standards.
- We swing from an inadequate self-image to a compulsive drive for achievement of an impossible ideal. We cannot be average like everyone else. Average is not enough.

As we begin to assimilate the Workaholics Anonymous Program of Recovery we find the grip of perfectionism and procrastination loosening. We admit we are powerless over this outdated method of coping with life. We come to believe in a Power greater than ourselves, and we make a decision to turn our will over to this Higher Power or God of our understanding. With the help of our W.A. group or sponsor, we continue to engage ourselves in the Steps. We come to know the root causes that drive our perfectionism and procrastination. Without effort, we find ourselves free at last to see life as progress and a process of maintaining a spiritual connection that guides us beyond our old ideals. Looking back, our lives in recovery are "beyond our wildest dreams."

# W.A. STEP STUDY GUIDE

## Overview: Recovery from Work Addiction Through Working the Twelve Steps

*The study of the Twelve Steps of Workaholics Anonymous is the core of personal recovery and progress. At first this can seem daunting. But the Steps are not meant to be studied alone. This is the time to ask for the help of a sponsor or to join a Step study group. Many of us have found the reading of related portions of the Big Book of* Alcoholics Anonymous *(Chapter Five, "How it Works," Chapter Six, "Into Action," and Chapter Seven, "Working with Others") helps us understand the Step question. We also read from the related Step chapter from* The Twelve Steps and Twelve Traditions *of Alcoholics Anonymous, with word substitution for work addiction, as a way to begin working each Step.*

### The Problem

Workaholism takes many forms. Among them: deriving our identity and self-esteem from what we do; keeping overly busy; neglecting our health, relationships, and spirituality; seeing everything as work-related; having no desire to do anything (work avoidance or burnout); procrastinating; postponing vacations and rest; doing unnecessary work; worrying; perfectionism; avoiding intimacy; being controlling.

All these are ways we cope with the pain of having lost our sense of being and of not feeling good enough. Overscheduling our lives with activities is how we run from ourselves. We keep busy to blot out our feelings. We enjoy the adrenaline highs that come from intensity and rushing to meet deadlines. Maybe we are praised and promoted at work for being responsible and hard working. We may even be employed by a workaholic company that uses praise and promotion to encourage our addiction. Yet we have paid an enormous price for these "rewards." We have traded self-awareness for burying our pain in work and worry. We have endangered our health and destroyed our relationships. We may have often felt, "Is this all there is?"

Because there are many misconceptions about workaholism, recognizing it may take a long time. It is both a substance (adrenaline) and a process (overdoing) addiction and is not limited to our paid work life. We can also be workaholic in hobbies, fitness, housework, volunteering, or in trying to save the world. All of these may appear admirable, but if they mean self-abandonment due to incessant doing, it is work addiction.

Since this is a progressive disease, ultimately we become more driven until we hit bottom. Our bottom may come in the form of a serious health problem or an ultimatum from our partner, employer, or a friend. At some point, "workaholic" is no longer a label we prize. We realize that we have to change.

To help guide us in our recovery, there are the Twelve Suggested Steps of Workaholics Anonymous. Because our work addiction is so entrenched in our lives, the process seems overwhelming. How much time will recovery take? We are already too busy! What do we do with our commitments and responsibilities?

## The Solution

As our pain intensifies, we begin to gain willingness—willingness to admit that we are addicted to work, that our lives are unmanageable, and that our way hasn't worked; willingness *not* to have all our questions answered immediately or to expect a quick fix; willingness to say, "I'm sick. I want to recover and I need help." In Workaholics Anonymous, this admission of powerlessness is Step One. We have found it helpful to take this Step and those that follow with others in W.A.

From this initial willingness comes more willingness. Step Two tells us that a power greater than ourselves can restore us to sanity. This power can be God, Higher Power, the Universe, the W.A. group—whatever is our source of strength.

Step Three involves making a commitment to turn our will and our lives over to God as we understand God. Letting our Higher Power guide us requires giving up control, *not* being irresponsible. Our will now becomes a tool to turn self-will into willingness. For those of us who pride ourselves on being self-sufficient and strong-willed, taking this Step involves a new way of thinking.

In Step Four we make a written inventory of ourselves in relation to our workaholism. We include both our shortcomings and our assets. We ask a W.A. member for help on how to do Step Four. By taking a close look at ourselves, we become acquainted with the lovable person we truly are, the person we have lost in busyness.

Because many of us feel shame about how our work addiction has hurt others, and ourselves, it is healing to do Step Five and talk to an understanding person. This person can be anyone we choose. When we share our secrets, we often find that others have had similar experiences.

Steps Six and Seven ask us to prepare ourselves inwardly to make amends to those we have harmed. In Step Eight we list those people and in Step Nine we make amends prudently. After these Steps are completed, many of us discover that a great burden has been lifted, that we have a sense of freedom and peace.

Recovery from workaholism is not a cure, but a lifelong process. We are granted only a daily reprieve contingent upon our maintaining our abstinence and growing spiritually. In Step Ten, we continue the process begun in Step Four — awareness of our feelings and taking responsibility for our words and actions. Taking Step Eleven strengthens our conscious contact with our Higher Power, begun in Step Two, by having us stay in touch through prayer and meditation.

Step Twelve tells us we can maintain and expand the spiritual awakening we experienced in doing all the preceding Steps. We can do this by carrying the W.A. message of recovery to workaholics and by practicing these principles at work, at home, on vacations—everywhere.

The best way for us to keep from sliding back into old habits is to share about our W.A. recovery with others. "We can't keep it unless we give it away." We carry the message by being an example of a recovering workaholic in our daily activities as well as by giving service in W.A.

Following the Steps brings us in touch with our inner wisdom and our spirituality. As we learn to accept ourselves as we are, we experience a new attitude toward work and activity. We enjoy our work more and find ways to work more effectively. When work has its proper place, we find time to have fun and to nurture our health, relationships, and creativity.

We welcome you to our program and wish for you the recovery, serenity, and self-enjoyment we have found.

# Step One

## Guide for Step One in Workaholics Anonymous

**Step One: We admitted we were powerless over work—that our lives had become unmanageable.**

These ten questions were designed to be answered in writing, one question a day for ten days, while working with a sponsor. It is also suggested they be written in a Step group. It takes time to face the full consequences of our affliction and how workaholism is manifesting in our lives. For many of us Step One is challenging but we have found if we don't honestly admit how powerless we really are over this affliction, we are doomed to continue our insane lives. For some of us we are well aware of our condition and in one setting we are ready to move on to Step Two where we begin to feel hope and a path to peace of mind. You are free to use these questions to stimulate your thinking about workaholism and how it affects you.

## *Step One Questions*

1. How has work stress and excess work and/or work avoidance affected my health?
2. What is the history of my workaholism, starting with my family history of addictive work and other addictions? What has my family of origin taught me about work? Including my first memories of work or activity, what is the progression of work addiction in my life?
3. What have I tried in the past to control my problems with work: changing jobs, taking classes, retreats, taking time off, reading self help books, etc.?
4. Free-write about what I am powerless over, and my feelings about powerlessness.
5. Using another workaholic's example of Step One qualifications, how would I quantify my workaholism? (See first Step One Story.)
6. How have my relationships or lack of them been affected by my work problems?
7. What seems unmanageable in my life? How has this addiction diminished my life?
8. How would I describe my relationship to money and power?
9. How would I describe the criticism I direct to myself, on my negative thinking and poor self-esteem? How do these drive my decisions?
10. How do procrastination and perfectionism and love of power affect my life? How have I been deceptive and tried to cover for how out of control life feels?

# Step One Story: *Quantifying My Unmanageability*

As part of my Step One writing, my sponsor encouraged me to quantify the impacts of the disease of work addiction in my life. Answering these questions helped me see the depth of my unmanageability, how deeply the disease had affected my life. Over the course of my Step One writing, I estimated each of the following:

- Number of times I studied late at night
- Number of times I sat in a bathroom stall all night (at graduate school) working on a paper
- Number of times I worked all night in my current job
- Number of times I worked all night
- Number of times I worked until late evening
- Number of times I worked until early morning
- Number of times I made mistakes due to being tired
- Number of times I worked all night and all the next day
- Number of days I didn't see my infant son, because I was working late
- Number of times I came home too late to spend time with my kids ("bucking bronco"), but went ahead and spent time with them anyway (contrary to my spouse's wishes)
- Number of times I said I'll be leaving by ___ or I'll leave in ____ minutes, but didn't (I worked longer)
- Number of times I got home after dinner had already started (with grandparents present)
- Number of times I would stay up even later, after getting home late
- Number of times I consumed a lot of caffeinated pop
- Number of calories consumed eating sweet foods when tired or stressed
- Number of hours spent watching TV to escape
- Number of years lost in building relationships with my spouse and children
- Amount of lost wages due to probation or lack of promotion
- Number of times I have given excuses (lies) for being late
- Number of hours I have made people late or kept people waiting because I was late
- Number of times I procrastinated about doing tasks for one of my "moonlighting" jobs
- Number of fatigue-related accidents I have experienced
- Net profit from "moonlighting" jobs

- Cost (interest expense or lost interest income) of not submitting expenses for reimbursement in a timely manner
- Cost to send things by express mail
- Cost of health problems due to work addiction
- Cost of eating in employee cafeteria versus at home
- Number of hours of life lost due to overwork, illness, TV watching, errand/shopping during work time, reading the paper (or other publications for personal reasons) at work
- Number of times my tax returns have been way overdue
- Number of projects that have been late
- Number of times I have been late to work
- Number of days I have avoided one or more tasks
- Number of times I have tried to hide the fact that I was eating in my office
- Number of times I have tried to avoid getting caught arriving late to work and to hide reading the newspaper on the job
- Number of times I've been in a panic or whirlwind
- Number of times I have been reprimanded (e.g. for being late, taking too long, not communicating my whereabouts, completing projects late).

# *Step One Story: Insanity, Feeling, and Sanity—A Step One Writing Process*

It didn't dawn on me how unmanageable my life had become until my friend searched out a recovery program for workaholics and gave me the contact information. The turning point came while on a weekend vacation with her in L.A. I had wanted to remain in the passenger seat of her parked car "to prepare my notes for the following week's workload" as she attended an hour-long recovery meeting.

By the time I read the W.A. flyer (answering "yes" to all but three questions), I knew that I had a problem. The memories of poor choices started to flow. Sponsors are few in my W.A. program, but after attending meetings for a couple of months, our program grew enough to develop seasoned sponsors. My sponsor encouraged me to work the Steps. In Step One, I identified where I was powerless over this deadly disease and how my life had become unmanageable. Below I've outlined the process I went through while identifying my powerless behavior.

1. With a small notebook in hand, I went about my normal day jotting down moments when/where I found myself powerless over work or activity. My problem

was clearest to me when my intention did not match my actions. The most obvious entries were when often I lost track of time and neglected self-care, such as staying at work during late evening hours and eating my lunch in the mid-afternoon instead of at noon.

2. In the evening at home I sorted the list into three columns, answering the following questions:
   -What was the **insane activity**?
   -What were my **feelings/emotions** during the time of the activity?
   -By contrast, what would have been a **sane action plan**?

Below is an example of my list:

| Insane Activity | Feeling/ Emotion | Sane Activity |
|---|---|---|
| Leaving work at 8pm | Tired, anxious, hungry | Leave work at 5pm; begin to wrap-up at 4:30 (not 5pm) |
| Eating Lunch at 2:30 | Hurried, under pressure, very hungry, cranky, irritable | Eat lunch at 12pm; leave work environment to avoid temptation to return to work early |
| Departing late to an event | Rushed, anxious, angry at conductor/traffic over slow speed | Plan on arriving _ hour before event begins, leave extra early, commit to meeting friends earlier for event |
| Three events on one weekend: Saturday- long bike ride; Sunday - brunch date in morning and Super Bowl party in afternoon | Excited, rushed, exhausted at night, hungry at times. No time to organize, prepare, or wrap-up | Choosing one social event for the weekend. Allowing unscheduled time for unexpected self-care and nourishing activities (such as walk on the beach, café stop, etc.) |

As the weeks progressed, my list began to grow and I was forced to take a hard, honest look at my choices. It was very disheartening to realize my powerlessness.

3.  At this point it was extremely important to have support. My sponsor was encouraging and compassionate. Through her, I was able not only to see the signs of this disease, but also to be gentle with myself as I took note of my choices. She kindly reminded me that my addiction is a chemical addiction, like alcoholism. I was addicted to the adrenaline rush my body experienced while maintaining the desire to be busy constantly.

4.  Practicing gentleness. The easiest way for me to determine whether an activity was sane is by asking myself what kind of advice I would give a four-year old child in my care. Ninety percent of the time, I would suggest eating, resting and taking care of her body, *before* attending to a task or a planned event. I just never followed this advice before Workaholics Anonymous.

A synopsis of my W.A. Step One process would include:
1.  Recording behaviors in a notebook.
2.  Sorting behaviors into three columns: insane activity, feelings/emotion, and sane activity.
3.  Getting support through sponsorship or with other W.A. members.
4.  Being gentle with myself.

Slowly, I began to see my vulnerabilities and realized battling this disease cannot be done on my will power alone. I needed guidance from someone that could help create sanity in my life. I was ready for Step Two.

# Step Two

## *Guide for Step Two in Workaholics Anonymous*

### *Step Two: Came to believe that a power greater than ourselves could restore us to sanity.*

Step Two introduces us to the concept that a power greater than ourselves alone provides hope for our sanity and balance. For workaholics accustomed to self-sufficiency and pride in self-reliance, this can be difficult to understand. In the beginning some will think a power greater than ourselves indicates a religious entity, but it does not. We are free to determine what restores us to sanity. We come to believe in a "Deeper Power": a loving guidance that helps us to deal with the addiction of workaholism.

There are almost as many names for Higher Power as there are W.A. members: universal wisdom, Higher Power, deeper power, the great spirit, great mystery, God, Goddess, and many more. For some of us, our W.A. group is our Higher Power.

We have tried many other solutions: changing jobs, changing schedules, quitting work altogether, hiding from life. Nothing helped for more than a short time. Belief in a power greater than us is the antidote to our disease. We find ourselves believing in other things: the goodness of our fellow human beings and the positive aspects of life. We find the courage to reach out to others and get the help we need to recover.

For many of us, faith is a foreign concept. It is not necessary to take Step Two all at once. If you are willing to believe in a power greater than yourself and allow that belief to grow in you over time, you will be surprised at how your world expands.

Many of us come to Step Two with baggage. We are disillusioned with the religion of our childhood; we do not believe in a Higher Power; or perhaps we believe, in our suffering, that God has abandoned us. Workaholics Anonymous does not tell us we must believe in any particular concept of a Higher Power; however, we have found that we must believe in something beyond our addicted mind that restores us to sanity.

## Step Two Questions

1. Using the work I did in Step One, I can draw a line down the center of a piece of paper, labeling one side "sanity" and the other side "insanity." What are examples of how I know when I am behaving sanely or insanely? What is a list of anything I do or think that is destructive to myself or to others such as: compulsive behavior, obsessive thoughts (resentments, anxiety, worry, depression), or trying to control others?

2. How have I come to believe change is needed? What have I tried in the past to control work binges, pressure, or procrastination before coming to W.A.?

3. How do false pride and shame avoidance influence my asking for help when I am feeling overwhelmed and powerless?

4. Since my willpower hasn't helped the consequences of my workaholism, am I willing to look for a power greater than myself to restore me to sanity?

5. How did I initially relate to the concept of a "Higher Power"? How has my attitude changed?
6. If I do not believe in a Higher Power, how can I "act as if"?
7. How do the tools, the telephone, meetings, sponsorship, meditation, and service restore me to sanity?
8. How do I experience belief as reliance on a Higher Power, not defiance?
9. What actions am I willing to take that others have told me worked for them?
10. How do I describe the experience of the presence of a Higher Power in my life?

## Step Two Story: Gardening as a Metaphor for a Higher Power

Gardening has been a great teacher for me. Early on, I would buy some packaged garden soil, spade up some ground, mix it and plop down my seeds. Without too much luck. Or, only with luck would anything sprout and prosper. Gradually I figured out that a garden needs to be in harmony with its location (sun/shade), the time of year (how much sun can be expected), the soil temperature (early/late in the year), condition of the soil (wet/sandy etc.), water (keep the seeds damp but not wet), and the plants chosen need to be suited to this year's garden. These are just a few of a multitude of considerations. The best planning will not guarantee a garden, as there is an interworking of all these forces that is complex and miraculous. In fact, failure is the norm, not the exception. As with most things, the more you know, the more you realize there is to know until, finally, I learned humility and wonder when thinking about a garden. The opposite to being a good gardener is to use will power (I will grow this here, now) and reasoning alone (if I do this and this, this will result). Will has its uses, as it is what gets me down on my knees weeding or sowing. Reasoning can help to avoid the obvious mistakes, like planting sugar cane in a cold climate. But, alone, they do not make a garden.

Somewhere I came on the concept of "feeding the soil, not the plants." This made immediate sense to me, as I had noticed that when the soil feels right to the hand, the plants are happier, too. If we feed only the plants, they become too tall and fall over, are susceptible to disease and insects and often have lots of leaves, but not the root, seed or fruit that we are looking for. Untended, the soil will not absorb or retain water and loses the character that small and large plants need. Plants grown this way have greater food value.

I am coming to apply this philosophy to my life, especially the spiritual side. Instead of relying on my will power and rationality, which were the tools I was taught as a child, I am trying to take an attitude similar to my gardening. It goes like this:

> I don't assume that wanting something will make it happen.
> I try to be patient and not immediately analyze each impasse to find a resolution.
> I try to pay attention and watch for signs that things are going right or wrong.
> I try to be flexible and not to keep doing the same thing over and over, without any result.

My main principle is to feed the soil/soul by providing proper rest, food, play, love, friends, music, mental stimulation, and healthy support. At least these. Then comes the selection of what to plant, or how to direct my life, which needs to take into account my appetites, strength, and energy. Then there is pruning of old stuff, so that it does not crowd or shade this year's garden. This old growth is retained anger, past trauma and old stress; this must not be dug up and discarded, but needs to be brought into something I can work with and around.

Also, there is the weeding, to avoid the competition of addictions, being rushed, not having time for the continued care of the seedbed/soul or the time to enjoy what is growing in the garden.

This is as close as I can come right now to the concept of a Higher Power. The power is both outside me in the miracle of life and inside me as a small voice that leads me to question the forces of will and reason. This power feels mysterious and unknowable. It was either given in my genes or it comes from elsewhere.

## Step Story: Steps One and Two and A Higher Power

From the beginning, I was drawn to accept Step One. Even before attending my first meeting I had known there was something wrong. I was working all the time, even though I wished I could relax and be comfortable with myself and with others. As an excuse, I always said to myself: "that's the way I am." It finally became clear to me that I was unable to change. Each time I "turned over a new leaf" another one was revealed that looked just like the one before. There were plenty of reasons to make changes, both in terms of my peace of mind and my relationships with loved ones, but the pattern of being obsessed by working resisted all my efforts to change. I had reached a place where I expected to experience peace: my children were on their own as young adults, my health was good, and I had reasonable financial security. Yet the work addiction lost none of its power.

When I first went to a W.A. meeting, I had an immediate recognition: this was something that I had been looking for. I am seventy-eight years old. I was young enough in spirit to aspire to a fuller life, despite the years spent in getting set in my ways. One of these long held patterns was my extreme self-reliance, which shows up in my always having been self-employed. Another was a belief that reason and logic were my best tools for solving life's problems. Reliance on logic was part of my early education and a method I had used successfully to hold my family and business together. However these attitudes were keeping me from seeing any evidence of a Higher Power. Having accepted Step One that I was unable to achieve sanity on my own, I believed I could move on to Step Two, only if I could honestly grasp the concept of a Higher Power. I tried to go around Step Two thinking: "it will come," but actively seeking a Higher Power left me frustrated. I tried prayer, but it seemed artificial. I was embarrassed that I could not feel what I was saying. I began to meditate regularly and started the day off in a more serene way and felt as though I was moving in the right direction. However, each time I would hear the Higher Power addressed at meetings, I felt personally lacking as though something was missing in me. Recently, I reflected on the progress I have made since coming to W.A.: connecting to family in a stronger way, being more able to listen, not working compulsively, reaching out by volunteering at a local school, not taking on new projects at home. I was getting positive feedback from family and friends who had noticed these changes. In going over the recent past, I stumbled on a powerful thought: some kind of magic has occurred, some sort of catalytic event has brought me to W.A. and made me receptive to its message. This was not the result of my old problem-solving ways of perseverance and analytical logic. It seemed to come from another source altogether, and I sense that it was a manifestation of what I can call a Higher Power. I had been looking for something showy or dramatic, almost a vision, and had failed to see that what had happened was a remarkable thing. It makes me wonder how many other events in my life were like this, but went unrecognized. It is another kind of knowledge, one that does not rely on willfulness or reasoning. I am not yet steady enough on my feet to rely on it, to use it in prayer, or to say a whole lot about it; but it feels like a beginning in the development of my spiritual life. This realization makes me want to be more alert so that I won't miss similar truths that come my way.

# Step Three

## *Guide for Step Three in Workaholics Anonymous*

### *Step Three: Made a decision to turn our will and our lives over to the care of God* **as we understood God.**

The key to success in starting Step Three is willingness to turn our lives over to the care of a loving Higher Power. "Let go and let God." This can be difficult for workaholics who are used to success depending on self-will alone. We have been self-reliant to a fault. A will of steel has gotten us through long workdays and sleepless nights. If we turn our lives over to the care of a Higher Power, we aren't sure who we will become.

Yet we have found through experience that giving up our illusion of control is the sure path to serenity and recovery. When we turn to our Higher Power, we are able to let go of the outcomes of our endeavors and enjoy the process of living.

In moments when difficult feelings arise, we are tempted to turn back to self-reliance. Our fear tells us we need to take charge of the situation, that we can't trust God. We learn in W.A. that it doesn't matter how many times we take back our will and our lives as long as we turn them over again. Eventually, we realize that our Higher Power is always watching over and protecting us, whether we are aware of it or not. We can choose to live in anxiety and fear or we can open our eyes to the reality that we are cared for and loved at every moment.

It is often recommended that people read through Step Three, pages 60-64 in the Big Book of *Alcoholics Anonymous*, and the chapter on Step Three in the A.A. *Twelve Steps and Twelve Traditions* as preparation for doing writing on this Step.

## *Step Three Quotations*

### We had a new Employer....

"When we sincerely took such a position [on Step 3], all sorts of remarkable things followed. We had a new Employer. Being all powerful, He provided what we needed, if we kept close to Him and performed His work well."

## Third Step Prayer

*"God, I offer myself to Thee—to build with me and to do with me as Thou wilt. Relieve me of the bondage of self, that I may better do Thy will. Take away my difficulties, that victory over them may bear witness to those I would help of Thy Power, Thy Love, and Thy Way of life. May I do Thy will always!"*

*Both quotations from page 63 of the chapter "How It Works" in the Big Book,* Alcoholics Anonymous.

## *Step Three Questions*

1. Consider the phrase "Let go and let God." This can be difficult for workaholics who are used to success depending on self-will alone. In what ways am I willing to adopt a new attitude about work and business?

2. What barriers remain that block my relationship with a Higher Power? Anxiety over giving up self-determination? Difficulty trusting? Unworkable definition of a Higher Power? Old habits? No experience with a caring Higher Power? How does surrendering to a power greater than myself feel to me?

3. Create a balance sheet. On one side list all the reasons for believing in God. On the other side, I list my reasons and beliefs that keep Higher Power out of my life.

4. How do I "play God"? What is dependence and how can dependence on a Higher Power lead to greater independence?

5. How do I describe the God of my understanding? Do I need a more loving, forgiving, available experience of a Higher Power—what would that look like?

6. How do my work and activities create an illusion of power and control?

7. Am I still trying to handle each problem myself, or am I asking for the help of coworkers and my Higher Power for guidance?

8. What are the signs that tell me I am working from ego, willpower, and pressure? What are the signs that tell me when I have turned my will and my life over to the care of God?

9. Do I invite the presence of God by thinking of God as my employer? Do I begin each day with a prayer listing what I feel

grateful for, asking how I can be of service? Do I take time to cultivate a relationship with my Higher Power? How do I use the Serenity Prayer?

10. Do I misuse willpower, bombarding my problems with it instead of attempting to bring it into agreement with God's universal wisdom? Do I pray for what I want rather than using meditation and other spiritual experiences to become teachable and open to the support of a caring Higher Power?

## Step Three Story: Living in Divine Flow

### A HUMAN DOING

At some point our feelings become submerged in our non-stop activity. We lose touch with our being and become a human doing.

This transition comes gradually. As long as we are enmeshed in schedules, goals, and quotas, we don't notice that our sense of self is missing. We can't even feel our numbness. This is not like the cry of pleasure deprivation— "Is this all?" —after a grueling week. Rather, this is the profound loss of being that comes after years of not connecting with one's self and of turning a deaf ear to the pleas of our family and friends to stop killing ourselves with overdoing.

The pain of this loss may hit us during bed rest, a quiet vacation, or retirement—all of which were probably initiated against our will. Some of us describe it as the emptiness of unrealness, as if we were robots with a dead battery. Our reason for existence—our functionality—is gone and we're lost without it. We don't know how to live in a world we can't control by agendas, deadlines, organizational charts, and machines. We have no idea how to just be.

### RECOVERY

Recovering what we've lost takes time and patience. So does learning new ideas—generally the opposite of what we've believed:

We make haste by not being in a hurry.

We learn that efficiency is not effectiveness.

The more we take it easy, the more we accomplish.

The more overwhelmed we are, the more we need to take a break.

Worry causes problems, not vice versa.

The more we surrender to time, the more we become its master.

Freedom lies not in knowing we can do whatever we want, but in knowing we're doing what our heart leads us to.

The highest form of control is surrendering all control.

## SURRENDER

Once we have worked the Steps and surrendered our life and our will to our Higher Power, we begin to live not merely more slowly but "flowly." This means acting from love instead of ego, letting things unfold by effortless effort, and moving at a comfortable pace, allowing time to savor experience. When we stop resisting the flow of life and cooperate with it, we experience more energy—not driven energy or an adrenaline rush, but pure energy.

For those of us used to forcing, experiencing effortlessness may be the hardest thing we've ever done. We're not used to being receptive and want to take back control. Yet, by getting out of our own way, all is accomplished.

Living flowly helps us recognize our direction and thus make correct choices. We no longer suffer from "experience greed"—wanting to do everything—because we are content with what we have. Before, we feared contentment and valued dissatisfaction as a spur to ambition. Now we realize that as we move to our next stage, the unnecessary falls away. We no longer try to push growth. For once, we experience an absence of struggle and we enjoy it.

We eventually understand that it's useless to desire anything but God's will because nothing else will bring us the feeling of being in the right place at the right time, the feeling that what we're doing is what we're supposed to be doing. We may have achieved what we thought would make us happy, but without this feeling of rightness, there's only hollowness. We learn to want what we have rather than to be concerned with having what we want.

## HARMONY

Living flowly is being in rhythm—our mind, heart, and body act in harmony with divine power. We know when to be active and when to be still. Each phase is part of a whole and nourishes the other. We carry our stillness into our activity and our aliveness into our repose. We trust our being to guide our doing. We use our will to become willing.

We make a daily appointment with our Higher Power and listen to guidance. We schedule our priorities instead of prioritizing our schedule. Our priorities include breathers, time for just sitting, and time to make sure we are still connected with our being. We become the best boss we've ever had.

Living flowly means doing the work we are born to do—work we would do for free or pay to do if we had to. Work in which we lose track of time because we are filled with joy. And it means carrying this surrendered attitude into routine chores. We welcome such tasks because they don't absorb us totally; they create a fertile void from which we receive breakthrough ideas.

This mode of living connects us with nature and divine order. Regaining our lost sense of wholeness makes us comfortable with solitude and silence. Before, there was shallow chatter and busyness; now there is depth and presence.

## REWARDS

Living flowly gives us time to:

Recognize the messages of our emotions and body sensations
Retain our self-awareness and perspective and not become enmeshed in events
Hear intent as well as content and build empathy
Realize the impact of our decisions, speech, and actions
Act spontaneously and be more flexible in recognizing opportunities
Find meaning in routine events
Delight in surprise and revive our sense of wonder and playfulness
Enjoy small and simple pleasures
Remember our dreams
Celebrate, grieve, and put closure to experiences
Discover heightened relevance in synchronicity
Become a friend to time
Allow significant memories to emerge
Practice masterly inactivity

## GROWTH

This spiritual awakening may be bittersweet. We see how impoverished we've become. How much of the richness of everyday living we have denied ourselves! As we realize that regret is a sign of growth, it eases the pain.

Or we may become impatient and try to hurry the process. As society's pace accelerates, we may fear being left behind. Yet we can't speed up our slowing down. Later, we will sense our rhythm is perfect.

We look back at those crowded, blurry days as a bad dream. We feel we have been raised from the living dead—and we have. That human doing seems to be a stranger. How could we have been so cruel to ourselves and to those around us? Then we remember the payoffs: self-importance from being surrounded by piles of work; an adrenaline rush when we worked against deadlines; admiration for our untiring dedication; feelings of indispensability, self-sufficiency, and invincibility; the illusion that we could ignore time and space. These seem paltry rewards for the price we paid in self-alienation, broken health, and lost relationships.

We acknowledge the teachings of workaholism, grieve our lesson years, and celebrate our new way of living by keeping our conscious contact with our Higher Power. We nurture our mind, heart, and body. We cherish the people in our lives and stay grateful that we've been given a second chance through W.A.

# Step Four

## Guide for Step Four in Workaholics Anonymous

### Step Four: Made a searching and fearless moral inventory of ourselves.

The following questions are meant to be helpful to the recovering workaholic who is ready to work the Fourth Step. It is easier at this point to have a sponsor or to be working the Steps in a group with others who have worked the Fourth Step. These questions are meant as a guide. It is best to have worked the first three Steps; turning our will and our lives over to a power greater than ourselves helps enhance the "fearless" part of this inventory.

The inventory begins by listing our present resentments, guilts, and fears. In this Step, as we name our attitudes and write about our patterns, both helpful and unhelpful, we begin to understand ourselves better. As we move through our Fourth, Fifth, and Sixth Steps, and as we practice the other parts of the program—meetings, action plans, meditation, surrender, and getting help—we notice we have become freer of these character defects and more appreciative of our strengths. The promises of true serenity and a healthy, balanced life will be ours.

Many of us have begun by using the Step Four guidelines in the Big Book of *Alcoholics Anonymous*, pages 64-71. We write our answers. The following set of questions can be used as a guide. Further guidance is available in the Step Four chapter of A.A.'s *Twelve Steps and Twelve Traditions*.

# *Step Four Questions*

## RESENTMENTS

1. We begin by listing our resentments, fears, and shame. The columns described in the Big Book are very helpful. Part of an example follows:

| I am resentful at: | the cause, event: | Affects my *(Options include self-esteem, ambition, pride, security, personal relations, sex relations)* |
|---|---|---|
| Sam, my boss | fired me | Self-esteem Finances (security), pride |
| My partner | bugs me about work | Self-esteem Relationships |

Additional columns include identifying "My Part" and "Related Character Defects."

2. What were the patterns of resentment and anger in my family of origin? (E.g. silence then rage, retaliation, passive resistance and acting out, blaming others.)
3. What are common triggers for my anger and patterns of expressing it?
4. What is my definition of healthy expression of anger and resentments? In what ways have I been respectful and assertive with my anger?
5. How have resentments taken up space in my daily thoughts?
6. Can I express anger without blame or criticism?
7. Am I a conflict avoider, pleasing others at any cost?

## FEAR

1. How do I experience fear? What patterns of fear, worry, immobilization, procrastination, and anxiety do I have?
2. Is there a family history of fear and anxiety?
3. Where has self-reliance failed me?
4. What/whom do I trust? How has the experience of surrender, prayer, and meditation led to an increase of serenity?

## SEX

1. Reviewing my past experiences, have I been selfish, dishonest, or inconsiderate about my sexual behavior? Have I taken health risks? Have I aroused jealousy?
2. Do I take my considerations about sex to my Higher Power for guidance?
3. Do I use work to avoid sex? Am I too depleted by work to have a healthy sexual relationship? What has been my pattern of work and worry, and how has it affected my sex and love life? Am I jealously possessive?
4. Can I now enjoy non-manipulative sex?

## SHAME

1. What gets in the way of my accepting myself as a limited human being who makes mistakes?
2. Can I make mistakes and be imperfect and still be lovable and forgivable?
3. "We are as sick as our secrets." What major secrets do I have?

## OTHER QUESTIONS

1. What am I grateful for?
2. How am I a perfectionist? How does this feed my patterns of procrastination?
3. For what have I begun to forgive myself? What are some of the origins of my behaviors?
4. Whom do I still need to forgive?
5. What percentage of my thoughts are negative—fearful, resentful, self critical, judgmental? Am I sensitive to criticism? Make a list of examples of self-hatred and self-abuse.
6. Do I trust others or situations to work out?
7. How has pride affected my workaholism? How has my ego affected my work addiction?
8. To live in balance, I need to feel proud of my achievements and contributions. Make a list of them, letting the self-critic rest.
9. What is a list of my positive attributes (generous, caring, recovering, etc.)?
10. How have substances such as caffeine, recreational drugs, nicotine, and/or alcohol been a pattern in my workaholism?
11. How have food, debting, and/or gambling been a factor in my workaholism?
12. How do I set limits on the allocation of my time and energy?

13. Am I power hungry? How do I react when I don't get my own way?

14. How do I try to maintain control of situations and people? What is my pattern, and what was the pattern in my family?

15. In what ways have I been honest? In what ways have I been dishonest?

16. Do I let the needs of others take over while ignoring my own needs?

17. Have I been unavailable to my children or partners?

18. What is my relationship with time? Frequently late? Overscheduled? How does the reality of ignoring time serve me?

19. How have I avoided taking responsibility for my behavior? Denial? Blame? Distraction? Dishonesty? Rationalization? In what ways do I admit mistakes?

20. What is my relationship to money? Am I debting? Am I a money anorexic?

## Step Four Story: Tools for Gentleness, Coping Skills, and Character Assets

### Gentleness Collage

Before I began my Fourth Step writing, my sponsor gave my Higher Power and me an art project: making a Gentleness Collage. The assignment was to gather images, words, ideas, and yes—activities, that were ways I could be nourishing and gentle with myself. I got out crayons and pens, prayed, crafted words on paper, cut out images from magazines, drew, and glued. Some of the things in my gentleness collage included:

Sitting in the garden
Taking a nap
Walking in the nearby park
Picking a bouquet of flowers
Taking a soothing bath
Reading from comforting books
The qualities of kindness, compassion, fun, and joy
Images for inspiration and images reminding me of Higher Power

I placed my Gentleness Collage in a prominent place in my room. My sponsor suggested I be or do something from the collage after each time I work on my Fourth Step. My Gentleness Collage became my companion through my Step writing, reminding me that the Fourth Step isn't a litany of how bad I am (as my developmentally arrested inner addict tended to think) but a neutral snapshot of all resentment, anger, lingering feelings, and fear that stand in the way of my conscious contact with my Higher Power. It was a great way of practicing what was to become a living amends to myself, of being internally gentle with myself and cultivating a climate of compassion inside—a practice that I continue to deepen today.

### "Negative Coping Skill" Re-Languaging

I had a difficult time with the language of "character defect" in Step Four, both because my 1990's English language brain is only a cousin of the language of the original A.A. *Big Book* authors, and because I am a survivor of intense verbal abuse that I had internalized. "Character defect" seemed like character assassination instead of loving compassion. The phrase "character defect" connected with a sense of rigidity and fixity for me. My sponsor offered the phrase "negative coping mechanism" or "negative coping skill" as a substitute for "character defect." This alternative language helped me approach my extensive inventory with compassion for myself, with a sense that the behaviors were understandable coping skills that helped me survive tough situations that had outgrown their usefulness and had come to harm and hinder me from full living.

### Character Assets

Additionally, my sponsor suggested I log entries of my "assets" ("character assets") as well as my defects ("negative coping skills"), since the metaphor in the *Big Book of Alcoholics Anonymous* talks about taking a thorough inventory, as of a store, noting what's present and available—not only what's missing or 'rotten on the shelf.' So I added a column of assets (see below for complete list), which my sponsor had me use two ways. One, if the entry were about an asset or positive-feeling situation, I wrote the asset in the last column. If the entry were about a fear or anger, for example, with an underlying negative coping mechanism, I would not only note the negative coping mechanism (e.g., illusion of indispensability) but also the potential character asset that could be involved were I to have a healthy response or presence in a given situation (e.g., faith). As throughout my Fourth Step work, there were times I got stumped on what to put in these particular columns, and so I asked my sponsor for help and filled them in when I was doing my Fifth Step. In this way, my Fourth and Fifth Steps were a real learning opportunity for me in healthy living and positive possibility!

**Extra Columns**

I found as I did Fourth Step writing that on some items I had feelings and feelings about those feelings, layers thick. So my sponsor and I added some columns (which, it turns out, are remarkably similar to the *CoDependents Anonymous Big Book* columns). My sponsor also had me add a column next to "character defect" for "character asset," as described in the section above. All in all, here are the columns I used:

- **Person** (can include myself)
- **Feeling** (e.g., anger, fear, shame, gratitude)
- **Issue**
- **Affects My** (select one or more: security, ambition, self-esteem, personal relationships, sex relations)
- **My Part**
- **Negative Coping Skill** (a.k.a. "Character Defect")
- **Character Asset** (Potential or realized, also sometimes "Positive Opportunity").

Here are five columns that replace the first three columns above for extra-emotionally squishy items (from the *Co-Dependents Anonymous First Edition Big Book*, pages 44-45):

- **Person**
- **My codependent behaviors and reactions**
- **My feelings that drove those behaviors**
- **Consequences to the person, myself, and the relationship**
- **My feelings about my behaviors and consequences**.

I am so grateful to my sponsor for helping me learn to work my Fourth Step with compassion and gentleness!

# Step Five

## *Guide for Step Five in Workaholics Anonymous*

**Step Five: Admitted to God, to ourselves, and to another human being the exact nature of our wrongs.**

For many of us in Workaholics Anonymous, this Step can be a big stumbling block. Being perfectionists, we procrastinate. Many of us suffer from big egos. We use work as a way to distract ourselves from facing the reality of who we are and the pain of our past. To admit "to God, to ourselves, and to another human being the exact nature of our wrongs" can seem impossible. But if we have completed our Fourth Step inventory and have begun to apply the first three Steps to our lives, this Step will bring a sense of inner peace and self-acceptance never known before. We begin to feel truly connected to God and our fellow human beings. We feel forgiven and experience a healing humility. We become more honest and realistic about ourselves.

Some of us have done our Fourth and Fifth Step as part of a Workaholics Anonymous Step group. Others picked a sponsor from another program to give our Fourth Step to. Some of us have co-sponsored each other. Some have chosen to give away our Fourth Step to a counselor or religious leader. Some of us have worked this Step in other Twelve Step programs but have yet to do a Fourth and Fifth Step in Workaholics Anonymous. We put it off without realizing we are delaying receiving the benefits that this Step can provide.

For many of us, the relief from this process is immediate and lasting. We find our relationships at work and outside of work improving as well as our relationship to ourselves. The negative thinking that drives so many of our relentless work and planning decisions is greatly healed by doing this Step.

*The dammed-up emotions of years break out of their confinement, and miraculously vanish as soon as they are exposed. As the pain subsides, a healing tranquility takes it place. And when humility and serenity are so combined, something else of a great moment is apt to occur...even those who had faith already often become conscious of God as they never were before.*
From *(Alcoholics Anonymous)* Twelve Steps and Twelve Traditions, *page* 62

## *Step Five Questions*

1. With whom should I share my Step Five? My sponsor? Another trusted friend?
2. In what way can I admit my character defects to my Higher Power?
3. Recognizing that taking Step Five is an important moment in my life, how can I create space around this time in order to reflect, recover, and nurture myself? Do I want to do Step Five in one day or spread out over many small meetings with a trusted advisor?

4. After confiding my Step Four writing, what have I learned about the experience and myself?

## Step Five Story: Reaching Out for Help

When I first joined W.A., no one at my meeting was available to take me through the Steps. So I asked a friend to help me. This woman had been in another Twelve Step program for many years, and had helped others with the Steps. We had known each other about four years at that time.

When I finished my Fourth Step, I called to ask her if she could hear my Fifth Step. When I asked her, she took a deep breath. She admitted to me that she had overcommitted herself. She was going through a lot right then, and didn't feel as if she had the time any longer to help me with the rest of the Steps. She couldn't hear my Fifth Step. I wasn't actually all that surprised. As I had started to recover in W.A., I had started to see this problem in her life. In the few months I had been in W.A. up until that point, I had told a lot of people that I had to back out of a commitment I had made. Instead of being angry, I understood, and I told her that. I thanked her for her help and told her I was glad she was taking care of herself.

She was surprised. At other times that she had let me down, I had responded with anger. She and I could both see my recovery. I was grateful.

As soon as I hung up the phone, I got down on my knees, which I don't do very often, and prayed. I asked my Higher Power to guide me to the right person to hear my Fifth Step and to help me continue my Step work—if that was my Higher Power's will. Oddly, I seemed to be very confident that I would find the right person.

That night, I ran into someone whom I knew casually. I knew she was active in another Twelve Step program and had helped people through the Steps. I felt she could keep a confidence, and she seemed very non-judgmental. All these things helped me feel she might be the right person. I explained my situation to her—that I was in W.A., that no one at my W.A. meeting was available to help me, and that the person who had helped me up to the point of my Fourth Step was not available to continue. I asked if she had the time to help me. This woman said she was honored, and graciously agreed to hear my Fifth Step. We scheduled a time when we could get together.

Before that date, I sat down with my written Fourth Step. I needed to admit these things to myself and to my Higher Power. I prayed, asking my Higher Power to help me accept these things I had written down, and asking for help to believe that my Higher

Power also accepts these things about me. I looked at the first item, and just sat still. I said to myself, "Yes, I have that resentment. Yes, my Higher Power knows I have this resentment. Yes, this person hurt me. Yes, I reacted selfishly." I did this sort of thing with each item in my Fourth Step. At each resentment, I prayed for that person, using the prayer out of Step Four in the Big Book of *Alcoholics Anonymous*, page 67: "This is a sick person. Show me how I can be useful to them. Save me from being angry. Your will, not mine, be done."

This was painful. I had to go back to Step Two many times, to remember how I came to believe that there was a power greater than myself that loves me no matter what I have done. After sitting with each item on my Fourth Step, I felt more at peace than I had in a long time. I started to feel like my Higher Power WANTED me to abstain from compulsive working every day, no matter what. I started to feel like I had the help to do that. I started feeling more secure in my recovery.

When I got together with the woman I had asked to hear my Fifth Step, I was nervous. I didn't know her that well, and so I worried that some of the things I had to say would upset her, or that she would judge me. I decided I would just start, and if there were anything I wanted to skip over, I would do that. I could find someone else I trusted more for those things, if I had to.

We prayed together, asking our Higher Powers to help us. As I told her about the things on my inventory, she asked a few questions for clarity. In some cases I had not been able to see my part in something, and she helped me with that. She didn't say much, but she did not judge me. After going through everything, she said she felt I had been very thorough, and we discussed some themes that seemed to run through many incidents in my life. We discussed how we would proceed with Steps Six and Seven.

That evening, I took some time to just sit with myself. I asked myself if I had been thorough and honest. I felt I had been. I thanked my Higher Power for the gift of this woman in my life, and for helping me through this. I looked at the first five Steps and asked myself if I had taken them to the best of my ability. Did I truly believe I was powerless? Yes, otherwise I never would have done this Fifth Step. Did I believe there was a power greater than myself that was restoring me to sanity? Comparing my life before and after I came to W.A., it was clear that SOME power was restoring me to more sanity, serenity, and hope. Had I made a decision to turn my will and life over to this power? Yes. That is why I went ahead with Steps Four and Five. That is why I was taking suggestions. Had I made a searching and fearless moral inventory? Yes. And I had also admitted to a power greater than myself, to myself, and to another human being the exact nature of my wrongs.

I felt relieved. I felt grateful. I felt hopeful. This marked the beginning of starting to share my daily struggles with others every day, instead of letting things build up. I could see the benefit of reducing my isolation. I asked my Higher Power for help to continue.

# Step Six

## Guide for Step Six in Workaholics Anonymous

### Step Six: Became entirely ready to have God remove all these defects of character.

This Step requires the support of the first five Steps. We admit we are powerless over work and business and that our lives have become unmanageable. We have come to believe in a power greater than ourselves who could restore us to sanity. We have made a decision to turn our will and lives over to the care of a Higher Power we have come to understand. We have made a searching and fearless moral inventory of ourselves and we have admitted to ourselves and to God and to another human being the exact nature of our wrongs. There is usually a great relief from shame at this point. We are ready to continue the healing these Steps have generated so far.

This Step asks our willingness to have God remove all our defects. As workaholics we are often plagued with perfectionism and self-will. After working the first five Steps, we come to understand ourselves better. We realize that we are neither perfect nor secretly defective. We are human. Our character defects are made up of dysfunctional survival skills. We are hurt by our old patterns of thinking and reacting. At first we think we would happily remove any defects of personality, the faster the better. But this Step is not about our removing the defects but the willingness to have God remove all our defects of character. It is not about being more perfect but about being better able to do God's will as we come to understand that.

We begin Step Six by making a list of all our defects of character. We review our Fourth Step. An example of a list might be: I am afraid of rejection so I frequently isolate; I feel safer hiding my anger, but then I act out in self destructive ways; I can't say "no" because I am afraid of disapproval; I do not take care of myself, skipping meals, sleep, and exercise; I lose myself in the rescue of others. I seek adrenaline highs unconsciously; I am intolerant of change; I become controlling when I am fearful; I compulsively judge others rather than feel my shame or guilt.

We may notice a character defect we are not ready to ask God to remove. Perhaps because of fear of change, or loss of enjoyment, we are not sure how we would cope without it. We are reminded that we are being asked to become entirely ready to ask God to remove *all* our defects of character. The naming of our defects and our willingness to have them all removed is a process of trusting that God will remove them in God's time. All of us who have done this Step have experienced relief, sometimes quickly and sometimes slowly. We have become better workers and partners. We can admit our mistakes; we cease to struggle, to defend. We dedicate our lives to growth and change.

*Even the best of us will discover to our dismay that there is always a sticking point, a point at which we say, "No, I can't give this up yet." And we shall often tread on even more dangerous ground when we cry, "This I will never give up!" Such is the power of our instincts to overreach themselves. No matter how far we have progressed, desires will always be found which oppose the grace of God.... What we must recognize now is that we exult in some of our defects. We really love them.... The moment we say "No, never!" our minds close against the grace of God. Delay is dangerous, and rebellion may be fatal. This is the exact point at which we abandon limited objectives, and move toward God's will for us.*

*Excerpted from "Step Six" in A.A.'s* Twelve Steps and Twelve Traditions

## Step Six Questions

1. What character defects am I willing to release right now? How might my life be different once I have released these defects?
2. Which character defects am I unwilling to release at this time? What benefit am I still getting from these characteristics? What would it take for me to become willing?
3. Alternatively, scan through the Step Four entries and extract the patterns of defects. For each cluster of character defects, answer the following four questions:
    a. What does the defect do for me? (How is it working for me?)

   b.  What does the defect do to me? (What is the negative consequence of it?)

   c.  What would bottom look like with this defect? (What will happen at its severest if I do not allow it to be removed?)

   d.  What would serenity look like? (What will it be like if this defect is removed?)

   e.  Am I willing for this defect to be removed?

## Step Six Story: Not all Roses and Miracles

While doing my Fifth Step, certain problems I tended to have in all of my relationships became clear (mostly due to my sponsor pointing out these "themes"). As I continued to live my life, some of my defects, or unsuccessful ways of dealing with people, became even more obvious to me. I heard myself saying selfish and judgmental things, but I could not stop myself. Although it seemed strange, I was clearly powerless. I could not control what came out of my mouth, and it bothered me.

Furthermore, it became clear to me that no one else was in denial about these character defects—others around me had seen them in action for years. My selfishness and tendency to judge others were not secrets. Although perhaps I was seeing them for the first time, I could not comfort myself by claiming that no one else was hurt or affected. That was clearly not true.

This realization certainly brought me more willingness. I did not want people to think I was selfish or rude. (I had not yet gotten to the point where I did not want to BE selfish or rude.) However, it was also pointed out to me that Step Six did not involve me removing any of my defects myself. I was as powerless over my dishonesty, desire to control others, and unwillingness to admit fault as I was over my compulsive working.

Observing myself convinced me that I was quite powerless. But did I believe a power greater than myself could help me with this problem? Clearly some power had helped me with my workaholism. I had abstained from compulsive working for some time. But for certain defects, it was hard to believe my Higher Power would help me. Shouldn't I be able to control these things by myself? What was wrong with me? But that attitude was not helpful.

What helped was asking others in W.A. to share their experiences with Steps Six and Seven with me. Because my W.A. meeting was small, I asked people in other Twelve Step fellowships also. Some of the stories were truly impressive—defects removed through no direct action of the person at all, only humbly asking God to remove them. Other stories did not include clear divine intervention, only the taking of suggestions made by a sponsor. But many people had experienced relief, or at least improvement. This was encouraging.

Not all stories were roses and miracles. I heard one person say that God removed his character defects in the order in which it is useful to God and to others. I was not happy about that! Why can't God remove the one that I find the most troublesome at this time?

Like many things I have learned in W.A., it doesn't have to make sense for it to work. I decided to try asking my Higher Power to remove all my defects of character.

As I struggled with some defects, people in my life made suggestions. For instance, perhaps if I apologized as soon as I realized I was rude, I could stop right then instead of being rude all day. Perhaps if I prayed for the people I resented, I would treat them better. Taking suggestions required a whole new level of willingness. It involved more than just allowing my Higher Power to see that I was not perfect and needed help—more than just asking for help when I was alone in a room with my Higher Power. It involved taking action in front of other people.

Looking back over my years in recovery, I can see that I tend to go through various degrees of willingness with different character defects. If I stay close in touch with my friends in W.A., they often point out to me when my unwillingness to take a suggestion holds back my recovery. I've also found that if I'm not willing, I can pray for willingness. In some cases, when I am struggling with a difficult problem, I call several people until I hear a suggestion I am finally willing to take. Often taking that one suggestion seems to make me more willing to try some others that I had initially rejected.

But I have found that the part of Step Six that I forget most frequently is the part about allowing a Higher Power to remove the character defect. I don't have to do it myself. All I have to do is pray and take suggestions. The same power that helps me abstain from workaholism can help me with my other problems. I never have to do it alone.

# Step Seven

## Guide for Step Seven in Workaholics Anonymous

### Step Seven: Humbly asked God to remove our shortcomings.

When we are entirely ready to have God remove all of our defects of character through working Step Six, the next Step is to humbly ask the God of our understanding to remove our shortcomings. In Step Six, we workaholics fight our self-will and pride. In Step Seven, we can experience the value of humility. We are a people preoccupied with power and prestige in our own accomplishments. We usually believed we were the one shaping our own destiny, demanding recognition, admiration, and control over everyone, risking our health and perhaps the health of others. Our striving was to control time, people's behavior, and the outcome of everything. There was never enough time, money, or love. We were never enough. Our addiction to work or avoiding work shut down our feelings, both of joy and frustration.

Workaholics are not usually comfortable with humility. Yet this is the cornerstone to our becoming truly happy. Humility is the key to abstaining from compulsive work and worry. To be truly humble is to get really honest with ourselves and accept who we are. We are recovering workaholics with dysfunctional ways of coping, self-destructive patterns of thinking and doing, and shortcomings that have gotten in the way of our usefulness to the greater good. Humility is a cousin to surrender. We surrender our shortcomings to a loving God of our understanding, knowing they will be removed. We are putting God first, not ourselves. We do this not by wishing or thought but by positive prayer. Some of us even get on our knees and say the Alcoholics Anonymous Seventh Step prayer:

*"My creator, I am now willing that you should have all of me good and bad. I pray that you now remove from me every single defect of character which stands in the way of my usefulness to you and my fellows. Grant me strength, as I go out from here, to do your bidding. Amen."*

*From page 76*, Alcoholics Anonymous.

Some of us then list these shortcomings slowly and imagine in prayer what our life freed of these shortcomings could be like. In that time of "conscious contact" we can be greatly helped to experience our essential selves humbly living a new life free of our addiction and free of the characteristics that hurt us and hurt others.

## Step Seven Questions

1. Looking back over your Step Six list of character defects, are there some defects of character that I have already released? Are there other character defects I am ready today to turn over? What shortcomings am I honestly still attached to?
2. Character defects can sometimes feel like defining characteristics. Reflecting for a moment on who I am at my core, what is important about who I am as a person and the person I will be without holding on to my shortcomings?
3. How is my life enriched by the experience of humility and surrender?
4. How can I truly have the willingness to have God remove all my shortcomings? What are the obstacles to willingness? What simple action can I take to move myself toward willingness?
5. What can my sponsor, my meeting, and other W.A. program members do to support me in this process? How can I reach out for assistance in truly letting go? Can the experiences of others help me walk through this Step?

## Step Seven Story: From Contraction to Arms-Wide Embrace

One way my sponsor coached me to approach Step Seven was to consider why Step Six in itself was not sufficient. In Step Six, I become willing to have the source of all creation remove my negative coping mechanisms from me.

In working Step Six, I had combed through my Fourth Step—which of course, being a workaholic, I summarized in an Excel spreadsheet that had 400+ alphabetical, unique entries by character defect (negative coping mechanism, a.k.a. liability) and character asset. I scanned the entries. I was really ready to release some of the coping mechanisms, having fully understood how they harmed me. I pondered how others still served me and journaled on that. Upon further reflection, I became ready, in

Higher Power's time, to become a fundamentally different person than I had been as a practicing addict.

The reason why Step Seven is a separate Step beyond Step Six is that part of my spiritual awakening requires me to release my negative coping mechanism of "playing God" (related to other defects such as "center of the universe," egoism, egotism, self-will run riot, illusion of control, etc.). Just because I am willing to have the defects of character removed in Step Six doesn't mean that they will be instantaneously removed. Step Seven is a living out of Step Three, in which I've turned my life and will over to the care of the benevolent universe. Part of the motion of Step Seven is a motion of surrender. I approach my connection to the immense fabric of creation with an acknowledgment that I cannot skillfully run the whole universe (or even remove one defect by my own will alone)—in a word, "humbly." In this, I am engaging a larger flow of spiritual power, and use the W.A. tool of "Asking"—"*asked* God to remove our shortcomings." The healing in Step Seven is the release from the imprisoning isolation of workaholism's island of self-centered fear and illusion of control. In working Steps One through Six, I have learned that the end-run of the "playing God" pattern, which is at the core of my disease, is my being cut off from the larger flow of life, of intuition, energy, and guidance. It makes my life smaller and smaller, my vision and my body more and more constricted. Through working the Steps, though, this process of contraction and dis-ease on a daily basis is brought to a stop. The motion of Step Seven is an outward sweep of my arms to embrace a larger spiritual Source that has the power to lift the patterns of the illness. Humility does not need to be me, head bowed, feeling bad and wrong. Humility for me is really this outward swinging, arm-opening, heart-opening welcoming of the larger resource of energy, life force, balanced knowing, and deepening that comes from my re-connection with a power greater than myself. I put down the defects and I open to receive the daily blessings of balance and clarity, groundedness and wholeness. By working Step Seven, I open more deeply and wholly to Divine Will, so that source energy can more fully flow through me. I believe that is why the *Twelve Steps and Twelve Traditions* chapter on Step Seven speaks about going beyond pain-enforced humility and willingness to a heart-centered openness that promises having a different daily experience. The practice of surrender, of opening, at the heart of Step Seven is the healing and balm that nourishes our repatterning to health. And as my sponsor reminds me, that motion to partnership with Higher Power, condensed in the wisdom of Step Three and Step Seven, can be engaged as a practice of daily renewal, in prayer and in living from assets, one day at a time.

## Step Seven Prayer: Prayer to Be Free of Resentment

*If you have a resentment you want to be free of, if you will pray for the person or the thing that you resent, you will be free. If you will ask in prayer for everything you want for yourself to be given to them, you will be free. Ask for their health, their prosperity, their happiness, and you will be free. Even when you don't really want it for them, and your prayers are only words and you don't mean it, go ahead and do it anyways. Do it everyday for two weeks and you will find you have come to mean it and to want it for them, and you will realize that where you used to feel bitterness and resentment and hatred, you will now feel compassionate understanding and love.*

*Page 552, Big Book of Alcoholics Anonymous, Third Edition*

# Step Eight

## Guide for Step Eight in Workaholics Anonymous

### Step Eight: Made a list of all persons we had harmed, and became willing to make amends to them all.

After we have humbly asked God, as we are coming to know God as our Higher Power, to remove our shortcomings in Step Seven, we turn our attention to our relationships. In our past times of long hours, frantic deadlines, stress depletion, and burnout, we had little time to nurture healthy relationships with other people. Even as we begin to work and schedule more realistically, many of us discover we cannot deal with the pressures of life or the pain of our past. If we are to stay in a healthy relationship to work, activity and other people, we need to take an action on those patterns that bring harm to others and ourselves.

In this Step, we begin by making a list of all persons we had harmed, including ourselves, with our addictions and/or character defects. Most of us go back over our Fourth Step and list names we had listed there, including our own.

The next action of this Step is to become willing to make amends to all the people on our list. It means being willing to see our part in the problem. It means to have compassion for the other, to forgive them and ourselves. We begin to admit that we are human with character defects and that we make mistakes. We begin to experience the inner calm that comes with forgiveness. The Step calls us to become willing to make amends to "all" the people on the list. Most of us have found that real serenity comes when we can finally truly and completely forgive everyone and when we are not yet ready, we pray for the willingness.

This is a two-part Step, first the list, then the willingness to make amends. Amends can mean we are truly sorry. As we progress through the Steps, we admit our character defects with the help of our relationship with our Higher Power. Most of us define amends to mean a change in our thoughts and behaviors—a change in the way we live that will not harm us or harm others. Although it is very meaningful for others to hear us say we are sorry, a greater impact comes from them seeing the changes we make in life as the character defects and addictions are removed. Step Eight is not about deciding exactly what the amends will be, whether direct, indirect, or living. That is the activity of Step Nine. Step Eight focuses us on our spiritual condition, our willingness to do our part in healing from this fatal affliction.

## Step Eight Questions
1. Going back over my Fourth Step, whom have I harmed?
2. What are my patterns of doing harm to others?
3. To whom am I not willing to make amends? Do I understand how holding onto that resentment is hurting me?
4. Rank each needed amends by level of willingness: Am I completely willing, somewhat willing, not willing at all?
5. How have I harmed myself? Am I willing to make amends to myself?
6. Have I gotten help from a sponsor with this Step? What are other stories of strength and hope in doing Step Eight?
7. Am I willing to make amends for my part in the relationship problem?
8. How does progressing through the Twelve Steps in Workaholics Anonymous help maintain spiritual and physical changes?

## *Step Eight Story: Cultivating Honest Willingness*

I was hoping that all my character defects would be removed before I started on Step Eight. But it became clear that I would never get to Step Eight if I waited until I was perfect. A couple of months after my Fifth Step, I had experienced improvement with some of my character defects. There were instances where I could see that my changed behavior prevented what would have otherwise been an unavoidable problem with someone. I could see how my relationships had improved and I wanted to mend some of the previous harm I had caused. I discussed this with my sponsor and others in W.A. Most people agreed it made sense to start on an Eighth Step list.

I set aside some time one weekend and sat down with my Fourth Step. I started going through it, using it to remind me of the people to whom I might owe amends. I wrote down the names of people and organizations to which I felt I owed amends. I included anyone from whom I had stolen something, people to whom I did not deliver what I had promised (such as a work product), people whom I had clearly hurt, and people with whom I had bad relationships. After each name I wrote a brief sentence as a reminder of what amends I felt I owed. In some cases, I owed one person amends for several separate things. The list looked something like this:

> Marcie, coworker: Did not give her report I promised
> Eric, coworker: Never followed up with promised information
> John, coworker: Never followed up with promised information
> Mark, product vendor: Never followed through with purchase as promised
> Peter, husband: Promised to spend time with him and then worked instead; constantly told him what to do.
> Employer: Lied on my timesheet and so was paid for work I did not do.
> Jeff, roommate: Left my stuff all over the house, left the fridge a mess
> Mary, friend: Promised to make her a clock. Made it, but never gave it to her
> Teresa, friend: Promised to make her a piece of art. Never made it.
> Pat, friend: Promised to meet for coffee several times and forgot to go

Andrea, friend: Promised to buy her something, but when
    I took her to the mall I made her pay for it.
Lisa, boss: Gossiped about her behind her back
Laura, co-worker: Gossiped about her behind her back
Amy, co-worker: Gossiped about her behind her back
Barbara, co-worker: Gossiped about her behind her back
Caroline, co-worker: Gossiped about her behind her back

After I had finished making the list, I arranged to meet
with my sponsor. We went over the list. I told her very briefly
about each amends. Some, she had questions about. She asked me
details that did not seem important to me, like exactly what I said
to someone, or what I had done after I let them down. She asked
me about some people on my Fourth Step, or other people in my
life, who she thought might also need an amends, but who weren't
on my list. This discussion helped me determine when I really
owed each of these people amends, and helped me complete the
list.

Then my sponsor asked which amends item on the list
seemed like the easiest. Not the one I wanted to do the most or
that seemed the most urgent, but the easiest. She suggested my
friend Mary might be the easiest. I had promised to make her a
present (a clock), and had made it, but never given it to her. We
were on good terms, so all I had to do was call her up and arrange
to give it to her. This made sense.

I certainly wasn't willing to make all my amends right then.
But I thought I might be willing to make amends to Mary. My
sponsor and I discussed exactly what that amends might involve.
There were no hard feelings between Mary and me, and I hadn't
promised to get her the present within any specific amount of
time. My sponsor suggested that I discuss this in confidence with
a couple of other people with experience making amends, so that
I could get the perspective of others before I decided what I
wanted to do. She also suggested that I start praying for Mary
every day in preparation.

It seemed ridiculous to call other people and discuss this
with them, especially for such a little thing. Plus it was
embarrassing. How many people were going to know about my
stupid behavior? But I had learned previously that it could prevent
a lot of problems to discuss my plans with someone outside the
situation. So I prayed for willingness. I eventually thought of a
couple of people with whom I could discuss this. I called one of
them on the phone, and explained the situation. I asked if she had
ever had to make amends in a situation like that. She had not. But
she thought my plan of calling Mary and arranging to give her the

present made sense. I called someone else who said the same thing. So I called my sponsor, and discussed my plan with her.

When it came time to make the phone call to arrange to give Mary the present, I was a little scared. I had to get on my knees and ask my Higher Power for help to make the phone call, but once I did that, I was willing and I picked up the phone and arranged to meet with her.

I became willing to make one amends at a time. After making the amends to Mary, other amends seemed more possible. As I progressed to the more difficult and complicated amends, I spent more time discussing things with my sponsor, seeking out people who had made a similar amends to hear their experience, and contemplating my options. For each one, I first had to become willing to look honestly at what I had done to hurt someone. Then I had to become willing to consider all the different ways I could make amends—even the scarier, more direct ways. Then, I had to become willing to make the amends in the way that was the most generous and effective. For each amend, I had to pray for willingness at each point in the process. I also found it helpful to pray for the person I had injured. Then I had to trust that my Higher Power would provide me with the willingness and perspective to make this amends at the right time. Discussing my fears with others also helped develop my willingness.

The last amends I became willing to look at was the one to my employer for lying on my time sheet. I had worked free overtime for all my previous employers, but my current employer was the only one that had paid me for hours I claimed to have worked but had not actually worked—my first episode of long-term work avoidance.

One person suggested the first task was to sit down with my time sheets and my records and really look at how much I overstated my work hours. How could I become willing to make an amends if I didn't even know how big a financial issue it might be? I had a year's worth of records to go through. About once a week I set aside an hour to go through my records. Each time I had to pray for willingness. At the end of the hour, I put things away and asked for help not to think about this until the next hour I had set aside.

Thinking about this amends too much filled me with fear. Each time that fear came up, I told myself that I set aside one hour a week to work on this, and the rest of the time my Higher Power can work on it. All I had to do was my part, and trust that I would receive guidance and willingness at the right time. I didn't have to be willing to make amends right now.

I compared my timesheets to my records of computer use, my phone log, and my date book. Some weeks I had worked MORE than I had claimed. I wrote that down. Other weeks I had worked less than I had claimed. I wrote that down, too. I didn't try to do it perfectly—in some cases I had to estimate or guess. I didn't worry about that. I did the best I could with the information I had. It took me many months to complete this exercise. When I was done, I added it all up. I had been paid for many hundreds of hours more than I had actually worked. When I multiplied that by my hourly wage, I saw that I potentially owed my employer almost one-fifth of my annual salary.

I was very upset and called a W.A. friend right away. Just hearing an understanding voice on the other end of the line was helpful. My friend reassured me that I was still a good person, and that my Higher Power would show me the best way to make amends. I didn't have to figure it out now, nor did I have to figure it out myself. Again, I didn't have to be willing right now. I could trust my Higher Power to take care of that.

I contemplated various possibilities for how exactly to make amends. My employer had no idea that I had lied, and it was very tempting to contemplate never telling them. I accepted that the right thing to do might not become clear for a while. I actually spent more than four months discussing this amends with various people in W.A. and other Twelve Step fellowships, telling them the various ways I thought I could make amends, and listening to their suggestions. The suggestions varied widely, from not saying or doing anything, to telling my boss everything and cleaning out my IRA account to pay the debt.

One person asked me a very important question that hadn't occurred to me: who was actually injured? My firm, a nonprofit, was grant-funded to assist certain people in doing a particular task that would benefit society. Although I had assisted these people to do the task, I could have assisted many more had I actually worked those hours I claimed. Was my firm actually injured? Was the grant maker injured? Were the people I was supposed to help injured? Or is it society, who would have benefited from more people doing this task?

Through discussions with others and contemplative prayer, I came to a decision about which parties had been actually injured, and what I could do to change that. I also came to the conclusion that I did not need to live in poverty to make amends. I came up with a reasonable plan that would not negatively affect my financial responsibilities to my family and other obligations. Then, I prayed for willingness until I was willing to write that first check.

# Step Nine

## *Guide for Step Nine in Workaholics Anonymous*

### *Step Nine: Made direct amends to such people wherever possible, except when to do so would injure them or others.*

When we finish with Step Nine, most of us begin to experience the freedom our Promises had predicted. Freed from the wreckage of the past, we find ourselves free to start a new life of community with our family, friends, and co-workers. Although this Step takes courage, good judgment, and a Higher-Powered sense of timing, the rewards are great. Using our list from Step Eight, we reflect carefully on each person we have hurt. With the help of our Higher Power and our sponsor, we can discern whom we need to make direct amends to right away.

We remember that an apology is not an amends. An apology is helpful, but the Step is about how we are changing. We begin our amends by integrating into our lives the principles of the Workaholics Anonymous program. We make amends to our family by maintaining our own recovery, by being healthy and "showing up." We make amends to our co-workers by setting reasonable goals, being honest, maintaining our sanity, respecting time, etc.

Another caution is that this is not the time to unburden our guilt at another's expense just to clean our conscience. Nor should it be a veiled effort to let go of any festering resentments by bringing up old hurts. The other person may be more to blame than we are, but we stick to our own errors. Telling a spouse or a boss about someone else's misdeeds may compound problems. This is the time for us to explain how our work addiction impacted another, and how we are changing our life. We do not want to inflict new wounds while trying to correct past harms.

Although the outcome of working this Step provides a big piece of our serenity, how the other person reacts need not do so. We need to guard against the exhilaration of a surprising forgiveness from someone formerly hostile, just as we need to protect ourselves if the person to whom we make amends is cool and skeptical.

Being workaholics, we might procrastinate on taking Step Nine. We ask our Higher Power for guidance and courage. There are issues especially hard for us, like false pride covering up vulnerability and shame. We can discuss the underlying causes with our sponsors, and we can pray for an obvious opportunity to come our way. Some of us book end the call for our appointment with phone calls to program friends. Step Nine encourages us to make the amends in person; the Step doesn't say "whenever possible" but "*wherever* possible." But, if the opportunity for direct amends is not possible, we can write a letter. We seek an "attitude check" from a sponsor or spiritual advisor before we send it.

We make amends to ourselves. We forgive ourselves. We are powerless, we are human, and we can be restored to sanity by our loving Higher Power. We continue to integrate the program of Workaholics Anonymous into our lives. We might find ourselves saying, "I forgive myself for actions that hurt me and others that came from fear, vulnerability, resentment, envy, selfishness, and preoccupation, as my Higher Power forgives me. I am being helped to lead a new life, and I am grateful."

## *Step Nine Questions*

1. How can I take good care of myself during the process of making amends? What extra kindness can I show myself? What is the best way to space out the amends process to keep myself from feeling overwhelmed? Who are some people I can reach out to and share the feelings that come up during this process?
2. To whom on my amends list am I ready to make amends today?
3. How would I categorize each amends in terms of direct, indirect, or living amends?
4. How has my life as a result of coming to W.A. become an amends to myself and to my past?
5. To which people on my amends list might I never be able to make direct amends? In what ways might I make these amends?
6. Will any of my amends harm the person or others? If so, what alternative amends might work in this situation (i.e. writing a letter that is not sent)?
7. What might be a good time and place for each amends? How can I plan what I'm going to say to each person to ensure that my apology, not my resentment, comes through?

## *Step Nine Story: Freeing Amends*

Making amends was the most healing Step for me, and the Step that made the most difference in my life. Each amends was a practice session for me in learning how to have right relations with others. Once I learned how to admit my faults, take responsibility for my behavior, and make up for the harm I caused, I no longer had to live in fear of not being perfect. I now know from my own experience that no matter what I do, I can always find a way to make amends. I spend a lot less time paralyzed with fear.

For each amends I needed to make, I started by praying for the person I had injured. Somehow this action, over time, lessened any resentment I had towards them and seemed to lessen my resistance to admitting my fault. I also sought out people who may have had to make a similar amends. I listened to their experience, and what the results of their amends had been. In many cases I couldn't find someone who had the exact same amends to make, but by asking around I found people who had something similar for most of my amends. It was also helpful to talk to people who had been hurt by someone like me. I got to hear what the consequences of my actions might have been, how I might have affected someone, and how I might be able to avoid hurting someone further.

I didn't necessarily make amends exactly the same way that others did in similar situations. In most cases, I spoke to several different people who did very different things to make amends for the same type of behavior. I felt some of those people didn't make as full and generous amends as they could have. And when I heard others discussing their experience, I felt they had really gone overboard. For some, I wondered if they hadn't caused more hurt to someone. One of the biggest gifts I got from Step Nine was the ability to understand that what is right for others might not be right for me. This doesn't mean they did their amends wrong, just that I had to look deep within myself and decide, for me, what was required to make up for the hurt I caused and establish right relations with the person I injured. As useful as it was to talk with others, ultimately my decision was between my Higher Power and myself.

In a way, Step Nine was the first time I had to bring my changed attitudes and behavior into the world of real relationships with people outside of W.A. I had to admit my faults to someone who was actually affected by me. I had to search inside myself for generosity, and let go of the attitude that everyone owed me something.

Particularly important was the consideration that I was not to injure anyone else. Telling the president of my company that my boss let me get away with egregious behavior might harm my boss by getting her fired or disciplined. Or would that be just letting her live with the consequences of her actions? Each situation is different, and in this case for me it was not clear-cut. I decided that I had to take action using my best judgment right now. I could always go back and make amends again if I see later that I should have done more. After praying for guidance, talking to others in W.A., and waiting a few weeks to contemplate this, I decided not to tell the president of the company about my behavior in order to avoid injuring my boss.

Most amends involved both making up for past behavior and changing my behavior in the future. So for some amends I had to go back to Steps Six and Seven. One of my big amends was to my husband. I had blown him off many times so that I could work more and more hours. I wanted to apologize and tell him I would change, but I knew it would just hurt him more if I apologized and then went back to my old behavior. Instead I started by asking if we could spend one hour a week together. He consented, and I went to any lengths to make sure I could show up for that hour, asking my Higher Power and W.A. members for help.

This amends also involved not getting angry with him that he didn't want to spend more than one hour a week with me. Someone pointed out that I had basically abandoned him while I worked compulsively. Is it any wonder he sought out other activities and obligations to fill his time? I can't expect him to give all that up just because I've decided not to work compulsively any more. Honestly acknowledging to myself and my sponsor how my past behavior may have affected and hurt my husband, and humbly asking my Higher Power to remove any character defects related to my relationship with him, helped me to have more compassion for his struggles and how I may have caused them, and to avoid harming him further.

After many months of showing up for him that one hour a week, it seemed it was time to acknowledge to him that I knew I hurt him when I was working compulsively, that I was wrong to do that, and that I would do everything I could to avoid doing that in the future. I discussed this with others in W.A. and prayed, asking for guidance. I considered how much it would hurt him if I did this and then went back to compulsive working. In the end, I decided to go ahead and have that talk with him. After I said those things, he said he was grateful to hear it. He also pointed out to me other ways my compulsive working had hurt him, things I hadn't even thought about. Fortunately, I had been praying for him and had some practice accepting my faults. Even though I was tempted to argue with him and tell him I didn't think I hurt him that much, I listened instead. Our relationship has improved greatly. Without W.A., I doubt we would still be married.

Some amends on my list fell into the category of ones that I could only reasonably make if I ran into the person. These were people whom I had hurt emotionally, but who were no longer in my life. Seeking them out would most likely bring up an old hurt and disrupt their life unnecessarily. For these, I prepared just as if I was planning to seek them out to make a direct amends. I prayed for the person, and discussed with other W.A. members what I would say to them if I ran into them. In some cases I asked a W.A. friend to act out the amends with me, so I could practice saying the words "I was wrong." This helped me feel more confident going about my daily life. I knew if I ran into the person, I wouldn't have to leave or hide. I could say my piece and accept whatever they said in return.

Some amends I have not yet been able to complete. For instance, I owed an old roommate some money. I had not been in touch with her for several years, but I sent a check to her last known address. The letter wasn't returned to me, but the check was never cashed. I tried other ways of finding out where she was, but couldn't find her. So I must be content with knowing that if I ever come across her, I can pay her then. Whether that happens is up to my Higher Power.

The more amends I made, the more evidence I had that admitting my faults improved my life and relationships. I can now usually apologize and make up for my wrong shortly after I do something hurtful or inappropriate. I no longer have a lot of people in my life with whom I have bad relations or whom I have to avoid. The freedom Step Nine has given me is really wonderful.

# Step Ten

## *Guide for Step Ten in Workaholics Anonymous*

### *Step Ten: Continued to take personal inventory and when we were wrong promptly admitted it.*

The Tenth Step is a *daily* maintenance Step as are the remaining Steps. Our experiences have revealed that daily practice of these last three Steps is essential to a balanced life and continued growth and renewal. In addition, we use them to recover from workaholic slips into toxic work binges. Practicing a daily Tenth Step starts our day and our new way of life from a spiritually and emotionally stable place. We will continue to do things that create problems, and events may happen that can throw our newly abstinent and sane life into turmoil. We are humans, not saints. But we can look back over our day and inventory our fears, false pride, envy, self-pity, and resentments. These are our old patterns of negative thinking. We can inventory attitudes and characteristics that were barriers to joyful, healthy living and reliance on our Higher Power that day. This is how we grow and change into sanity.

Twelve Step literature describes several kinds of inventory: a spot-check, daily, or intensive inventory. A spot-check is useful throughout the day to clean up hasty action or words that have caused harm. The spot-check helps us to identify and clear up blunders as soon as the event occurs. Many W.A.'s conduct their daily Tenth Step regularly in their evening or morning prayer and meditation time. Some write it down, others review the day with a sponsor or program friend. We notice when our behavior harmed or blessed those around us. A Tenth is a miniature Step Four through Nine. Similar to a Fourth Step, we notice both assets and liabilities in our behavior. The A.A. *Twelve Steps and Twelve Traditions* explains:

*"In all these situations we need self-restraint, honest analysis of what is involved, a willingness to forgive when the fault is ours, and an equal willingness to forgive when the fault is elsewhere. We need not be discouraged when we fall into the error of our old ways, for these disciplines are not easy. We shall look for progress, not perfection. Our first objective will be the development of self-restraint. This carries a top priority rating. When we speak or act hastily or rashly, the ability to be*

*fair-minded and tolerant evaporates on the spot. One unkind tirade or one willful snap judgment can ruin our relation with another person for a whole day, or maybe a whole year. Nothing pays off like restraint of the tongue and pen. We must avoid quick-tempered criticism and furious, power-driven argument. The same goes for sulking or silent scorn. These are emotional booby traps baited with pride and vengefulness. Our first job is to side step these traps. When we are tempted by the bait, we should train ourselves to step back and think. For we can neither think nor act to good purpose until the habit of self-restraint has become automatic."*
Twelve Steps and Twelve Traditions *by Alcoholics Anonymous p.91*

The intent of this Step is to conduct a daily self-search but not to experience additional remorse and self-criticism. We review our day to give ourselves appreciation for our progress and credit for things well done. We acknowledge where we need to take an action that is due. We cannot afford to risk our serenity with long-held negative emotions. We ask God to reveal what part we played in our upset. We pray for willingness to forgive others and ourselves. We promptly make amends. We do not blame others for our negative feelings or actions. With this inventory we admit and correct our part. Some of us write a daily gratitude and appreciation list as well as list our fears and resentments of the day. We practice this Step in order to live in peace.

## Step Ten Questions
1.  Have I been afraid, resentful, controlling today? Did any of my character defects flare up today?
2.  What actions in my day might require correction or amends? How can I make the amends that I need to make in order to maintain my spiritual fitness? How can I show myself forgiveness for my faults and accept my imperfections with self-love?
3.  How can I create space and time each day for Step Ten? Where is a good place in my home to practice Step Ten?
4.  What prayers or rituals would I like to use?
5.  What positive actions can I acknowledge today? What help have I received today? What help have I given to others today?

## Step Ten Story: "G" for Generous
I think that taking a daily written inventory has been a key factor in my continued abstinence and the happiness and joy I now have in my life. It has helped me change from judging my day

based on how much I got done to focusing on gratitude and evaluating my progress based on "behaving in accordance with [my] moral principles in every situation."

If I happen to have a day or a few days when I do not set aside the time to take a written inventory, I just base my next inventory on the events that have passed since my last one. There is no need to berate myself for not doing it perfectly, every day.

Each thing I write down as part of my inventory also involves prayer. The first thing I write down is "Thank you." I start by thanking my Higher Power for helping me to abstain from compulsive working to the extent that I was able.

Then I think about the previous day. I consider my actions. I look for times that stick out because I was angry or had a bad interaction with someone, or because I worked compulsively or strayed from my abstinence plan. Then I consider—did I act selfishly, trying to get my own way or hurting someone because I was focused on my own needs above theirs? Then I write down a short phrase about the incident under "S" for selfish. Was I dishonest? Did I lie? Then I write it down under "D" for dishonest. Did I act out of fear? Did I do something or avoid doing something because I was afraid? Then I write it down under "F" for fear. For me, every time I work compulsively, it is because I am acting out of fear or selfishness, or because I was dishonest with myself or someone else.

For each thing I write down, I say a prayer of thanks and ask for help. For instance, "Thank you for helping me see where I was selfish and took the last donut. Please help me be generous today," or "Thank you for helping me see where I lied to my boss. Please help me to tell him the truth today."

If I need to make amends (for example by telling my boss the truth), I think about how that will happen and what exactly I will say. Often I need to call another W.A. member for help in deciding what to say, and to help me become willing to set things straight.

Then I go back over my day again and look for times when I was generous, especially when I wanted to be selfish. Did I give up my seat on the subway? Did I thank my spouse for making dinner? Did I answer the phone when someone called? I write a short phrase under "G" for generous. Then I consider where I was honest. Did I want to lie but I told someone the truth instead? Was I tempted to tell my boss I could get done more than I reasonably could, but instead I was honest? I write that under "H" for honest. Then I look for times when I walked through fear to do the right thing. Did I ask for help even though I didn't want to? Did I call a new W.A. member? (That could also go under "generous.") Did I try a new thing? These go under "C" for courage.

Again, I say a prayer of thanks for each item. "Thank you for helping me to be generous and answer the phone," or 'Thank you for helping me to be honest with my boss."

Instead of berating myself for FEELING selfish, I thank my Higher Power that I did not act on it. Instead of berating myself for ACTING selfish, I thank my Higher Power for helping me see what I did, and ask for help to make amends and do better today.

I then make a list of all the people I resent. I pray for them: "Please give them everything I need in life, everything I would want for myself." When I start thinking about my resentment during the day, I can say this prayer again and remind myself that I have set aside time each day to think about my resentments (my Tenth Step time), so I don't need to think about it now. Praying for these people seems to reduce my resentment and help me have more compassion for them. Even if I don't want anything good for them, I can agree that if they got everything they needed, they probably wouldn't be behaving in a way that bothered me so much.

My written Tenth Step usually looks something like this:
1/1/05 Thank You

Selfish
- I did not call a member of my W.A. group (also out of Fear)
- I would not let my spouse have the TV remote.

Dishonest
- I told my boss I could finish the report by Wednesday (action-tell boss truth today)

Fear
- I did not answer the phone when it rang. (Also Selfish)
- I did not read my email at work.

Generous
- I went to the drug store for my husband.
- I went to bed on time.
- I left work on time (also Honest)

Honest
- I called in sick because I was sick (also Generous)
- I was honest on my time sheet
- I told my group I needed help avoiding a bottom line behavior (also Courage)

Courage
- I called a new person in my W.A. group

- I asked someone at work to show me the new computer program

Resent
- Mom
- Ted
- Jack
- Lucy

What I pray goes something like this: "Thank you for helping me abstain from compulsive working yesterday to the extent I was able. Thank you for helping me see where I was selfish and acted out of fear, not calling someone in my W.A. group. Please help me to be generous and walk through that fear today.... Thank you for helping me be generous and go to the store for my husband.... Please give Ted everything he needs in life, everything I would want for myself...."

After thanking my Higher Power for each incident where I was generous, honest, or courageous, or where I saw that I was selfish, dishonest, or acted out of fear, and praying for those I resent, I thank my Higher Power for "all the gifts in my life" and go on with my day.

I often find it helpful to discuss my Tenth Step with others. In fact, when I first started doing a Tenth Step, I discussed each item with someone over the phone, usually once a week or sometimes even more often. This helped me avoid beating myself up, and helped me see what exactly was going on. For instance, sometimes I have a problematic interaction with someone, but I don't know why. Was I acting selfishly? Or out of fear? Or both? Usually someone else in W.A. can help me figure this out. I have also sometimes put an incident under "Fear" when it really should have been under "Courage," and discussing my Tenth Steps with someone else helps me make sure I give credit where it is due.

After years of doing this, I feel I have trained myself to be grateful. Every time I leave work on time, I say thank you. Every time I'm polite to someone I don't like, I say thank you. Every time I am rude, I can still be grateful that I noticed it and can make amends. It wasn't that long ago that I didn't even notice that I was rude, or if I did, I justified that the other person deserved it. My relationships deteriorated, and I didn't know why. Now my relationships are improving, and I can see that doing a daily inventory is one of the main reasons why.

# Step Eleven

## *Guide for Step Eleven in Workaholics Anonymous*

### *Step Eleven: Sought through prayer and meditation to improve our conscious contact with God, as we understood God, praying only for knowledge of God's will for us and the power to carry that out.*

Prayer and mediation are our main sources of conscious contact with our Higher Power, the God of our understanding. How can we turn our will over without knowing what God's guidance will be for us? We workaholics can struggle with this Step. For many of us, in the beginning, if we pray at all, our prayers are quick, desperate requests for help. We think there is never enough time to meditate. We have little patience for sitting still. Our mind, in the silence of meditation, is undisciplined and the "to do" list or self-critic takes over. In the beginning, we might think meditation is the skill of mystics. For those of us in recovery who, for whatever reason or belief, have not come to experience a personal relationship with the Loving Spirit of our understanding, this is the next Step. The result is the promised spiritual awakening.

Our willingness to practice meditation and prayer begins the most healing and soothing experiences of our recovery. With practice and patience we come to know our time of conscious contact as a relief from our critical, effort-filled minds and our toxic bodies. We incorporate it as a daily part of our Action Plan. We find we need the light and love of our contact with our Higher Power. We discover the nourishment and guidance of that contact. It is good for our minds, bodies, and souls. So how do we start?

We can begin our instruction with the words on the Eleventh Step in the A.A. *Twelve Step and Twelve Traditions* (98-99):

*The actual experience of meditation and prayer across the centuries is, of course, immense. The world's libraries and places of worship are a treasure trove for all seekers. It is hoped that every A.A. [workaholic] who has a religious connection, which emphasizes meditation will return to the practice of that devotion as never before. But what about the rest of us who, less fortunate, don't even know how to begin?*

*Well, we might start like this. First let's look at a really good prayer....*

*"Lord, make me a channel of thy peace—that where there is hatred, I may bring love—that where there is wrong, I may bring the spirit of forgiveness—that where there is discord, I may bring harmony—that where there is error, I may bring truth—that where there is doubt, I may bring faith—that where there is despair, I may bring hope—that where there are shadows, I may bring light—that where there is sadness, I may bring joy. Lord, grant that I may seek rather to comfort than to be comforted—to understand, than to be understood—to love, than to be loved. For it is by self-forgetting that one finds. It is by forgiving that one is forgiven. It is by dying that one awakens to Eternal Life. Amen."*

*As beginners in meditation, we might now reread this prayer several times very slowly, savoring every word and trying to take in the deep meaning of each phrase and idea.*

We take these words in with each breath. Our breath is our connection to the sacred and our body temple. It relaxes us and prepares us to be uplifted and held by spiritual energy. It helps to imagine being in a beautiful place in nature. In time we learn to quiet our mind and relax our body.

We can imagine finding a Divine Presence. We use our breath to bring the Divine close or even into our body. When we begin to feel peace, light, and love-filled, we have made "conscious contact." This is when we can begin our conversation with our Higher Power. We experience spiritual meaning flowing through us. As we find our way to this special state of mind, we can ask to know God's will for us.

You might say this is just imagination, *"there is nothing the matter with constructive imagination; all sound achievement rests upon it. After all no man can build a house until he first envisions a plan for it. Well, meditation is like that too; it helps to envision our spiritual objective before we try to move toward it"* (page 100, A.A. Twelve Steps and Twelve Traditions).

This description is a tiny beginning to an amazing life of meditation; it can take many forms. We all have to find our own way. We can seek out classes, groups, and teachers. In seeking, we find what works for us. All forms lead to the same place—conscious contact with Divine love, wisdom, and grace.

The other hazard facing us is unconsciously projecting our will in a meditation into the search for God's will. How do we guard against using "well-intended unconscious rationalizations" for behaviors we want to justify? Perhaps the best answer is we use *discernment*. We ask ourselves if it lives up to the Eleventh Step prayer. Before making big decisions, we use our imagination again. We reflect, with Higher Power's presence, on an internal rehearsal of the outcome of big decisions. For a time of discernment, we check our physical body's reaction, as it is a great truth teller. We discuss our situation with our sponsor or a spiritual advisor. We grow to trust the wisdom we experience in meditation when we experience the love and forgiveness of the Eleventh Step prayer and align our will with the intention of that prayer.

Besides all the health benefits of meditation such as relaxation, reduced blood pressure, renewal after a stressful day, enhanced immune response, increased awareness of physical problems that need attention, there is one added benefit. Regular meditation helps us see the bigger picture, what is really important—things such as charity, truth, justice, and love. We find ourselves feeling chosen and special, a child of God. We belong to something greater than the small world of our work. The hostility of human affairs becomes less important. We find peace of mind.

## Step Eleven Questions

1. What am I grateful and thankful for today?
2. When in my daily schedule will I pray and meditate? What time of day works best for me? Where is a good place for me to meditate and pray (space at home, in nature, build an altar)?
3. In what ways have I taken back my will and my life from my Higher Power today?
4. Am I willing to turn it back over?

## Step Eleven Story: Breath and Gratitude

There are days when I don't want to take the time to sit still, pray, meditate, and read W.A. or other spiritual literature. But my experience is that if I am not willing to do this, I will work compulsively. If maintaining and furthering this relationship with my Higher Power is not the most important thing in my day, I go back to my old ways, and getting things done becomes the most important thing in my day.

For me, Step Eleven starts with asking my Higher Power every morning to help me abstain from compulsive working that day. At the end of the day, I thank my Higher Power for helping me to abstain from compulsive working to the extent I was able that day. I don't have to have a perfectly abstinent day to thank my Higher Power for helping me do the best I could.

When I came to W.A., I also started meditating for twenty minutes every day. I look at meditation as a practice session for sitting still and concentrating. I sit, and I attempt to focus on my breath. Whenever I find my thoughts straying from my breath, I see how gently I can bring my thoughts back to my breath. I don't get upset about straying thoughts—they are to be expected. The more I practice this, the better I become at sitting still and concentrating on the task at hand throughout the day. Some days, it is harder to do this than others. That's just the way it is.

My criterion for successful meditation is not how many breaths I was able to focus on. As long as I do my best to sit still, I check that off as a successful meditation. Some days I only end up focusing on one or two breaths for the entire 20 minutes. Other days I focus on many more before my thoughts stray. But that doesn't matter. It's just practice.

Prayer and meditation have been crucial in getting me through some very difficult days. Sometimes something happens that upsets me greatly and I cannot function. I have found that sitting still and focusing on my breath, if only for one or two breaths can help me calm down and be more useful during those stressful moments. I also meditate while waiting in line—one of my least favorite activities. I no longer have to go to a different store or restaurant if there is a line. I can wait now and save myself the effort of finding a line-free store.

Some days I have a great amount of difficulty focusing at work. I don't want to do anything except chat with my coworkers or surf the Internet. I have found that prayer can greatly alter the course of my day on those occasions. First, I pray, asking my Higher Power for help to do the next task. Often this gives me the ability to do that one task. Then I thank my Higher Power for helping me do that task. Then I pray, again asking for help to do the next task. Sometimes I have to break the tasks down into tiny subtasks: Ask for help and get the report out of the file box. Thank my Higher Power. Ask for help and open the report cover. Thank my Higher Power. Ask for help and read the first sentence. Thank my Higher Power. I have gotten through entire workdays doing this for every task, and a day that would have been fraught with dishonesty and procrastination turns into a somewhat productive day at work.

I also say prayers every day thanking my Higher Power for the gift of all the people in my life. I name them individually: Thank you for the gift of Peter in my life. Thank you for the gift of Amy in my life. I started doing this because I felt so alone, and it has really helped. I now remember that I have people in my life who care about me.

Another type of prayer that has helped me tremendously is praying for people I resent. I am the kind of person who tends to get a lot of resentments towards people. They don't say hello the right way, or do exactly what I want, and I resent them. So I routinely pray for almost everyone in my life every day. I say "Thank you for watching over Janice. Thank you for being with her in her hour of need. Thank you for showering love and light upon her." I have found that over time, praying in this way for people who bother me results in me not being so bothered. It doesn't always lift the resentment completely, especially if it is a particularly big resentment, but it usually helps get things to the point where I can have positive interactions with the person and not spend a lot of time plotting my revenge. In addition, it seems the more I do this, the fewer people I get resentments against in the first place.

Sometimes I get frustrated with Step Eleven. I ask my Higher Power for knowledge of her will for me, but I don't get an email telling me what to do. Instead, I must use my best judgment and consider whether a planned action is selfish, dishonest, or if I am planning to act out of fear or resentment. I can ask myself how I can be most useful right now, rather than how I can get my way or get what I want. I can discuss possibilities with others, and often my Higher Power seems to speak through others, but I still do not ever receive direct guidance from my Higher Power.

However, over the years, I have found that I am making better and better decisions. I still slip up a lot, but I am making more decisions that are "in accordance with my moral principles." I feel I have an idea of what my moral principles are. I am making fewer decisions that place me in a position to be hurt. And I am spending less time obsessing about my past actions and more time considering how I can be useful to my Higher Power.

## Step Eleven Story: Message from My Deeper Power—"M Therapy"

In the beginning of my recovery I was trying to cope with the toxic depletion I felt after a week of work. During a meditation this wisdom popped up. It has served me well over the years. I seem to need to plan three "M"s in a day to recover from burnout but the results are a wonder to me even now. Your "M"s might be different. The secret is to list things that are a transformation to your mind and body. The goal is to come back to your recovery spirit-self that desires healthy food, a balanced life and feels sane and sleeps well.

My list of "M"s is: meditation, measured meals, moments in nature, movement (like yoga or aerobic), making love, mass (or spiritual service), meetings (Twelve Step), music, and massage.

# Step Twelve

## *Guide for Step Twelve in Workaholics Anonymous*

### *Step Twelve: Having had a spiritual awakening as the result of these steps, we tried to carry this message to workaholics, and to practice these principles in all our affairs.*

What is a spiritual awakening in Workaholics Anonymous? We find the answer in Step Twelve of *The Twelve Steps and Twelve Traditions:* "*We believe we are now able to do, feel, and believe that which we could not do before on our unaided strength and resources alone.*" Looking back, as a result of practicing these Steps, we *have* become transformed. It seemed to happen without effort. We have a new energy, we are at peace, and we are sane about our compulsive work and activity. Our life has been restored. The presence and guidance of a loving God awakens us to our higher selves, to our body, mind, and spirit. We have the help of a fellowship of people with whom we can share the truth, and they love us all the more. We have received a sense of grace, and it now seems like a free gift. Life does throw us off track every once in a while, but we can face those bumps with our newfound program tools and our W.A. fellowship.

Naturally we want to give back some of what we found in Workaholics Anonymous. We all, newcomer and long-timer alike, feel something special about helping someone find recovery in Workaholics Anonymous. It helps us all to watch the lives of other sufferers move from despair to hope, from insanity to sanity. Who can help someone find recovery from work and activity addiction better than we can? We know what it was like and what life is like now.

How do we carry the message of Workaholics Anonymous? There are many ways. Changing our lives is the best message of all. Going to meetings or starting a meeting, making phone calls, or providing sponsorship are as helpful to us as they are to others. We reach out to tell our story to a fellow sufferer.

Accepting a service position at the group or Workaholics Anonymous World Service Board Organization is an opportunity that can be challenging to a workaholic. Many of us in early recovery are eager to simplify our lives. Yet we have found participating with other work addicts and volunteering to help the fellowship has strengthened our program of recovery. We are more likely to practice a program of surrender and sanity when we take a service commitment among fellow recovering workaholics. This helps us put into practice that last part of Step Twelve—*"We practice these principles in all our affairs."* We begin to live and breathe the W.A. program of recovery. We practice our tools and principles to maintain our spiritual awakening so we can be of better service to our family, friends, and coworkers.

Workaholics cannot abstain completely from work; we are at risk for slips and relapses. Even in retirement we can overschedule ourselves. We need the last three Steps to maintain our program of recovery. When we find ourselves slipping, we increase our use of the W.A. tools, especially meetings, meditation, the Tenth Step inventory, and phone calls to help get us back to sanity. It is an ironic truth in recovery: the service we give services us.

*... But today, in well-matured [W.A.'s], these distorted drives have been restored to something like their true purpose and direction. We no longer strive to dominate or rule those about us in order to gain self-importance. We no longer seek fame and honor in order to be praised. When by devoted service to family, friends, business, or community we attract widespread affection and are sometimes singled out for posts of greater responsibility and trust, we try to be humbly grateful and exert ourselves the more in a spirit of love and service.... Service, gladly rendered, obligations squarely met, troubles well accepted or solved with God's help, the knowledge that at home or in the world outside we are partners in a common effort, the well-understood fact that in God's sight all human beings are important, the proof that love freely given surely brings a full return, the certainty that we are no longer isolated and alone in self-constructed prisons, the surety that we need no longer be square pegs in round holes but can fit and belong in God's scheme of things—these are permanent and legitimate satisfactions of right living for which no heap...of material possessions could possibly be substitutes. True ambition is not what we thought it was. True ambition is the deep desire to live usefully and walk humbly under the grace of God.*

*From the* Twelve Steps and Twelve Traditions *of Alcoholics Anonymous, "Step Twelve," pages 124-125, with word substitution in brackets*

# Step Twelve Questions

1. What benefits do I get when I offer service to others? How does service enhance my recovery?
2. How can I offer service to my meeting or to other workaholics?
3. Where does service fit into my abstinence plan? Am I in danger of being compulsive in helping others? Am I compulsively avoiding service?
4. Can I offer assistance to others without ego, seeking nothing in return? How does the act of serving with humility further my own recovery?

# Step Twelve Story: The Miracle of Abstinent Service

## "Having Had a Spiritual Awakening as the Result of These Steps..."

I do believe I have had a spiritual awakening as a result of working the previous eleven Steps. This spiritual awakening, for me, consists of two connected parts: changed behavior, and changed beliefs.

My behavior changes include:

I am now honest with my employer about the hours I work. (Previously, I lied on many occasions, either claiming to work more than I had to hide my work avoidance, or claiming fewer hours than I had worked to hide my compulsive working.)

I am much more honest about how much I can expect to get done in a given amount of time. (Previously, I would tell others I could get a project done when, in reality, there was no way that could happen. On those occasions I was usually lying to myself also.)

I pray every day. (Previously, I prayed less frequently.)

I meditate almost every day. (Previously I had never meditated every day for more than a few months at a time.)

I perform a written moral inventory of my behavior almost everyday. (Previously I had done this only once a month or less.)

I enjoy life more. (Previously life felt like a struggle every day, which I tolerated so that I could achieve "retirement.")

My belief changes include:

I believe that my purpose in life is to serve this power greater than myself that has restored me to sanity. I believe that any action I am considering can be weighed in light of that purpose. (Previously, I thought my purpose was to achieve things and change the world.)

I believe every human being deserves to enjoy life every moment of every day. (Previously I believed everyone deserved to suffer continually because I suffered so much.)

I believe I am responsible for earning my own living. (Previously I felt my parents, family, and employer owed me a living.)

I believe, based on my experience, that prayer helps me. (Previously I did not think it could.)

I believe, based on my experience, that spiritual growth can help prevent and mitigate many of my current problems. (Previously I believed that pushing for my own way was the only way through my problems, and controlling others was the only way to prevent them.)

I believe that everyone deserves to rest as much as they need. (Previously, I believed everyone should work constantly.)

I believe everyone is equal in the eyes of my Higher Power. (Previously, I believed that some people were more worthy of love, recovery, attention, or a livelihood than others.)

I believe I am extremely fortunate to have everything I have today. (Previously I had very little gratitude and generally felt that I deserved more of everything except rest.)

There were no shortcuts for me to a spiritual awakening. I had to take all the Steps, as suggested. I could not force it. The Steps took time, and they took longer than I thought they "should." I didn't take the Steps to get a spiritual awakening. I took the Steps so I would not die of workaholism. But, looking back, I can see that by taking all the Steps with the help and advice of others, I have had a spiritual awakening that has contributed to my recovery and my happiness.

## "...We Tried to Carry This Message to Workaholics"

Shortly after I came into W.A., I saw workaholism everywhere. I thought almost everyone I worked with was a workaholic, as were my friends and spouse. My relationships with others became strained when I tried to explain to them how their behavior was "workaholic" and how I had the solution. I had forgotten tradition 11: this is a program of attraction rather than promotion. Once I stopped judging, and focused on my own recovery, my relationships with others became better. No one around me had to stop working compulsively, or to recognize his or her own workaholism, for me to recover. I simply stuck to my abstinence plan, and remained willing to go to any lengths to abstain from compulsive working. Some co-workers and friends noticed some changes in me, and some even asked how I am able to leave work on time. I simply told them how I did that. In many cases, I did not even tell them I was in W.A. Sometimes I just explained how certain things I did helped me leave on time—such as meditation, prioritizing, and substituting. Some people expressed how difficult they found it to do such things without support, and I told them about the support I receive in Workaholics Anonymous. Only a few of those people actually came to a W.A. meeting. But that brings me to another important thing for me to remember: carrying the message is successful if I remain abstinent. My success is not judged on whether others start recovering from workaholism.

I have to keep my own abstinence a priority when working with others, especially with people whom I sponsor. I need to use the tool of substitution every time I commit to Twelfth Step work. If I say I will be available to talk to someone on the phone, or meet with them to discuss a Step, I have to think about where that time will come from—what will I give up? Even if I am giving up watching T.V., I need to be clear with myself about what will come out of my schedule to accommodate any new commitment. I try to be very clear with those I sponsor about how much time I have for them. I don't have as much time as I would like to give them. But I don't believe it helps them if I overschedule or over-commit in order to give them more of my time. A big part of carrying the message is being an example. They, like I, need to see that it is possible to help someone and still maintain abstinence and serenity. For me, sometimes this means not returning phone calls for a day or two, or not being able to hear a Fifth Step right away. If I remember that they have a Higher Power (and it is not me) and that they have other resources besides me, such as literature, other members of the fellowship, and all the tools, I can avoid the ego-trip that often results when I start believing that other people in W.A. need me right now, and no one else can help them right now. That is simply not true.

Sometimes I put time into working with someone, and they don't take any suggestions, they complain that nothing works for them, and they continue to work compulsively, or in other ways frustrate me. It is easy to get angry with them. But I have found this is not helpful. Instead, I try to focus on being grateful that I am able to take suggestions. Why am I more willing to take suggestions than they are? That cannot be explained. I can just be grateful and remember that my job is not to make them do anything. All I have to do is listen to them and tell them what worked for me. That is really all I have to offer. I cannot promise them that what worked for me will work for them. I have found with most people, our relationship is better if I limit myself to sharing my experience and avoid giving advice or trying to get them to do anything. When particularly troubled by someone who continues to work compulsively, I remember the story about Bill W., co-founder of A.A. He stayed sober in New York for a period of time by working with other struggling alcoholics—none of whom got sober. But working with those alcoholics who never got sober helped HIM stay sober long enough to find Dr. Bob, who co-founded A.A. with him. This helps me remember that the people I sponsor don't have to do anything in particular for the interaction to be helpful to me. If all I get out of it is gratitude that I am not where they are, that is enough to help me abstain from compulsive working for one more day.

I also have to avoid thinking that I cannot ask others in the fellowship for help because I sponsor them or because they ask me for help, have less time in recovery than I do, or any other reason. That is also not true, and very dangerous for my recovery. Everyone in my local group has less abstinent time than I do. If I hadn't continued to ask all of them for help, I would not be abstinent today. Every time I have a slip I am tempted to avoid telling anyone I sponsor. I wonder if they will think the program doesn't work if I tell them I have a slip. But it helps to remember that it has helped me tremendously to hear other people talk about their experience of having a slip-and then getting back on the wagon. My relationship with those I help in recovery is one of equals. Over time, all of the newcomers I have helped have helped me, and I now have mutually supportive relationships with them.

## "...We Tried to Practice these Principles in All Our Affairs"

What are these "principles" to which Step Twelve refers? I think it may be quite fortunate that these principles are not listed in Step Twelve. Each of us is free to look at our own experience with the Steps and determine what principles we see there and which are important to us.

By looking over my experience, I can see what principles are important to me, and what has worked for me and what has not. The principles that I see embodied in my experience with the Twelve Steps include:

**Honesty.** Particularly honesty with myself about everything, including my limitations and others' limitations. This doesn't mean unnecessarily telling someone something that will hurt them.

**Not doing it alone.** It is very tempting for me to stop checking in with others about my motives, Step work, decisions, and struggles. But I have found that refraining from asking for help results in me lying to myself, hurting others, making bad decisions, and working compulsively.

**Generosity**. This includes generosity to others and myself. If I am generous in taking care of myself, I find I am better able to be generous with others. For me, generosity is the opposite of selfish behavior. Answering the phone when I have time, going to bed when I need to, and just saying thank you are all generous acts.

**Compassion**. For me, compassion is the opposite of resentment. Resentment often fuels my workaholism. Thus, my recovery seems to depend upon having compassion for the struggles of people who hurt me. This does not mean I continue to put myself in a position to be hurt, but that an adequate response to injury can consist of taking measures to protect myself and others, and does not need to include revenge. The most effective way for me to acquire compassion seems to be by praying for the person I resent.

**Taking responsibility for my own actions.** For me, this involves checking out my actions and decisions with others ahead of time, and making full and generous amends when I am wrong or when I have injured someone. This also involves being honest about priorities. When I neglect to do something, it is not because I didn't have time, but because I prioritized something else.

So what does it mean to practice these principles in all my affairs? Like most addicts, I find it easier to be honest, generous, and compassionate in some situations than in others. I can be compassionate towards someone I sponsor who has just lied to their spouse, but it is much more difficult to be compassionate when my spouse lies to me. I have no trouble checking in with other W.A. members regarding my Step work, but want to keep it to myself if I am inching towards working compulsively.

Practicing these principles in all my affairs means that I continue, every day, to attempt to make progress in practicing these principles. I'm not perfect, and I don't have to be perfect. There are times when I fail miserably. I have found that if I am selfish and dishonest, I can ask for help to stop. When I do that, things don't get so out of hand. Every day I have the choice to clean up my past and ask for help to do better today. The more I do that, the better I sleep, the better my life is, the happier I am, and the easier it is to stay abstinent.

# Artistic Responses For the Twelve Steps

**Step One**: Build an altar to your unmanageability. Select and add an item to represent every major aspect of your unmanageability. Light a candle on your altar and spend ten minutes for seven days in a row in silent contemplation of your Step One Altar. Sit lovingly with yourself and gaze at the aspects of your disease with acknowledgment. Journaling can be a useful activity after the silent meditation.

**Step Two**: While not displacing your Step One Altar, build a different altar, this time an altar about your Higher Power. Select and display tangible items that represent aspects, qualities, and traits of your Higher Power. Are there symbols of your belief that you can add to the altar? Select some more items, those that represent the best/biggest/most powerful/loving aspects of Higher Power you could wish for. In order to do this, you might want to write a "help wanted" ad for your Higher Power, or visualize going to the Higher Power boutique and trying on some new Higher Powers. Light a candle and spend ten minutes a day for a week with your altar. Feel free to add items to the Altar as inspiration guides you. Journaling can be a useful activity after the silent meditation.

**Step Three**: After completing Steps One and Two, conduct a ten-minute meditation with your Step One and Step Two altars. Then take each item, one at a time, from your Step One Altar and place it on your Step Two Altar. Imagine you have angels/guides/guardians/helpers assisting you in carrying each item to your Higher Power. Place each item beside an object on your Step Two altar that has the power to take care of the Step One item. When you have completely cleared your Step One Altar and given your life and your will and all aspects of your disease over to your Higher Power, spend ten minutes a day for a week contemplating in deep, restful peace and serenity the nourishing feeling of support and letting go from not having to worship at the Altar of Unmanageability any more. Some people find it helpful to include something to symbolize your whole life and your whole will to place in the loving care of Higher Power by placing it on the Higher Power altar.

Alternatively, build and collage/decorate/decoupage a coffee canister or other similar container to make a "God Can" expressly for turning things over. Decorate both the inside and the outside of the can with your favorite images of transformation. Create beautifully decorated note paper that will then be all ready for writing things down to turn them over. Stickers, stamps, go to town!

Now, as it says in *Alcoholics Anonymous*, "we can only clear the ground a bit" (Third Edition, page 55) unless we continue with Steps Four through Nine to have ongoing spiritual relief.

**Step Four**: In order to take a fearless and thorough moral inventory, it is often great to start with developing a Gentleness Tool. You can use this artwork to describe a resource for Gentleness with Self. These sheets can be hand-bound with dental floss or string into a wonderful Gentleness Book. Step Four entries themselves can be done with crayon or colored pencils on paper using one of the suggested formats. Have your sponsor give you fun stickers for each completed entry. Draw smiley faces and give yourself "A+"s. Another way to augment the Step Four experience is to make a collage of your best self, highlighting all your assets. Select pictures and words that represent your best assets and glue them on poster-board to represent your vision map.

**Step Five**: Light a candle and make an altar when you meet with your sponsor. Dress as an altar. Wear beautiful clothing, all the colors of the rainbow, or floral and festive prints to your Fifth Step. You are the living miracle. Celebrate it! Another idea: burn your Fourth Step entries as you share them in Step Five (although this can make the defect synopsis in Step Six more difficult).

**Step Six**: Write each key defect on a piece of origami paper with the four questions answered: 1) What does this do for me? (How has this defect served me?) 2) What does this do to me? (Describe negative impacts.) 3) What would my low point with this look like? And 4) What will emotional/spiritual/mental serenity look like as this defect is removed? Add the words from Step Six that are assets or positives to the collage mentioned in Step Four.

**Step Seven**: Fold the origami papers into little boats and let them float away on a river or pond as you become willing and ask your Higher Power to remove them.

In **Step Eight**, draw a picture on a three-by-five card of each person, place, or thing, institution, or incident to which you have caused harm. Use pens and colored pencils. Outline each card with a color for your willingness. Yellow is not willing; Blue is somewhat willing; Green is very willing. As you pray and become more willing, update the edging colors to update the color codes. Green is for go. Any amends with a Green edge means you are ready to work Step Nine.

**Step Nine**: Stack the cards from Step Eight in priority order of amount of harm caused. (Usually your "self" card will be at the top of the list.) In your daily prayer and meditation, every day for two weeks, take each three-by-five card and pray for each card (including yourself) every good thing you can think of that you would like for yourself. As you do this prayer, draw golden light or a halo around each card's figure. By the end of two weeks, the cards will fairly glow.

**Step Ten**: One possible artistic tool to use for a daily Tenth Step is a sketch of your day. Draw yourself and your Higher Power and list how you collaborated today. What were the healthy choices represented today? Write a "recycle" list of everything you'd like recycled or scrubbed away from the day, and highlight in orange any actions you need to take as a way of making amends.

**Step Eleven**: Create a prayer and meditation space for yourself. Perhaps it's a hand-knitted, warm prayer shawl or a sweet corner of your living room or den that has a quiet space, possibly a beautiful cloth, live plants, etc. Decorate your prayer and meditation space so you can enjoy spending time there. Customize it so that it is just right for you. Do a collage of what Consious Contact looks like and post it in the space. Spend time in your special place daily.

**Step Twelve**: Draw a gratitude list in which each service opportunity or life modeling of your recovery is a star-bursting firework. Write rays of all the positive things you learn, contribute, receive, and/or get to enjoy through each firework of "carrying the message" and "practicing the principles in all our affairs." All together, this is the firework show of your spiritual awakening.

# MEETINGS

## How to Contact us and How to Find or Start a Meeting

You can contact Workaholics Anonymous as described below:

Workaholics Anonymous World Service Organization
P.O. Box 289
Menlo Park, CA 94026 USA
Messages: 510 273-9253
Email: wso@workaholics-anonymous.org
Web site: www.workaholics-anonymous.org

Meetings are listed and updated on our website. Information, introductory literature, and applications for our World Service Organization Conferences are on our website as well.

We have an excellent newsletter *Living in Balance*, published several times a year. You can subscribe by mailing your request to the above address.

Recovery from workaholism is spreading across the globe, including international meetings and a German-language fellowship. As we are a growing Twelve Step program, some of us may not have a meeting nearby. There can still be recovery. Here are some ideas about how to get a program of recovery.

1.  We have found sponsors or spiritual advisors familiar with the Twelve Steps to help guide us through the Steps.
2.  We have attended the Workaholics Anonymous World Service Conference. This is a great way to meet other recovering work addicts and to deepen our program.
3.  We sign up as a W.A. Individual ("Loner") Member. "Loners" will receive the Newsletter and will be given the names of other Individual Members who wish to be contacted.
4.  There are online and telephone meetings. Check the W.A. web page for information.

5.      Daily reading of our literature and a phone call to discuss our daily action plan has helped many of us, including those who do not have a meeting nearby.

6.      Start a meeting, once you get two or more interested. Write W.A.-W.S.O. at the above address for a meeting starter kit.

# Suggested Guidelines for Workaholics Anonymous Recovery Meetings

*[Please adapt for your own group purposes.]*

*Pass out the suggested readings: The Characteristics of Workaholism, Signposts of Workaholism, Tools of Recovery, How Recovery Happens, The Twelve Steps of Workaholics Anonymous, the Twelve Traditions and The Promises of W.A.*

"Welcome to the _____ meeting of Workaholics Anonymous. My name is _____ (first name) and I'm a workaholic and your present secretary of this group. Will all those who wish to please join me in a moment of silence, to do with as you wish, followed by the Serenity Prayer?

"God grant me serenity to accept the things I cannot change, courage to change the things I can, and wisdom to know the difference."

*(Read the Preamble}*
"Workaholics Anonymous is a fellowship of individuals who share their experience, strength, and hope with each other that they may solve their common problem and help others to recover from workaholism. The only requirement for membership is a desire to stop working compulsively. There are no dues or fees for W.A. membership; we are self-supporting through our own contributions. W.A. is not allied with any sect, denomination, politics, organization, or institution; does not wish to engage in any controversy; neither endorses nor opposes any causes. Our primary purpose is to stop working compulsively and to carry the message of recovery to workaholics who still suffer."

"Now is the time we introduce ourselves by our first name only. Please let us know if you are here for the first time or visiting from outside this area so that we may welcome you. My name is _____.

"I will pass around a list for names and phone numbers. This means the signers are willing to talk with you about the program between meetings.

"Are there any W.A.-related announcements?"

## POSSIBLE GROUP READING

*Ask volunteers to read:*
  1. *How Recovery Happens*
  2. *The Twelve Steps of W.A.*
  3. *Characteristics of Workaholism*
  4. *Signposts of Workaholism*
  5. *The Tools of Recovery.* "The tools can be read in any order and you may pass at any time."
  6. *A Tradition of the month*

## SPEAKER/TOPIC

The format of this meeting is _____.

*[If it is a speaker meeting or a meeting that reads from literature, the speaker, Step, or literature is shared at this point, or other topic introduced.]*

"We ask that we avoid cross-talk. Avoiding cross-talk means that when we speak, we address the meeting as a whole. We speak in the first person and do not give advice. Please do not share again until everyone who wishes to has had an opportunity to share. We keep the Twelfth Tradition of anonymity in mind, placing principles before personalities.

"The meeting is now open for sharing. The topic is _____."

*At about 15 minutes before closing, the Secretary may say,* "Would any of our newcomers wish to share?"

## CLOSING

*At the end of the meeting:* "Our meeting is now completed. If you didn't get an opportunity to share, please stay after the meeting and talk with someone."

"By our Seventh Tradition, we are self-supporting, declining outside contributions. I will pass the basket. If this is your first meeting, please don't contribute. The money we collect goes to pay for rent and literature, and to support our outreach to other workaholics." *(Pass the basket.)*

"A member will now read *The Promises of the Program.*"

"In order to preserve each member's anonymity, we ask that all you see here and all you hear here stay here. The opinions expressed are personal ones. Please take what your like and leave the rest."

*Thank those who read during the meeting. Repeat welcome to newcomers and to any who are celebrating a birthday or anniversary of abstinence.*

"In closing, we are thankful to have this opportunity to grow in respect for ourselves and to learn a healthy attitude toward our work. No matter how deep-rooted and desperate our workaholism, no matter how hopeless our problems seem, we start from where we are. By living the program one day at a time, we begin to experience the freedom and happiness it offers. As we grow closer to our Higher Power, we find we have become transformed. We have what we always sought, love and peace of mind. What seemed impossible is now a reality. If we continue to take action on our program, one step at a time, we find life becoming richer and more joyful."

*(Secretary distributes copies of the closing prayer.)*

"Let's end our meeting with the _____ prayer." (*Meeting choice, for example the Unity Prayer, the Serenity Prayer, the Third Step, Seventh Step, or Eleventh Step Prayer.*)

# Meeting Stories

## *Meeting Success Strategies*

Our local meeting is doing a number of things that we thought we might share with the other groups.

At the beginning of the meeting, the chairperson asks if anyone has any "successes" they would like to briefly share so that we can clap and cheer for members making progress towards abstinence from compulsive working. This consists of brief statements ranging from "I left work at 5pm every day last week," to "I got to the meeting on time." After each statement, the group claps, pounds on the table, cheers, and stomps. We started doing this because another Twelve Step group meets downstairs from us and we could hear them clap and cheer every week. We wanted someone to clap and cheer for us! Where else will someone cheer for you just for leaving work on time?

We also wanted to read some "promises" at the end of the meeting, so the chairperson chooses to read either the last two paragraphs of the pamphlet *Recovery from Workaholism: The Twelve Steps of Workaholics Anonymous* ("Following the Steps brings us in touch with our inner wisdom and spirituality....") or the last three paragraphs of the pamphlet *Turning Work into Play* ("Contentment becomes a natural part of living....")

We don't have set topics for particular weeks, but usually use one of two formats. When a newcomer is present, we usually go around and each member tells a little about their story: what it was like, what happened, and what it's like now. If there is no newcomer, the chairperson usually picks some literature to read, and we go around the room, each person reading a paragraph or two and then sharing on that paragraph, and then passing the reading to the next person, who reads a paragraph or two and then shares if they wish. This format seems to help some of us who have short attention spans and have trouble listening to a long reading.

## *Successful Meeting Highlights*

The Tuesday night meeting in our city has been going strong for about five years. In the three years since I joined the program, the size of the meeting has grown from 2 - 4 people most weeks to 4 - 8 regular attendees. We have grown tremendously in our strength and unity as a group through planning and putting on two "W.A. Days" attended by members from other fellowships in the region and by helping to put on last year's World Service Conference. Our meeting has a rotating format. We have a speaker, games night, Step reading and open sharing, with a grab bag meeting when there is a fifth week.

Because we have a small meeting, we have found it helpful not to have a regular secretary. We do have designated key holders who make sure the room is open for the group. Each meeting, one of the attendees volunteers to act as secretary for the evening. This takes the pressure off and allows members to contribute more or less according to their level of energy.

Games night is a unique feature of our meeting and one of my favorites. We were inspired by another W.A. group's inclusion of play in their format and by experiencing recovery through play at the first W.A. Day. We tried a number of different types of play and fun and different meetings structures. Our current format includes brief shares (2 minutes each) followed by 30 minutes or more of non-competitive play. The game that has worked best for us is charades. By practicing the tool of Play and Fun, we have learned to laugh more and built our sense of community. Games night has strengthened my recovery by reminding me how fun it is to laugh and be silly. I leave the meeting wanting more of this good stuff and I have added more recreation to my life since we started this practice. Do other meetings find ways to bring Play and Fun into their group recovery?

Another unusual format is the Grab Bag. Each member puts a question or a topic into a basket. We then pull out the questions/topics and whoever wants to can share on each one. Shares are limited to two minutes so we can get to as many questions as possible. We have found this format leads to interesting and focused discussions of topics we might not otherwise have addressed as a group.

## Area Meetings Throw A Retreat

On July 20th at 1:00 p.m. the second (annual?) Regional Workaholics Anonymous Retreat got under way. Put on by the combined efforts of members of the two W.A. meetings in the area, this was actually a great advance for the recovery of all in attendance. Members of two other local meetings attended the retreat as well.

Several members from around the area went early to the busy retail and restaurant district near the meeting place for a deli lunch in the fresh air. Then attendees gathered at one member's home, signed in with our telephone numbers and email addresses, got our name labels and sat down for a round of two-minute check-ins. It was suggested that each leave a donation (ten dollars was suggested) for W.A.-W.S.O. in the basket provided.

An announcement was made that, with the election completed, three of the active posts on the board were still/again open, and every person present was encouraged to consider whether she or he might step into service.

The gathering opened with a W.A. meeting, with different members reading The Preamble, A Definition of Workaholism and The Twelve Steps. We passed the sheets of Principles and Tools around for everyone to share in the reading. One member from a local meeting was the speaker. Then there was time for three-minute (timed) sharing. After the Promises we took a break to have some tea or talk or take a walk or sit or whatever.

We gathered after the fifteen-minute break and sat down for a few introductory comments about meditating and then a period of silent meditation. This was followed by a second W.A. meeting, this time reading the Characteristics. After the sharing time we took another break of about fifteen minutes.

Then we returned for a laughing meditation. This is a regular part of many people's lives in India, often done in clubs or large groups. Those who participate find it quite healing. Physicians and psychologists find it a boon to mental and physical health. After a little explanation, we all sat (or stood) there and laughed for ten minutes. At the end we were breathless and happy.

People's minds were turning to food. Menus and envelopes were laid out for neighborhood French, Thai, Chinese, Mexican, Italian and deli take-out restaurants. We made our choices, put the cash in the envelopes and telephoned in the orders. One person took an envelope to each restaurant and carried back the order. It was an evening of fine dining. After dinner we shared in the cleanup and then chose to play Charades, to the continuing delight of all present, until we dragged ourselves away and headed home.

In the course of the afternoon one member volunteered to be the new Facilitator, one volunteered to be Treasurer of the W.A. World Service Organization. The regional retreat offered a day filled with inspiration, fun, fellowship, and recovery for us all!

# HELPFUL LITERATURE

## Characteristics of Recovery

1. We are able to speak with phrases such as: I don't know. I was wrong. I made a mistake. I'm sorry. I can't. I need help. I don't remember. I don't understand. So what? Who cares? Compared to what?

2. We are able to say: I hurt. I'm uncomfortable with what you said. I'm afraid. I'm sad. I'm lonely. I feel like goofing off. I feel silly.

3. We accept that others need not always be happy. We don't fight their feelings with logic or distraction.

4. We believe that many people can do all or most of what we do—as well as we can, or better.

5. We know that others have limits. We don't expect to predict the future or read minds. We know that failures and incomplete projects are part of the learning process. We realize that no matter how fast or efficiently we work, there are only 24 hours in a day.

6. We respect our body instead of fighting it. We realize that feeling ill or tired is part of the human experience. We rely on intuition and inner timing and rhythm.

7. We accept that everyone may not like us.

8. We can refuse responsibility or requests. We can say no without feeling guilty. We nurture ourselves and give from our overflow.

9. We delay, delegate, and lower performance standards, when needed.

10. We realize that it is okay to be inconsistent. We find our own mistakes a continuing source of humor.

11. While communicating, we notice people's states and respond to them rather than being solely focused on the matter at hand.

12. We value joy over efficiency. We understand the importance of rest and play. We think of work as part but not all of life.

13. We believe everyone has intrinsic value, whether they work or not.

14. We realize we are valued by how we treat others, not by what we own or produce or by how hard we work. We know that people don't care how much we know until they know how much we care.

15.   We realize we can't push growth. We know we can't change, control, or rescue anyone. We have reasonable expectations for ourselves and for others.
16.   We live in the present without regretting the past or fearing the future.
17.   We believe that others who are part of a joint venture share responsibility for bad or good outcomes.
18.   We accept change, the unexpected, and conflict as part of life.
19.   We trust our developing relationship with our Higher Power, and we embrace our goodness and serenity.

# Helpful Reminders

I refuse to rush; there will be enough time.

The slower I go, the more I do, the more time I have.

Think timelessness—sip not gulp.

Slow is beautiful and powerful. I move glacially.

Am I a human being or a human doing? Am I enjoying or enduring?

I don't have time not to have time.

When I take time, I make time.

I'm not livin' if I'm driven.

The body keeps score.

My life is full and underscheduled.

Rest is the best reward I give myself.

Success is the quality of your journey.

Enjoyment is my way of keeping score.

The goal is the excuse for the fun of the race.

Take an emergency leisurely.

I'm striving in contentment; my decision is letting go.

Work is the highest form of play.

Put it on your not-do list.

I do everything easily and effortlessly.

There is no place to go and nothing I have to do.

I can't help anyone if I can't help myself.

Spontaneity and surprise are the spice of life.

Even when offered the best, say "no" if you need to rest.

Simplicity means small and frequent pleasures.

Importance, not urgency; values, not goals; quality, not quantity.

The way to do is to be here now.

Recovery-related: rest, relaxation, recreation, renewal, and reconnection.

We must learn to be still in the midst of activity and to be vibrantly alive in repose. —Indira Gandhi

Don't succumb to production seduction.

We don't try to grow. We accept ourselves as we are, and we grow automatically.

My life is my career; my career is not my life.

Let go and flow.

Calm, breathing, and masterly awake.

Expect the unexpected.

The means determine the end.

My day is my work; my work is enjoying my day.

Critical mind/sick mind; positive mind/healthy mind; still mind/divine mind.

My highs come from my Higher Power.

Space out your appointments to avoid becoming spaced out.

When you simplify, you're not subtracting: you're adding time and space.

Live your life with broad margins. —Thoreau

Becoming a friend of time means treating it like a friend by devoting some time to it.... Make an appointment with time. —Jean-Louis Servan-Schreiber

God doesn't care about your ability, just your availability.

Everything can wait but love.

Underwhelm yourself.

My being is my doing; my overdoing is my undoing.

The more I play, the harder God works.  —Joseph C. Pearce
Regarding creativity: Do not try to think consciously. Drift, wait, obey. —Kipling

# Affirmations for Workaholics

1   The less I struggle, the more open I am to inspiration. The more I take it easy, the more I accomplish.
2   My Higher Power wants me to realize my vision of joyful work and a balanced life and gives me whatever I need to achieve it at the right time.
3   I do everything easily and effortlessly.
4   My life is full and underscheduled.
5   I now receive full assistance and cooperation from all persons necessary for realizing my work vision. I attract only loving people.
6   The more I risk, the safer I am.
7   I am more effective by being more selective.
8   The more I play, the more God works.
9   I have time to spare and time to share. Time is my friend. When I take time, I make time.
10  My top priority is doing my being. Before I do anything, I first do nothing.
11  I draw to myself everything I need for a joyful balanced life.
12  My doing my right work strengthens all my relationships. My work brings me closer to those I love.
13  When I take time, I make time. The more I take my time, the more time I have to take. I don't have time not to have time.
14  I am entitled to my right work and deserve the enjoyment, recognition, and health that right work brings.
15  I live by divine appointment with broad margins.
16  I am still in the midst of activity and vibrantly alive in repose. I take an emergency leisurely.
17  The slower I go, the faster I grow.
18  Even when offered the best, I say no if I need rest. Rest is the best reward I can give myself.
19  My body is my friend and my temple. I bless and thank it daily and obey its signals.
20  Emotions are information. I honor their important messages.
21  I love myself no matter what. I'm perfect just the way I am. I am enough. I have enough. I do enough.

22 People bring me important messages (angels in my life) when I listen or meditate carefully.

23 I work to live, not live to work.

# Our Favorite Slogans

Work Smarter, Not Harder.
Just for Today.
One Day At A Time.
First Things First.
Easy Does It .
Easy Does It, But Do It.
Let Go and Let God.
Live And Let Live.
Keep It Simple.
Listen and Learn.
Keep An Open Mind.
Don't Stop Five Minutes Before The Miracle.
If It's Not Broke, Don't Fix It.
The Three C's: I didn't cause it, I can't control it, I can't cure it.
The Three A's: Awareness, Acceptance, and Action.
Good Enough Is Good.
Sometimes, The Best Plan Is No Plan.
If It's Worth Doing, It's Worth Doing So-So.
It Feels So Good To Finish.
Progress, Not Perfection.
Progress, Not Perfection or Procrastination.
Life Begins After 5:00 PM.
Know When To Quit.
Avoid HALT: Hungry, Angry, Lonely, Tired.
Think.
Act, Don't React.
Give Yourself A Break.
Finish What You Start.
This Too Shall Pass.
How Important Is It?
We Came. We Came To. We Came To Believe.
Utilize, Don't Analyze.
Where There is Life, There is Hope.
But For The Grace Of God.
You Can't Run Your Life On Empty.
There Will Be Enough Time, Love, and Money.
Everything Can Wait But Love.
One Day At A Time.
One Day At A Time, One Minute At A Time.
Walking the Steps.

# How to Recognize Working Joyfully versus Working Compulsively

*If we could see ourselves when we are deep into workaholism—furrowed brow, clenched jaw, tense shoulders, perhaps sitting on the edge of our chair—we would immediately recognize that work addiction is unhealthy. But we are not familiar with what it would be like to work in a healthful manner. We need a model of working joyfully. This happens when we maintain our spiritual fitness.*

*Here is a list of how to recognize working compulsively versus working joyfully.*

| Working Compulsively | vs. | Working Joyfully |
|---|---|---|
| Very long hours | | Setting boundaries |
| Impossible standards | | Reasonable goals |
| Insatiable, never done | | Content with day's work |
| Tightly scheduled | | Room for the unexpected |
| Adding more work | | No adding without subtracting |
| Unable to estimate time | | Realistic time allotment |
| Non-stop | | Pausing for change of pace, focus, new ideas |
| | | |
| False deadlines | | Appropriate timing |
| Driven, adrenalized | | Feeling of being in flow |
| Sense of urgency | | Relaxed about time |
| Must complete work | | Can delay task |
| Confusing urgency with importance | | Able to prioritize |
| Reacting to pressure | | Following inner guidance |
| Mentally scattered | | Focused |
| Inefficient | | Effective |
| Mistakes: misplace, drop, spill | | Doing it right the first time |
| Rigid | | Flexible |
| Intolerant of new ideas | | Open-minded |
| Impatient | | Calm |
| Perfectionistic | | Learns from mistakes without blaming |
| | | |
| Tense | | Relaxed |
| Loss of humor | | Keeps a humorous perspective |
| Loss of creativity | | Flow of novel solutions |
| Overly serious and intense | | Able to be playful |
| Not enjoyable | | Finds work pleasurable |
| Abrupt with colleagues | | Responsive to others |
| Loss of spontaneity | | Open to the moment |
| Out of touch with feelings | | Aware of moods |
| Doing many things at once | | Doing one thing at a time |

| | |
|---|---|
| Body/mind out of sync | Unity of thought and action |
| Rushing | Leisurely paced |
| Jerky movements | Steady rhythm |
| Blurred perception | Vivid impressions |
| Unaware, mechanical | Mindful |
| Quantity-oriented (more is better) | Quality-oriented |
| Little delegation | Trust in colleagues |
| Racing the clock | In sync and respectful of time |
| Exhaustion | Happy tiredness |
| Struggle | Feeling of ease |
| Feeling of being a victim | Feeling completed |
| Neglecting health | Nurturing self |
| Can't hear body signals | Knows when to rest |
| Neglecting rest of life | Balanced life |
| Worry, over planning | Staying in the now |

# Workaholism and Other Addictions

In recovery, many of us have been truly baffled by the phenomenon of multiple addictions. In search of the ever-elusive promise of serenity, we may have come to W.A. after spending time in other Twelve Step programs. If we stay in W.A. long enough, we may discover the very depth from which all our other addictions spring.

If we are experiencing multiple addictions, it is important that we begin our recovery from the place where we have the most pain and dysfunction. If we were suffering from the torments of alcoholism it was there we needed to begin our recovery, seeking help through the fellowship and Twelve Steps of A.A. Once we got a handle on that addiction and gradually freed ourselves from the numbing effects of alcohol, we began to face life squarely—stone cold sober. Our once-frozen feelings began to emerge, and we often found ourselves ill equipped to handle them. We hadn't learned to deal with them. At this point, if we didn't relapse into our primary addiction, many of us crossed over into other addictions substituting drugs, food, sex, shopping, relationships, or work. We would use anything to bring on the desired numbness that we no longer allow our primary addiction to provide. We ended up feeling like Heracles fighting the Hydra: the moment we cut one head from the monster, two grew in its place.

The possibility of multiple addictions is very real for workaholics. The good news is that the Twelve Steps are a viable solution for all of them. If we "switched addictions" to compulsive work, then our new drug of choice became adrenaline (no need for crystal meth or speed: by living crazed-enough lives, we could synthesize our own!). For a while work seemed to fill the void in our lives, providing us with a sense of esteem we had never known before. After recovery from the despair and pain of something like alcoholism, it was very easy to be seduced by the false promises of work addiction. Work addiction, "the pain that others applaud," is the only addiction that is both socially sanctioned and financially rewarded. Suddenly we found ourselves being praised for our dedication, loyalty, persistence, and long hours. We became filled with a sense of self-worth and esteem and began to identify ourselves with our work. Driven by the harsh taskmaster of perfectionism, we constantly strived to do more, to gain the all-important approval of others. But our esteem was built on a house of cards. The first hint of criticism by a superior may have sent us into what seemed like an abyss of shame, self-loathing and despair.

The praise and success of the workaholic is a hollow victory when we realize we have come no closer to filling the horrible void we feel inside ourselves. We found that we could feel good only when being productive. We became as enmeshed with our work as we had been with our alcohol, drugs, and the people who enabled us. Work became the only way we could feel worthy, feel "OK" about ourselves. The void we felt inside was still living there, robbing us of any hope for the peace, wholeness or serenity that we had hoped to gain.

The hidden blessing of finding ourselves in a W.A. meeting was that it was a place where the core issue of addiction itself, could be openly discussed. We had finally found a safe place to confront the horrible dread that each of us carried secretly inside: that we were fundamentally flawed, inadequate, and unworthy. We found that in W.A. we could openly talk about our feelings of being completely alone, our terror of losing control, our feeling worthless unless we are doing something, and our overwhelming shame.

The void always comes with a story. It never arises in the middle of someone's life, unaccounted for. Many of us grew up in painful families; many workaholics were adult children of alcoholics, workaholics, or people with other compulsive behaviors. In these circumstances we quickly learned that the most important thing in life was survival and safety. The joy and enthusiasm for living, which is the birthright of every child, is squelched in these circumstances. We may have sought safety by trying to be perfect, by getting perfect grades, being helpful, always staying busy, and never allowing ourselves to let down our guard or relax. Experiencing only conditional approval from those around us, we became "human doings" instead of "human beings," feeling no sense of identity or value except through our accomplishments. This "hole in our soul" drove us to find the soothing anesthetic that addiction promised. Although for a time addiction could deaden the pain, it was a solution that never lasted for long. Many of us eventually found that own lives, even in recovery, had become part of the same, ongoing nightmare.

It is important in recovery to be able to talk about these memories and feelings from the past. Many of us found it difficult to speak about these core issues in other (non-W.A.) Twelve Step programs. For example, the opening comments of an A.A. meeting often request that sharings be kept strictly to the topic of alcohol. Even when members do risk sharing other issues important to their recovery, they may feel it is not a safe place to do this. The result may be several years of sobriety without the serenity that true transformation in recovery can bring.

Recovery from addiction is much more than stopping destructive behavior. W.A. recovery is about exploring the "horrible alone" that lies underneath all our other addictions. It was in W.A. that we could safely begin acknowledging the futility of using work to fill the void inside of us. Then, through working the Steps and accepting the support of our Higher Power, the hole began to shrink.

Work addiction is an insidious disease that can easily sidetrack our entire program of recovery. If we believe that we alone are responsible for fixing everything, even this disease, then we need to exercise great caution. No matter what the reason, workaholics need to be cautious about rushing. Rushing, in the name of recovery, to a multitude of Twelve Step meetings can create more problems in an already too-busy schedule. It is important to remember that the first three Steps require "being" and not "doing." We have to stop "doing" long enough to give God some elbowroom, to really transform our lives. This may well be the hardest part of recovery in W.A.: we really have to let go, in order to let God.

A word of warning: W.A. is not a time-management program. Some people come to W.A. looking for a more efficient way to manage their schedule, and see the tools of recovery as a way of staying in control and not having to surrender. This clinging to control is like the alcoholic who comes to A.A. hoping to learn how to be a social drinker. The end result for both is relapse.

Unrecognized and unchecked, work addiction virtually ensures that we will always be, in A.A.'s terms, "H.A.L.T. (Hungry, Angry, Lonely, and Tired) and thus continually at risk for relapse in our other programs. Many of us have found that once our work addiction is addressed the other addictions mysteriously cease to be a problem. It is truly remarkable. We recommend you give it a try!

# Living With a Workaholic—For Friends and Family

This chapter is for people with a workaholic in their lives. Perhaps you are just now becoming aware of workaholism and some of its consequences, a newcomer to addiction and recovery. We want to share with you the experience of other partners of workaholics, both before recovery and during early recovery. The effects of workaholism can be just as devastating for partners as for work addicts themselves. We hope you will find reassurance and support for yourself, whether the workaholic in your life is in recovery or not.

Sharing their experience in this article are recovering partners or spouses of work addicts, and also other family members who have lived with a workaholic (perhaps a parent). Recovering persons living with a work addict often refer to themselves as "co-workaholics."

### Before Recovery

Many recovering co-workaholics say that in early recovery their lives often got worse before they got better. They say they often used to feel recovery had failed because they had no experience of how life without the active addiction could be a good thing. And while they say getting past early recovery was almost always a crushing experience, they also share that it has been well worthwhile. They say the capacity to seek help and engage with support from outside the family was the most crucial step making possible long-term healing and growth.

Workaholism is often described as a disorder of several dimensions—physical, psychological, social, emotional, and spiritual. There's often an ongoing or recurring loss of control over excessive working and compulsive activity. Despite the adverse consequences, workaholics have a preoccupation and obsessive investment with work and activity. Along with this are distortions in thinking, particularly what is called "denial."

What do people mean by denial? The central contradiction of workaholism—denying the reality of the addiction while explaining it away at the same time—often necessitates dishonesty and secrets. Denial means not able to understand, not able to see things that are too threatening—it is an unconscious self-deception.

Many work addicts experience an ever-increasing need for intense activity and a corresponding increase in the denial of that need. As workaholism gets worse, changes occur in behavior and in thinking. (Work avoiders and work anorexics too are affected as much as compulsive over-doers.) For some workaholics, their sense of importance, powerfulness, and grandiosity—like intoxication— impairs their judgment. For others, anxiety and fear start to build around their ability to perform. Addicts hold two core ideas—a kind of "self-talk"—which they use to explain their view of themselves and the world:

"I am not a workaholic."

"I can control my work world."

Co-workaholics say their own behavior and thinking were affected by the disorder also. They say they joined the denial and contorted logic of the workaholic in order to gain reassurance and an illusion of control about the sturdiness of their relationship. They became preoccupied with the work addict and obsessed with the workaholic's wellbeing. One co-workaholic says, "Sometimes I would feel guilty and unworthy when my partner complained that I wasn't pushing myself as much as he did. I thought his over-involvement with work was all my fault. That his chronic avoidance of me meant there had to be something terribly wrong with me, and I couldn't seem to figure it out."

Some co-workaholics say they felt ashamed and began to close out the world, isolating their coupleship or family further. Recovering co-workaholics variously say they felt anxious, emotionally numb, insecure, powerless, and plagued by low self-image and a sense of hopelessness. Isolation made it even harder to ask for help and support when they "hit bottom." They say their capacity for genuineness and honesty was gone.

Depression and chronic under-functioning often became the norm. Relatives and friends were avoided or abandoned who did not support the compulsive busyness or the rationalizations of the work addict. The remedy for their distress was to try harder to control the workaholic, leading to mutual accusations and further disillusionment and despair. "I tried to fight it. I really tried. But it just seemed to make things worse."

Work addicts say their hostility towards change was very high. "I couldn't figure it out. I was rewarded by the world at large but despised by my own family." Work filled the void and deepened it; but while they were still over-working, the idea of resigning their perpetual busyness without a substitute was unthinkable. One recovering workaholic says, "There was no way

I was going to admit defeat. To do so was to become vulnerable, and I knew for certain that vulnerability always triggered attack." Why do partners and other family members go along with all this? Some say their intense need for attachment—and their fears of abandonment and aloneness—dominated everything else. "We were in shared denial."

## The Beginnings of Recovery

The beginnings of recovery can occur when one partner or family member "hits bottom." The denial and the resistance and the defiance can't be maintained any longer, or something else breaks down and a family member reaches outside for help. The pain of the addiction or co-addiction outweighs the considerable pain of recovery. One partner says, "Unfortunately, I wasn't aware of my partner's workaholism until after he hit bottom, which came in the form of his suicidal depression. I tried to control things and make them better—'fix it.' When my stomach was in knots I'd go for a walk outside the house. What helped during those horrible days was going to Al-Anon and to educational programs about addiction."

By the time the work addict halts her/his over-working, the co-workaholic and the rest of the family have been severely impaired. "I did manage to bury my emotional needs, but I wasn't able to bury my resentments." On the way to withdrawal from workaholism, things can get very bad and usually do, with increasing turmoil before the self-deceptions and other defenses ultimately cave in.

Co-workaholics say that their denial often lifted like a haze, slowly dissolving as they became ready to discern reality more clearly. One recovering co-workaholic says of her family, "It was something none of us were willing or able to talk about. We were trying desperately not to have the relationship we were having. Our rock bottom was delayed because we were all resigned to keeping everything together and patching over problems. Make nice. Good manners. We wanted to be a socially acceptable family."

The emotional acceptance of the end of the battle is what recovering people refer to as "surrender." Some recovering persons also refer to this as an admission of defeat or "ego deflation." Surrender, they say, is accompanied by their profound acceptance of loss of control. One co-workaholic says, "One day I realized I had no power or hold over the workaholic in my life. I finally saw I couldn't keep him in line, that I had to give up my efforts at damage control."

At the same time, they report that the beginning of withdrawal from workaholism is often very hard because the reality is so different from their expectations. Many co-workaholics also say it was difficult, awkward, even shameful to accept or look for a helping hand. "We both felt trapped and isolated. It was difficult to accept the fact that I couldn't do it alone." The introduction to recovery—becoming abstinent—is often full of disillusionment and disenchantment for all. This is especially the case if there's no one in the family invested in recovery. Abstinence is then likely to be what recovering people call a "white-knuckle" holding pattern. "We were in 'remission' rather than in 'recovery.' It was very hard to view workaholism as something that was harmful to my partner and to our coupleship, rather than a well-rewarded activity."

New abstinence is an intense, critical point. "Our family's recognition of workaholism was supposed to make everything better and put an end to upsets and fights. Instead it just seemed to leave a gaping hole, a great terrifying emptiness." Recovering co-workaholics and workaholics say early on they needed to sustain their fledgling recoveries from workaholism, which they did not know how to do. "I focused on just one day at a time, or even smaller increments, to get through. We needed to learn how to hold on."

In some recovering coupleships, both partners report that early on they felt only hopelessness. They had tried every measure they could think of in order to save their relationship, but nothing had worked for them. Some had tried therapy before recovery. "I was there because I was unhappy with him, and he was there because I was unhappy with him. It didn't work." They accepted that they were powerless to fix their irresolvable issues.

Finally, both had become willing, or were trying to become willing, to accept mutual responsibility for the destructive patterns in their relationship; both saw themselves as "identified patients" in the sense that they recognized that each of them needed help individually; and both accepted "loss of control" and were willing to accept outside help.

"When he went into recovery I was shocked. The therapist treating him told me to go to Al-Anon. None of it seemed to make sense. I kept going to work myself, while he was in bed all day for weeks and weeks. I started learning to take better care of myself, and learning to go places by myself. I was becoming less dependent on my partner and more dependent on myself. I was becoming less codependent." These two partners say they committed themselves to recovery—which was not the same as committing to each other. "We didn't know it at the time, but that wasn't possible until much later."

Co-workaholics often say that early in recovery they needed to learn to live with ongoing confusion and unpredictability as part of the strain of early recovery. Sudden outbursts were all too common. "If I became very anxious it helped me to remove myself both physically and emotionally from my partner." They say they needed to accept not knowing much about anything, which they say was often so upsetting and unsettling that they sometimes turned to short-term "fixes" and unhealthy behaviors harmful to recovery. "As a co-workaholic, here are things that I tried that didn't work: blaming, fighting, threatening to leave, ignoring, doing my own thing, working harder myself, over-eating to smother my feelings."

Some recovering partners say they found a couples therapist who guided and led them to put their attention and emphasis on themselves as individuals and *not* to try to "fix" their damaged coupleship. Yet, because these partners were fearful of the unpredictable future, or hadn't a clue as to how they might be restored to intimacy and commitment together, they say they were frightened that such a switch in their attention and energy would lead to the end of their coupleship. "Holding fast to one another in the midst of all this flux—that was one of our most critical tasks." Some couples new to recovery do grow apart and end up separating. Other times in early recovery, an unwillingness or an inability to accept the natural ambiguity and confusion have led to the end of the relationship, as one partner felt trapped and compelled to choose between recovery *or* the marriage/partnership.

Many co-workaholics say that in their coupleship one partner entered recovery alone and the coupleship lived with divisiveness between the old norm (active workaholism) and the new one (abstinence). In that scenario, they say, there were two versions of reality—there was no addiction and co-addiction in the partnership, and there was addiction and co-addiction in the partnership—in an atmosphere of constant stress while the partners were living in two separate worlds. This kind of rupture or disparity can go on indefinitely. Some couples find ways to stay together despite the ongoing heavy strain, while others end their relationship.

Some couples get to Workaholics Anonymous after considerable recovery from other addictions and co-addictions. One such co-workaholic says of herself and her partner, "We took an inventory of our lives together in a couples Twelve Step program. One of the problems we agreed on: we were both too depleted to be really present for our relationship, our friends or family. We wrote a spiritual contract that included going to a Workaholics Anonymous meeting together once a week. At the time I did not think it was a bottom—only that a friend had gotten relief in W.A. and I wanted my partner to get help. It was only after attending the meetings that I began to see the workaholic patterns I had myself."

To repeat: for many recovering co-workaholics in early recovery, reaching outside the family for support and then making continued use of that support for a lengthy period of time, was the single most important element in sustaining their process of recovery. "We had to accept that change is equal to action, and action is equal to accepting change." For "outside help" co-workaholics mention therapy, religion, and various Twelve Step programs.

One partner attended an addiction education and support group at her HMO; she says, "One of the premises, which I thoroughly agree with, is that the whole family is affected. If one person is to recover, the family needs to recover, too. The addict and the codependent both need education and support about their roles in the dysfunction or disease. Recovery changes the couple dynamic. When one person is recovering, the other must change also, if they are to stay together and be happy together." Nonetheless, nearly all co-workaholics report their initial resistance to outside help, including resistance to programs such as Al-Anon and CoDependents Anonymous—and resistance to Workaholics Anonymous as well, where there happened to be a nearby W.A. meeting. "At my first several meetings, I was just a guest rather than an active member."

People often report a rude awakening from their wishful thinking that abstinence and recovery were supposed to mean no more problems: "We figured that we'd be done and cured probably within six months, or twelve at the most. Now in hindsight it's clear that my recovery had barely started at one year and that our coupleship was just taking baby steps. I had been frustrated that I wasn't 'making him better.' We both felt we were 'running late' in recovery."

In early recovery many family members say they had a difficult time interacting. Some say they had no idea how to approach each other and feared making mistakes that could lead to feeling out of control or lead to relapse. Co-workaholics report they could not tackle problems, disagreements, or feelings head-on without ending up polarized in a battle over who was right and who was wrong—in essence, shaming each other and fighting over who was to blame. "I see now that I couldn't get to my own issues, because I was able to hide behind his flagrant ones." But an early focus on individual growth and responsibility, they say, prepared them to come back later as allies and to deal with differences or conflicts without getting totally out of control and without engaging in conflict avoidance.

## Progress in the Here and Now

The focus on their own individual growth and responsibility, say some co-workaholics, was sometimes at odds with the needs of their children. When they reached outside the family for help for themselves—therapy, religion, and Twelve Step programs—many co-workaholics had less time, energy, and focus for their kids. This was very difficult and painful: paying heed to their own self-reclamation needs while straining to meet the best interests of their children.

Some co-workaholics say that, even with resistance and impasses, they gradually understood they could not rely on their partner or the coupleship itself to fill a hole or heal them. "That's a task for the individual. In Twelve Step rooms it's sometimes said, 'We can't do it alone, but we alone can do it.'" Another says, "Al-Anon and CoDA are helpful in learning to 'put oneself first.'"

Co-workaholics who report their self-worth was vested in their work-addict partner—caretaking or controlling the workaholic—also say that early recovery was a time of deep sorrow, pain, and resistance to building their own separate individuality and separate recovery program. They say they wanted to sidestep the workaholism, to overlook it, and even ignore it—to focus on bettering communication and other facets of family life instead.

Another partner says, "Regarding my own recovery, now I focus mostly on myself. I spend much less energy on my partner's issues. The problem in both of us seems much deeper and more cunning than before recovery. I am aware of unconscious adrenaline-seeking behavior that can be stirred up even with things we agree to do as a couple on the weekend. I am aware of the problems of my mind that can turn future worry into catastrophes. For a while my own financial insecurities played into my partner's and fueled an illusion that money was the reason we needed to work so much."

Another co-workaholic says, "I went to my individual Twelve Step program and it was three years before I gave up the idea that I could get my partner to stop. And it was four years before she surrendered to her compulsive overworking. It was hard to look at myself and impossible to do it alone." Still another co-workaholic said, "I had a lot of fear that our relationship wouldn't survive all the changes in recovery."

For some co-workaholics, the recovering addict's recovery program was regarded as an unwelcome guest, a gatecrasher, a trespasser. Many non-Twelve Step individuals say they resented the recovering addict going to meetings or out for coffee or talking on the phone. What about their partnership? It's horrendously difficult to accept that the newly recovering person has plenty of energy and time for Twelve Step friends but no time for the coupleship.

Recovering co-workaholics say that attending their own meetings, connecting with other recovering co-workaholics between meetings, and switching their efforts onto their own recovery all helped in initial recuperation from the effects and consequences of work addiction. They say at meetings they heard how other people's experiences and problems were similar to their own, and that this helped them feel less alone and isolated and adrift. "If others have been there and survived, there is hope." As the self-deception and other self-protective measures lessened, co-workaholics and workaholics in Twelve Step programs set out to "work the Steps." This includes looking at one's own beliefs and behaviors and beginning a process of recognizing and accepting the reality before recovery as well as in the here and now. "I started learning how to be less critical of myself. I saw some of my own tendencies towards busyness, and in recovery I limited the number of projects I was willing to undertake. Now I recognize when I'm starting to get overwhelmed and I try to mitigate it."

Recovering people commonly say that early recovery often meant grief and defeat as much as optimism, and uncertainty and doubts as much as a return to any comfortable routines there might have been before hitting bottom. "In early recovery, it's important to realize you may be living together but you're not really much of a coupleship. You're polarized about practically everything. You have routines together, pay bills together, even sleep in the same room together, but there's no real sense of deep connection or bright future together, at least for the time being. Somehow you have to figure out how to stay connected while you're disconnected."

Partnerships in which both members began their individual recovery process say that they didn't end up getting back to the lives they had before recovery—this was a brand new experience.

Partners recovering from the consequences of workaholism and with significant progress in recovery often point out that it was not within their capabilities to have an intimate and committed relationship together without solid, stable individual groundwork first. In early recovery, they say, "It wasn't that we didn't communicate well together—we didn't communicate at all. There just wasn't any connection. I had faith that our shift together would happen in time. He had to emphasize and concentrate on his recovery. I wasn't kidding myself that all our problems had gone away. I figured we'd get to the other stuff later on. But I didn't feel frantic or rushed. There was progress in the here and now."

These partners say that their shared recognition of workaholism and the vocabulary of recovery served to hold them together until they could direct their energies back toward themselves as a couple. One co-workaholic suggests, "Believe your partner if he or she states, 'I'm a workaholic.'" Another says, "Even though each person has to put his or her primary program first in order to maintain health, the coupleship needs to be strengthened and nurtured too." Some couples turned to therapy in order to satisfy their needs to express angry feelings while protecting themselves from the dangers of uncontrolled argument.

When both partners arrange their coupleship around programs like Workaholics Anonymous, CoDependents Anonymous, and Al-Anon, the family gains from the outside buttressing of mutual new attitudes about workaholism and actions in recovery. "Meetings gave me support and encouragement, and, of course, a place to share my pain. I came away each time with hope, peace, love, and growth." Early on, however, the future can look pretty bleak: "It was scary for us in the beginning because we didn't know any couples who were both in recovery. Our society is organized around production and consumption, not connection and relatedness. Now after a long time in program, we've seen lots of couples separate or get divorced—or simply give up and accept the status quo—because they were unable or unwilling to accept mutual responsibility for the health or disorder of their coupleship."

Wanting to finally have persistent troubles "done and over with" is also common, say many recovering co-workaholics: "We told ourselves we should have gotten past all this by now." Some problems indeed are often better, but they aren't fixed. "In early recovery, it was invaluable to hear that other couples had experienced the same kinds of problems we were now having, and to be able to see the positive changes they had made. 'Progress, Not Perfection' was one of the slogans."

Another partner says, "After some time in recovery I have adjusted to a lower standard of living. My paychecks from my part-time job are no longer just the extra but about half of our combined income. It took years to become accustomed to not having my partner in Corporate America. I now appreciate more what we do have together, and I appreciate that we really have to work as partners to have a good standard of living."

## The Evolving Adventure

A few co-workaholics say their lives improved almost at once in early recovery, and that things just kept improving from there. While true for some, most others report that recovery was a gradual, evolving adventure where change and progress became evident only in hindsight. They say it wasn't recapturing something they had in the past yet had lost; instead, it meant wide-ranging adjustments and unforeseen transformations which only slowly evolved into a new sense of assurance and wellness. Later in ongoing recovery, they say they were better able to work on their coupleship and the rest of their family once the partners were solid in their individual recoveries.

Some recovering couples say they were well into recovery before the work addict was able to "show up" emotionally for the relationship. "He isn't as driven as he used to be, and he's somewhat more available to me. But he still resents getting interrupted in the middle of a project." And some co-workaholics say they were astonished to find out that they themselves had not been emotionally available or open to an intimate, committed relationship. They say that looking back they realized the unavailability and distance of their actively workaholic partner had felt familiar and comfortable to them. They say movements toward greater closeness and connectedness in later recovery often felt unfamiliar and uncomfortable but were worth the effort.

Some partners say that several years into recovery they could see in their coupleship healthy developments that were simply not even conceivable in the first year. "We work as partners more to plan large expenditures. We have more time together. We plan our calendars together. I can more clearly communicate my needs, and he more willingly alters his behavior to meet them. We enjoy our days off together. We've learned to be more flexible with our schedules. On our days off we may have ten things to do—but we're both willing to see how things go and to stop pushing to get everything done. Putting rest as a top priority."

Trust, warmth and mutual responsibility were restored only gradually, in fits and starts, evolving slowly and occasionally with slips back into the old, painful patterns. Their period of difficult adjustment and repair lasted more than ten years, according to some. But eventually, they say, they've become a healthy family, with a stable relationship, shared values and goals, more affection and love, and solid individual recoveries as distinct selves.

Finally, even with several years of recovery, many co-workaholics say they are still active in their program of recovery. They say that their ongoing involvement in outside support—Twelve Step programs, therapy, religion—helps them keep the focus on themselves as individuals while avoiding isolation or falling back into the old destructive patterns. "We socialize and share a lot with other recovering couples who are working to change themselves in order to stay together." They say they haven't "graduated" from healthy reliance and dependency on their support system. "We alone can do it, but we can't do it alone."

Another partner says, "Things are different. I left a very workaholic job and work part-time now. My partner has more responsibility but takes vacations, comes home early many nights, we get regular exercise, we help each other prioritize and make a realistic action plan, we are happier and have energy for each other, our family and friends. Our agreed plan of action is to keep those commitments to our spiritual contract, which nine years later still includes a weekly meeting of W.A." They've learned from their own experience that recovery is certainly possible and definitely worth it.

# Technology and Work Addiction

The Twelve Steps and the W.A. Tools for recovery suggest simplicity in living. Through these tools we are reminded to do one thing at a time and to be present for our tasks, other people, and ourselves. We are cautioned against doing many things at once, as our attention becomes fragmented. We are encouraged to allow time for enjoyable activities and play.

These Tools, together with the Twelve Steps, are invaluable to recovering workaholics because they help us set effective boundaries around work. Following the Steps and using the tools requires diligence, patience and willingness. It is therefore important for us to be aware of the hazards we face every day that threaten to rob us of our peace of mind and sabotage our recovery efforts.

We live in a habitat of ever-increasing technological complexity. As we are met with yet another new techno-gizmo we "need" in order to proceed with our lives and jobs, it may feel as though we encounter stress at every turn. In the effort to keep up with the quickening pace of life of our friends, family, and coworkers, some of us may have sacrificed simplicity for convenience. Those whose work addiction is active tend to live in a rush-about world, where multitasking is touted as a great virtue. For workaholics in recovery it is important to be aware of the way we use technology, and how it impacts our lives.

Technology has evolved to bring us much more power on an individual basis than ever before. This increase in power, although certainly desirable in many respects, brings with it the responsibility of choosing when and how to engage that power. In years past, some predictions were made that technology had the potential to become so powerful for the good in our lives that we would be able to cease working and just sit back and let machines do the work for us.

However, the promised "technotopian dream" has yet to arrive. Instead of living in a world where technological inventions do all of our work, which admittedly sounds at least a little naive, the empowerment that has evolved has led to some uncomfortable options for those of us with this disease. Our society has created a world where we can carry our work with us twenty-four hours a day, seven days a week. The line between work in the workplace and work we are expected to do after hours has certainly blurred. The cell phone and the laptop computer have made the portable office a reality. As a result we need never be too far from our work. Some of us are employed by corporations that expect us to work before the official workday begins, through lunch, and at home. Our technological developments have made excessive work easy, even convenient, such that those with poor boundaries are finding themselves indulging in a greater quantity of interaction but of course this can easily translate into a reduction in the quality of individual interactions.

W.A. warns us not to turn our home into a work place, but with the portable electronic office this warning can easily be dismissed. The "convenience" of cell phones now allows work-related calls to intrude at any hour into our personal lives and recovery time. Through technology, work has been invited into every corner of our lives. The ability to use telephones in any location now seems to justify their use in every location. Not only are we able to turn our home into a work place, but the local coffee shop, grocery store and restaurant as well. Without clear work boundaries those in our presence may be expected to wait as the technological intrusion of a cell phone or pager pre-empts an actual live conversation between people! Portable computers and telephones become enablers for workaholics who are already looking for an excuse to work around the clock. We may also become as dependent on and obsessed with our technological devices as we are to the work itself.

Our attention becomes fragmented when we do many things at once. We live in a world where the images on the television screen change at a very rapid rate, and we have to adjust ourselves to a state of perceptual speed-up. News broadcasts on our television screens are now split into several sections, requiring that we piecemeal out our attention even further. Pagers and cell phones seem to attach to us like invisible tentacles between us and our work, with power to summon us at any moment and interrupt any activity, should we leave them on. We can start the workday the moment we start the engine of our car, conducting "pressing" business over the phone as we drive. After work, playtime becomes tentative, provided no important phone calls interrupt our activities.

How can we mitigate the obstacles which technology poses to our progress in recovery? The solution to this problem may be a very close rereading of the Steps and tools for recovery, and an honest assessment of how the misuse of technology may compromise our recovery. If we are powerless over work itself, we may also become powerless over the tools that connect us with our work. We may argue that we have to work, that we have to use technology, that it is everywhere, and that we cannot avoid its intrusion into every corner of our lives. And to some extent it is true that technology is certainly part of today's reality in many areas formerly left untouched by it. However, using these facts as excuses for us workaholics to keep working compulsively and avoid taking full responsibility for our recovery would be an example of rationalization or disease-based reasoning.

If we make unconscious contact with technology, then we run the risk of becoming less human and more like robots. However, if we hold love above all other priorities, connecting with our own creativity and with others as well, then technology can be directed to enhance and expand our human-ness.

Today the tools of technology can help us to do many amazing things that were not possible at all for people of even recent generations. We can solve incredibly complex engineering and design problems to benefit all peoples, have doctors who are in another part of the world operate on us while we stay at the local hospital, or hear the voice and see a live picture of someone from another continent while we sit in our living room. Such events would have seemed, to our grandparents, as impossible as a trip to the Sun and back! Technology used consciously can help us to be more creative in art, in science, and in literature; to record and reflect upon our world and actions more accurately; and, yes, even to schedule more effectively and to express love between ourselves and others. It is certainly true that many companies use electronic communication to "overconnect" employees to their work, and electronics certainly can never surpass face-to-face connection with others. However it is the intent of the people involved that determines whether technology use will be indiscriminate or not. Companies, like individuals, are free to use the power of technology to enhance our human condition or require employees to endure less than human practices. If we find ourselves addicted to being over-connected, we may indeed need to give up such devices—at least for a while—to create a deeper connection to ourselves and to our Higher Power. Some of us form guidelines in our abstinence plans that involve having work-free time that includes not checking work email, turning off cell phones, and/or not receiving work calls (the wonders of "caller ID"). Others set times of abstinence from all electronics. Some of us W.A.'s, if boundary setting with others fails, may give serious consideration to letting go of jobs that use technology to pressure us.

Refreshingly, the Steps and Tools do not require the use of the latest technology. They do, however, require time, insight, discernment, patience and practice. There is precious little time or room for any of these in a rush-about world. Recovery requires that we go slower instead of faster, and at times shut off our gadgets. It requires us to do one thing at a time and pay attention to our Higher Power, the world we live in, and the people who care about us.

The Twelve Steps offer the way for an honest assessment of just how we have been living. They also offer us a solution involving trust in a Power greater than ourselves, greater even than technology. Fortunately, our Higher Power has no monthly service charges for an always-on, high-speed connection. It is all here, waiting for us, no moving parts, no batteries required!

# To Employers and to Helping Professionals

I am writing to you as an employer and a helping professional and as a workaholic. You no doubt are reading this book because someone recommended it to you or because you care about a workaholic.

Before I came into recovery I wouldn't have noticed the characteristics of a workaholic. I probably thought they were exceptional workers since they were willing to stay up all night and work double shifts. Multitasking, staying late, working weekends and vacations, accepting that things were always in crisis: we all thrived on it. We bragged about the drinking and drugs we needed to calm down and to get going each day. We were proud of the hard work and sacrifices. We worked for driven organizations; we were all a team. Peak performance was expected and tight deadlines were unfailingly met. "Workaholism" was a foreign word. What's funny is at the time I worked for a health care organization.

Books have been written on the organization and society as addict. Workaholism is found in many organizations, including some you might least suspect, such as schools, clergy, and nonprofits, as well as ones you would suspect, such as law firms, technology companies, and Fortune 500 corporations. Hard work, independence, and money are admired cultural values, so is pulling yourself up by the bootstraps. Workaholics come from all areas of life, including single mothers, laborers with two jobs, self-employed workers as well as type "A" corporate managers. The research also points to several patterns of workaholism, from the stereotype of the driven employee consistently working sixty to eighty hour weeks to the more surprising portraits of work anorexics and binge-and-crash adrenaline junkies who thrive on and are unconsciously committed to never completely finishing projects or to only relinquishing a task with maximal drama.

I wish now I had known more then. Some good people's lives could have been helped. I've seen heart attacks and strokes occur at work as a result of workaholism. I've known a number of workaholics who were hospitalized for depression or who actually committed suicide. There were many serious accidents and divorces. Nearly every employer and helping professional feels a moral responsibility for the well-being of their employees. But we were and still are in denial as professionals and as a society. Workaholism is not identified as a problem, but the consequences of it are. Until a workaholic is facing serious health risks or has made a huge mistake due to fatigue and stress, we stay part of "the harder you work the more you get" club. We are rewarded for practicing our disease. We were powerless to stop ourselves. It wasn't until I got in recovery myself that I could see the insanity in others.

To my surprise there is a world of recovery out there. I know now about the hope and help of Workaholics Anonymous meetings. The tools and literature were once like a foreign language to me. I would have told my fellow sufferers how the meetings were helping me stop the self-destructive cycle.

Workaholics have to find balance in a workaholic world. We need the regular help of a program of recovery in order to keep our sanity. The best thing to do is to help others get into the program of Workaholics Anonymous. If you have a staff member or patient with an issue, tell us if you think our problems may be due to workaholism. If so, we are hurting the organization as well as ourselves. You may want to look at excessive overtime as part of the pattern of the disease. Ask if we are ready to have a normal life. You could give us a copy of this book, *The Workaholics Anonymous Book of Recovery*. If we are having a workaholic slip, ask how the meetings are going, what Step we are on, and do we have a current sponsor? People in recovery appreciate interest in our program since it has a meaningful influence in our lives.

Workaholics in recovery make great employees. We are hard working, loyal, and creative, yet the driven, stressed, inflexible aspects of the disease are lifted as workaholics seek recovery. As you read this book some of the ideas may seem strange to you but they have worked for us. If you believe your organization has a workaholic climate, a whole change can take place toward health and sanity if more employees get into recovery. This could be the beginning of a new life.

# The Work-Binge Sales Pitch

The book or the TV show:
MIND: Just two more pages to the end of the chapter./The show is almost over.
BODY: 2 AM, my eyes are tired, and I can't concentrate.
Action: Put bookmark in book, turn out light, go to bed./Turn off TV and go to bed

Exercise:
MIND: You haven't yet had your daily exercise.
BODY: 11 pm, sneezing violently, eyes tearing.
Action: Take vitamin C, lemon and hot water, take warm bath, go to bed.

The Desk:
MIND: Just one more task.
BODY: 10 PM
Action: Put item on list for tomorrow, rest.

The Commitment:
MIND: But you said you would go. They're expecting you.
BODY: 8 AM, Splitting headache after three hours sleep.
Action: Cancel date, take aspirin and warm bath, go back to sleep.

The Deadline:
MIND: You made a commitment. You gave your word.
BODY: 7 PM, exhausted.
Action: Go home, rest, and then reschedule.

The Boss:
MIND: The boss is counting on you. He said you always come through. He said you have never disappointed him. That the company couldn't operate without you. That the show must go on and you're a trooper.
BODY: 10 PM, ready to drop.
Action: Go home, rest, and reschedule.

The Co-Workers:
MIND: She said if you want something done, give it to a busy person.
He said, "You're so capable. How do you do it all?" You can't let them down. You can fit in that extra project they handed you.
BODY: Sorry, can't help you out, I'm on overload. You'll have to ask someone else.
Action: Smile and hand back the work.

The Voices:
MIND: No one can do it the way you want it done. The company will go broke without you. You're almost done—why not finish it all now? You're slow, lazy, inefficient, irresponsible. It's urgent, important, vital. Do it now! Tomorrow never comes.
BODY: I can't. No. That's not my responsibility. It can wait. I'm only human. I don't know how. It's not my department. I need to rest. All I can do is my best. I can't work miracles. It'll be there tomorrow. Tomorrow is another day. I need help. I don't understand.
Action: Meditation and prayer and a dance in the garden.

# The Gifts of Rest

Most workaholics discount or ignore rest, thinking it wasteful and unproductive. Rest includes getting enough sleep at night, naps and breaks, silent time alone, or just sitting or lying still. Strolling along the beach or reading an engrossing mystery may be relaxing, but they are not restful. And neither is lying awake worrying.

Rest is the most important "activity" we do. Here are some of the gifts of rest, if we accept them:

1. Physical and mental RENEWAL. No matter how pleasurable the activity, you will enjoy it much more if you are rested. If you are tired, you will have to draw on adrenaline for energy. Even if offered the best, say no if you need rest. Rest is the best reward you can give yourself.
2. Experiencing our BEING. Being alone with ourselves without the distraction of props or activities. Appreciating the pleasure of solitude. Learning the art of self-enjoyment.
3. SLOWING our pace. Regaining a healthy breathing rhythm.
4. INTEGRATING the interconnections and impacts of our actions and those of others.
5. Quietness to listen for GUIDANCE from our Higher Power. Reminding ourselves of our spirituality and to get out of the way of God's plan for us. Noticing when we have shifted from flow to effort, from God's will to self-will, from letting go to trying to control.
6. Gaining PERSPECTIVE by a temporary withdrawal. Unwinding from being overly focused. Seeing where we lost our vision. Noting what we do that is unnecessary. Reminding ourselves to be selective. Being silent to reflect on the deeper meaning of events, speech.
7. Putting space into our day to SAVOR each event. Digesting impressions. Freshening our perceptions. Unwinding from being overly focused.
8. Catching ourselves before we RELAPSE into ego and self-will. Keeping awareness of our emotions and body signals, including energy level. Changing our thoughts to healthier ones. Regaining our patience, flexibility, humor, wisdom and creativity.
9. When ill, allowing our body to HEAL itself.
10. Cooperating with the universal RHYTHM of ebb and flow, winter and summer. Treating time as a friend.

# Reprioritizing Values

|            *Recovery Values* | *Addiction Values* |
|-----------------------------:|:-------------------|

### DOING:

|                       PROCESS | OUTCOME           |
|------------------------------:|:------------------|
|                    EXPERIENCE | MANIPULATE        |
|                         ENJOY | ENDURE            |
|                            BE | DO                |
|                   PARTICIPATE | PERFORM           |
|                         SAVOR | GULP              |
|                QUALITY. DEPTH | QUANTITY, LENGTH  |
|                 FLOW, SMARTER | EFFORT, HARDER    |
|                       RELAXED | INTENSE           |
|                     EFFECTIVE | EFFICIENT         |
|                      FLEXIBLE | RIGID             |
|                     IMPORTANT | URGENT            |
|          SURRENDER, SURPRISE  | CONTROL           |
|                        SIMPLE | COMPLEX           |
|                        VALUES | GOALS             |
|                        IN AWE | SHUT-DOWN         |

### RELATING:

|                    UNIQUENESS | COMPARISON        |
|------------------------------:|:------------------|
|                    PRINCIPLES | PERSONALITIES     |
|                     COOPERATE | COMPETE           |
|            BOTH/AND, WIN-WIN   | EITHER, OR        |
|                 RELATIONSHIPS | THINGS            |
|                INTERDEPENDENT | INDEPENDENT       |
|             LIVE AND LET LIVE | RESCUER           |
|                     CONSENSUS | MAJORITY          |
|                       RESPECT | ADMIRE            |
|                     DEMOCRACY | HIERARCHY         |

### TIME:

|                          TIME | MONEY             |
|------------------------------:|:------------------|
|                 UNDERSCHEDULE | OVERCHEDULE       |
|                           NOW | PAST, FUTURE      |

# Turning Work Into Play

## Attitudes

As workaholics, we have used work and activity to deny our being and escape our feelings. Overdoing may have been our only means of gaining approval, finding our identity, and justifying our existence. Play, compared to the all-important role we give to work, may seem trivial and superficial. We may feel so guilty playing that we make our play into a work project so we can feel useful.

Or perhaps we were raised with the idea that work is drudgery (the daily grind, the rat race) and play is frivolity. We use one as a respite from the other.

In either case, we don't take play seriously. Work is what we do for money; play is what we do for enjoyment. Work is serious. In fact, the more painful it is, the more we prove to ourselves that we have earned our pay. The ideal of being paid for playing seems ridiculous.

We may be self-employed and have the idea that we cannot charge much because we love what we do or that we are justified only by suffering. But buyers don't care about our struggle; they only want to know if a product fits their needs. In fact, if a book or film is produced in joy, that feeling shines through and attracts buyers.

Some of us have realized that spending most of our day to earn money to have a few hours of enjoyment is absurd. We have come to understand that our attitude toward play and work can be the same. No matter what we do, we can do it with a playful, creative, experimental spirit of enjoyment instead of focusing on the outcome.

## Rewards

Many of us are in our right field, one that uses our talents; others are not so fortunate. Or we might be doing the work we love, but in a workaholic setting or manner. In all cases, we came to W.A. because, whether we realized it or not, we were working out of ego, not love. We worked to be distracted, to be admired, to be loved, to be validated, to be stimulated, and to take pride in how much we had done. Sometimes we worked to fail because failing proved we were not okay and that felt comfortable.

Sometimes we worked for extrinsic rewards: a second house, a partnership, and a bigger paycheck. We may have begun the work because we liked it, but once we connected what we did with such rewards, the rewards became more important than the work.

Whatever our situations, we had destructive attitudes toward both work and play. Our work was done by us, but not through us. We may have been doing our right work, but it wasn't done rightly. We set impossible deadlines and forced projects before their time. We followed killing schedules and wondered why we recoiled from doing what we once loved. Or we found ourselves unable to work, paralyzed by our perfectionism, and took refuge in addictive behavior.

## Recovery

In W.A., we know that our Higher Power is our employer. By doing the Steps, we turn our life over to the care of God. We ask for guidance on what to do and when and how. We realize that our bodies and minds have limits, that we must nurture them with rest, healthy food, and exercise.

We learn that any activity no matter how pleasurable can become tedious if overdone. We understand that tired work is wasted work because we often have to redo it.

Enjoyment in the process becomes our criterion. Often we can use our will to continue working, but not with enjoyment. If, instead of concentrating on output, we ask ourselves, "If I keep on, will I enjoy it?" we will find the answer is often no.

Once we grasp the idea that we deserve to savor what we do, we will no longer have to ask. We won't have to wait till our eyes droop and our neck aches. We'll know long before that to turn off the computer, close the book, put down the phone, or store our tools.

This change takes time—to stop thinking of how many items we're accomplishing or what reward we'll get for the work and to stay in the present and truly experience our feelings.

What we are doing is growing a healthy self, one that savors life right now instead of dreaming of future rewards. Once we get in touch with our feelings, we become clearer about what we want.

## Workplace Changes

That clarity changes how we see our environment. Suddenly, we notice that there are other people in the workplace who do the same work, but sanely; that we don't have to overdo or try to become indispensable to keep our job. We begin to be treated differently as we establish boundaries. We don't enable anyone and no one enables us.

We might be the one who sets the pace. When we change the expectations, we might be amazed at how the level of creativity and cooperation rises.

Or, we might realize that we must leave. Our job doesn't use our talents, is alienating, and meaningless. We may find that our values have changed. We are no longer willing to work in ways we find harmful, unethical, or demeaning.

We might work for a cause we believe in but in a way that contradicts our recovery. We now believe that in order to be of highest benefit to society, we and our workplace must be healthy examples.

We begin to shift our focus from results and getting what we want to behaving in accordance with our moral principles in every situation. Thus we have found a new standard for what constitutes success.

## Outside the Workplace

Our new way of thinking attracts us to like-minded people. We find the position that is looking for us or we create it.

Turning work into play affects the rest of our life. Because we are gaining satisfaction from our work, we no longer feel driven to accomplish. We no longer need to own more to reward ourselves for the drudgery of work. Our health improves when we believe we are entitled to excellent self-care.

Contentment becomes a natural part of living. Ironically, we achieve more and we do it more easily. We don't need to get or do enough because we know we are enough. The feeling of inner emptiness and the craving for self-importance disappears. Work, as proof of self-worth, doesn't work anymore.

Our relationships change. We attract people who have firm personal boundaries—people who like themselves, are independent, and not controlling. We no longer need to be needed or earn friendship by caretaking. When we give, it's after we've taken care of ourselves. What we give is of higher quality because it's given freely without resentment.

When, instead of flogging ourselves, forcing a project before its time, we work refreshed, at the moment of ripeness, everything falls into place. Work itself, like play, has its own reward, because work is now play.

# Where the Time Goes

| There is NEVER TIME TO: | BUT ALWAYS TIME TO: |
| --- | --- |
| put things away | search for them |
| do things right | correct them later |
| drive safely | get into accidents |
| be patient | apologize for rudeness |
| ask a question | suffer from assumptions |
| follow your car manual | get lengthy repairs |
| heed body signals | have illnesses |
| listen | ask for a repeat |
| make extra keys | be locked out |
| read the instructions | ruin a new appliance |
| prioritize your work | stay after quitting time |
| monitor your fuel gauge | run out of gas |
| rest or relax | burn out or break down |
| ask directions | get lost |
| make a checklist | run home for an item |
| cool our temper | have a heart attack |
| meditate or pray | worry |
| have a dental check up | have a tooth extracted |
| follow a budget | get into debt |
| mend a rip | buy a new garment |
| share feelings | see a therapist |
| balance your checkbook | call about bounced checks |
| choose friends wisely | end painful relationships |
| select healthy food | endure malnutrition |
| wait for guidance | suffer from self-will |

# Recovery from Time Debting

Symptoms of work addiction for me have included living a compressed life, "rushing to beat the clock," and always having too much to do. Many of these symptoms are also addressed in another program of recovery. Debtors Anonymous offers strategies of recovery from time debting that I have found useful to deepen recovery from work addiction. Borrowing from D.A. concepts, more detailed strategies emerge to support the W.A. tools of underscheduling, pacing, and substituting. The following is introductory literature from a local meeting of "Time and Money" Debtors Anonymous which outlines the parallels between workaholic behavior and time debting:

*"The suggested focus of this meeting is on how our relationship to time affects our finances, and vice versa. As time debtors, we look at how our disease of compulsive time debting affects our*

*relationship to money, work, others, and our own self-care; often, the relationship that suffers the most is the one we have with ourselves. Specifically, time debtors frequently live with a chronic lack of sleep, exercise, play and relaxation, spiritual practice, and/or proper medical attention. Some of us also have trouble maintaining our personal relationships, meeting our professional commitments, or keeping up with our household responsibilities. Additionally, we may have issues around eating poorly, driving dangerously, and mismanaging our money and other resources. In short, time debting usually creates or contributes to unmanageability and an overall absence of balance in our lives.*

*Compulsive time debting can include any or all of the following behaviors: workaholism, perfectionism, promising too much, over-committing, not following through, under-delivering and chronic tardiness. Time debting can also take the form of avoiding responsibilities and commitments by procrastinating; "losing track of things" (deadlines, bills, important papers, verbal agreements, etc.); creating paper chaos; or wasting time in compulsive activities (such as watching TV, playing computer games, reading, cleaning, "puttering," and the like). We may experience constantly feeling frantic about time or always being overwhelmed. Some of us develop a dependency on the rush of adrenaline produced by attempts to meet our time commitments."*

So what does the outside of my life look like right now after six and half years of workaholism recovery informed by my recovery from time debting? I work part-time from home telecommuting at a "paying job" while I am cultivating and exploring new interests. Ironically, W.A. helped me so much in learning about how to sanely cooperate with divine will in coordinating time, energy, and resources that I now have a job doing that for whole work teams! In this latest position, when I recently transitioned to part-time work, at first I did not adequately engage the W.A. tools of underscheduling, pacing, and substituting. I had the perception of a sudden surplus of time, twenty hours I had been working and 10 hours of commuting all freed up—30 more hours per week! I quickly (unconsciously) filled up my days, a lot of it with short-term service commitments (nonprofit organizations and under-resourced organizations that feed my disease's characteristic illusion of indispensability—a great workaholic stash if there ever was one!) and odd jobs. My sponsor has guided me to have a "**72-hour hold**" guideline for considering adding to my schedule anything greater than a one-time, two-hour commitment. During those three days I check with my sponsor, friends in program, and my Higher Power and Inner Wisdom. When I was in time vagueness around my job transition and sloppily thought "Oh, I have lots of time," I was not rigorous with the "72-hour hold" principle, and I got into trouble. Then I became aware of what had happened: I could tell my life was too full when I had that "squeezed" feeling with my time. In the past two months I have re-engaged with a form of **a commitment moratorium** (adding no new commitments—often useful in unmanageability situations—a more strenuous form of the "72-hour hold"), while simultaneously exploring a **commitment reduction** (the process of reducing the number of hours I am committed to do volunteer or paid work). In order to do this I created a **commitment log**, where I was able to gain awareness of all the time and energy commitments, formal and informal, I actually had (and had been in vagueness about). Thank goodness the new commitments that I had over-added were in the days-weeks range of commitment, instead of the years/decades range of obligation. This situation reminded me of when I first came into program. In early recovery, I eventually became willing to use these tools of substitution and underscheduling, plus prayer and meditation, to ground my time and energy in a surrender experience—the "turning it over" that people speak about in Step Three.

These are parallel tools to the Debtors Anonymous (D.A.) Tools of Recovery of Record Maintenance, Spending Plan, Debt Repayment, Awareness, Pressure Relief, and Abstinence, applied around time and energy, as well as paper chaos, to seek relief from the progressive and fatal nature of the disease of work addiction. Working a program in Debtors Anonymous with a focus on recovery from time debting, I've learned to think of being behind or being late as a form of debting, where I have "overspent" my time or energy and now am beholden to the past, either through backlog (activity debt: unfinished activities or commitments; self-debt: inadequate time for sleep, exercise, relationship, creativity, medical attention, or self-care that harm me physically, emotionally, mentally, and or spiritually) or indentured to activity commitments in the future that exceed my capacity ("time/activity/commitment overspending" if you will). And in Debtors Anonymous, record maintenance is one of the tools newcomers use to gain awareness about where their money, or in this case, time and energy, is getting spent. Newcomers are directed to keep records for at least 30 days of all their income and expenses and any portions of debt that they pay, according to certain prioritized spending categories. So I have "kept records" on my time spending. First and foremost, I have kept records of how many hours I have worked at my jobs for over six years, on a daily basis. This includes being specific down to the minute, including taking breaks and meals, and recording when I leave work.

There are concomitant parts to this practice—how do we count hours when we lunch with coworkers without compulsively clocking or ignoring if we're really in a work discussion; how to "count" travel time for work trips or events; how to accommodate work-related conferences (when the hours really add up in a short space of time); how to not obsess and worry about work while not at work. For this last issue, I often visualize my Higher Power leading me out the office door at the end of my work day, waving good bye, and promising to take care of everything until I return.

Without keeping records of my time spent at work, how would I be able to know if I'd been abstinent and in alignment with my bottom lines? I have also often record-kept my hours of sleep, where unmanageability or "sleep debting" can trigger toxic adrenaline cycling. These time logs are things I review five days a week with my sponsor. As in other forms of recovery, I have become aware of the triggers of my disease and have become willing to have Higher Power guide me in a different way of being, including avoiding triggers altogether. It is rare for me to go to volunteer/booster meetings where there are lots of tasks and people looking for other people to take them on. (Don't even ask me all the times my disease has sidestepped the 72-hour hold by taking on a lot of little—less than 2 hour—service commitments that still added up to trouble!)

Sometimes, in addition to work and sleep logging, I have tracked breaks, resting, yoga/walks/exercise, and fun/wellness/self-care time. My record keeping, especially at the beginning, focuses on wherever I'm having (Step One) unmanageability. And at times I have kept records of all my time, in all sixteen Debtors Anonymous categories, to really surrender myself. It is an especially helpful tool if I am considering adding something new to my schedule. It helps me get concrete and specific about what I am currently spending time on when I am praying about a substitution plan. What I learn again and again from time record keeping is that my own addict's internal story of how I'm spending my time—"That project is eating up all my time"—(aside from the victim-thinking) is often inaccurate. It is usually a lie, and only record keeping leads me to rigorous honesty (e.g. "Oh, in fact, that project is only actually taking 1.5 hours per month."). Addict thinking: "Oh, that's easy, *it will take no time at all.*" (Now, of course, in workaholism and time debting recovery, we should hear a "yellow alert" go off whenever we hear those words, but it doesn't always happen.) The reality of record-keeping: That activity has lasted for five weeks so far and taken 3.2 hours the first week and 2 hours a week since then. Not surprising that my fantastical thinking and reality might have too much distance between them, since the disease is cunning, baffling, and powerful.

What happens in Debtors Anonymous for me around recordkeeping is that I become the scribe for Higher Power. My emotional attachments, filters, and baggage loosen up and often fall away, and I can live in reality. I am reminded of what one program friend suggests to me occasionally: "Don't use your mind for anything important today." Another friend (simulating a voice over a bullhorn): "Put the work {obligation, worry, avoidance, etc.} down and take three steps back." What my mind thinks and what is objectively true are not coincident. All this information, awareness, and honesty help me work with my sponsor and Higher Power to formulate a **time spending plan**. Through guidance and learning what is "enough," I am able to pro-actively co-create a daily plan for my time and energy. This planning has worked differently at different times, anything from a daily check-in with my sponsor about the twenty-four hours ahead, to mapping out service, volunteer, work, and recovery commitments on a weekly and monthly basis (and even annually for vacations and big fun), ensuring space for nurturing, fun, creativity, relationships, and downtime. Here is the simplified version of the categories I use sometimes to track my time, modified from the sixteen suggested money record maintenance categories of D.A. This is the first column of a spreadsheet that then has a column for each day of the week. Sometimes I've tracked throughout the day, other times I've used this as a form of Tenth Step inventory at day's end. Some of the guidelines I use for non-work time are to track time to the nearest 15 minutes (so I don't become compulsive about record keeping), and counting sleep from the night before (which helps me see how abundant rest and sleep sets me up for the day). For all categories, I include time spent traveling to or from an activity as part of the "time cost" of that activity.

## 1- Spirituality
Prayer/Meditation/Sponsor
Spiritual Reading/Program Literature
Service/Sponsees/Phone
Step work (including Daily Tenth)
Meetings

Creating/Writing/Journal/Art
Recordkeeping (hours, financial, yoga)
Out In Nature
Other/General Spirituality

## 2- **RESTORATION** Shelter/Body/Rest
SLEEP
Cleaning
Rest, Nap, Elevate, Breaks
Yoga-Move-Walk-Bike
HOUSE
## 2.5 Inflow
WORK
Transportation to and from Work
Other

## 3- **Divine Nourishment**
Food Shopping (including transportation)
Food Prep
Breakfast
Lunch
Dinner

## 4- **Transportation**
Getting Gasoline/Maintenance/Repairs

## 5- **Self-Care**
Bathing/Shampooing
Feelings
Quiet Time

## 6- **Clothes**

## 7- **Medical/Wellness (Doctor, Chiropractor, massage)**

## 8- **Entertainment**
Going out with Friends
Movies
Books/Reading/Library
Processing
Intimacy

## 9 - **Beloveds/Gifts**
Cards, email, letters, gifts

**10 - Education**

**11 - Vacation**

**12 - Personal Business - opening and sorting mail, getting office supplies, etc.**
**13 - Dependent Care**
 Time with family
 Walking the dog/Time with pets/Cleaning out the litter box

**14 - Savings**
 Extra Energy, Naps etc.
 Lollygagging
 Senseless Fun
 Restorative Yoga

**16 - Currency – "Debt Repayment"- Clearing up Backlog, Amends, and Paper Chaos**

*17-OTHER*

**Total Hours (should equal 24)**

Over time, with the help of Higher Power, my sponsor, and program friends, I can detect trends and patterns. Overspending time on service or work—Category 1—while underspending time on entertainment—Category 8—is a workaholic classic. Sometimes I've added up my projected commitments if I'm planning ahead for a given week, and my plan has exceeded the actual number of hours in a week by twenty-five to forty hours! No more "innocent" strategies of "Well, I'll just stay up a little later/get up a little earlier to finish that." The time spending plan and time record keeping allow me an objective view. My time spending plan has come in handy when something new comes up: anything from a gardening project to a service position, moving from full time to part time work, taking on a writing endeavor, or even deepening in my experiencing the balance of time for creativity, spontaneity, and fun. It helps me get out of vagueness so I can, with my Higher Power's help, develop a plan of action. It is a map for matching my time and energy to my values. In time debting recovery, the parallel for financial solvency is time currency. Record maintenance and formulating a spending plan for wellness lead me day by day to honesty and serenity. The keywords: Gentleness. Spaciousness. Surrender.

# Abstinence: Top Lines and Bottom Lines

## ABSTINENCE

One definition of W.A. abstinence is:

*"...To abstain from compulsive working, activity and worry. For many workaholics, abstinence means far more than relief from compulsive working on a physical level. It also means an attitude that comes as a result of surrendering to something greater than ourselves. Abstinence means not only freedom from compulsive working but also freedom from compulsive thinking and worrying. Each of us is free to determine our own way of being abstinent according to personal needs and preferences."*

Unlike substance addictions where abstinence is clearly defined by stopping the use of the substance, work addiction takes many different forms. Workaholism may manifest in blatant and subtle ways.

How do we know when we are abstinent and when we have lapsed into active addiction? Each workaholic needs to define abstinence for him or herself. Bottom lines are a helpful tool in defining individual abstinence.

## BOTTOM LINES

Bottom lines define the point where we cross over from abstinence to work addiction.

The behaviors that trigger and signal workaholism are different in different people. The first step in developing our own list of bottom lines is to go back to Step One: we admitted we were powerless over work and activity. We sit quietly and write a list of the unmanageable behaviors or actions that we take or have taken when we are active in our workaholism. It is helpful to go over this list with a sponsor or other W.A. member.

The next step is to pick one or two items from our list and create bottom lines that will give us guidelines for abstinence.

Here are some examples of bottom lines for abstinence that workaholics have surrendered to:

- I do not work (including housework and volunteer work) more than six out of seven days.
- I do not work more than forty-five hours per week.
- I do not start work and will stop work when I am hungry, angry, lonely or tired ("H.A.L.T.").
- I do not schedule a new commitment without checking with another W.A. member first.

- I do not bring work to the table during mealtimes.
- I do not allow work to encroach upon the time I commit to be with my family.
- I do not blame others for my stress.
- I do not rush or drive unsafely, even if I am late.
- I do not take on a new commitment without giving up an old commitment. A specific bottom line example of this might be: I do not take on any new commitment greater than a one-time, two-hour commitment without putting it on a "72-hour hold" during which time I pray and speak with my sponsor, creating a plan to substitute out something else of equivalent time and energy.

Bottom lines can also be written in the affirmative to capture baseline behavior that we learn is critical to sustaining our abstinence:

- I sleep at least seven hours a night.
- I pray and meditate every day.
- I attend at least one meeting per week.
- I read literature for at least ten minutes per day.
- I meet with my sponsor at least once per month to go over Step work.
- I make a program call at least five times per week.

As the principle of practicing gentleness reminds us, we are gentle with ourselves and patient in our efforts, knowing that our new way of living requires much practice. Bottom lines are meant as a guide to help us see when our behavior has crossed the boundary from healthier to less healthy. We don't use our lapses as excuses to beat ourselves up; rather, we view them as reminders that we are not perfect and must continue to work our programs one day at a time.

As workaholics, it is important that we not follow our program of recovery with the same blind zeal for work that brought us to our knees in the first place. We start simply; we can always add more bottom lines as our awareness grows.

When we create our first list of bottom line behaviors with the help of our Higher Power and program friends, we select actions that are achievable for us at the current time. If we find we are consistently unable to achieve one of the behaviors on our list, we adjust it to reflect that we can, with Higher Power's help, live in the here and now. Bottom lines should be hallmarks of our success rather than set-ups for failure.

Our bottom line behaviors will change over time, as we grow in our recovery and more becomes possible. We have found that recovery is contagious: the more we have, the more we will want.

## TOP LINES

Top line behaviors represent our goals and visions. For example, a person with a bottom line of "I do not work more than six out of seven days" might have a top line of "I will take off two days a week."

Top lines represent our aspirations. They give us goals to work toward. Our success with our bottom lines gives us hope that we will, in time, reach our top lines.

Over time, top lines become bottom lines. For the W.A. in the previous example, "I will not work more than five out of seven days" may shift from being a top line to an easily achievable bottom line. The new top line might be "I will work no more than four out of seven days."

Some examples of top lines are:

- I will take a vacation that has nothing to do with work of any kind.
- I will spend one whole day every week doing something fun with my children.
- I will put my health before my work.
- I will sleep at least eight hours every night.
- I will eat my meals sitting down in a relaxed manner.
- I will have at least one day each week with no to-do list.
- I will have two days off in a row per week.
- I will not work more than nine hours in a day or more than forty hours in a week.

## CONCLUSION

While we workaholics find we have much in common with each other in our disease, the actions and behaviors that lead each of us into our addiction are different.

Bottom lines are the signposts guiding us toward abstinence. Top lines are the signposts marking our paths toward recovery and freedom from worry. Top lines are important because they show us where the path of recovery is heading. While our bottom lines help free us from pain, our top lines promise joy and fulfillment.

Bottom lines and top lines allow us to create a structure within our program of recovery that is tailored to our individual patterns. We follow the direction shown to us by our evolving top and bottom lines with the help of a Higher Power, a supportive

W.A. community, a sponsor or co-sponsor, and our own desire for sanity and serenity.

# The History of Workaholics Anonymous

Like all Twelve Step groups, there was a time when this fellowship did not exist and had to be started by someone willing to be first in service. It was in the early 1980's that a number of people began to recognize that their pathological use of activity was affecting them like an alcoholic's or addict's abuse of substances. Some of them formed Twelve Step groups modeled after Alcoholics Anonymous (A.A.) as they found each other in the workplace, at home, or on the playing field.

In 1983, one of the first formal efforts to create a fellowship around work addiction recovery began in New York when a corporate financial planner and a schoolteacher met. They formed Workaholics Anonymous (W.A.) to stop working compulsively themselves and to help others who suffered from the disease of workaholism. In their first meetings, spouses joined them and in retrospect were the first Work-Anon group, seeking recovery for family and friends of workaholics. Since this nascent W.A. group welcomed spouses to join their meetings, they did not form a separate Work-Anon organization.

Over the next several years, people in California (some without knowledge of the New York effort) were also recognizing work addiction as an illness and began to hold meetings in their communities. Over time, several work addiction recovery groups were established in Southern California. Eventually members from Los Angeles and San Diego merged with the New York effort and began collaborating on carrying the message and on the creation of literature. Meetings also started up in several communities in Northeastern and Southwestern areas of the United States. Magazine and newspaper articles appeared about the W.A. meetings.

In the late 1980's an entirely separate Workaholics Anonymous organization developed in the San Francisco Bay Area. A nurse who had been acquainted with A.A. in Tucson, Arizona, noticed that her compulsive, intense working behavior affected her health and her relationships even more severely than alcohol had. She sought help at the Dry Dock, San Francisco's A.A. center. She established W.A. as a nonprofit California corporation in 1987. With the emergence of a coast-to-coast connection, this Bay Area group of fellowships gradually became known as W.A's first organization.

Requests for information came in from other countries. Groups formed around the world. However, despite being based on the Twelve Step approach, each group had a different Definition of The Problem, the Characteristics, Tools, Meeting Format, Promises of the Program and what to include on its Literature list. As more members and groups discovered each other's existence—and their striking similarities—many asked for sharing of ideas, development of a unifying meeting format and a uniting approach for responding to public inquiries about workaholism.

On March 31st of 1990, after a countrywide exchange of letters among several of the first W.A. groups, four W.A. members and two of their "Work-Anon" spouses converged to meet for the first time in St. John's Presbyterian Church basement in West Los Angeles. Having come from fellowships in New York, Los Angeles and San Diego, they titled their meeting the "Workaholics Anonymous First World Service Conference."

At this initial gathering, these pioneers shared the history, progress, and future hopes of their respective fellowships, and identified a number of common recovery problems. These included how to reach the practicing workaholic whose spouse is the one inquiring about W.A., how to deal with referrals from medical doctors and psychotherapists, how to substitute telephone support where attendance at W.A. meetings was impractical, how to respond to inquiries from people who had no Twelve Step experience, how to develop a meeting format for fellowships of only two or three people, and how to confront the fact that workaholism was not accepted by traditional American culture as a widespread and serious disease.

Four pioneers assumed the responsibilities of the new organization and mutually pledged to hold their offices until elections could be held at the next nationwide conference, tentatively scheduled for May of 1991. During 1990 these four pioneers of the first W.A. World Service Organization (W.S.O.) sought permission from Alcoholics Anonymous and the A.A. Grapevine to adapt the A.A. Preamble, Twelve Steps, and Twelve Traditions; began to develop new Articles of Incorporation and Bylaws; assembled a starter kit for new meetings, including a suggested meeting format, checklist of Characteristics, Tools of Recovery and the Promises of the Program; compiled a roster of all the known W.A. meetings worldwide; communicated with each W.A. group; began compiling an ongoing list of approved recovery literature and started gathering stories of workaholic recovery for eventual inclusion in a W.A. Book.

On November 7th, 1992, enthusiasm was high as participants, representing many of the 63 fellowships, including ones in Canada, Germany and Japan, came to the Second W.A. World Conference at Summit Medical Center in Oakland, California. About thirty people attended from California, Colorado, Florida, and Pennsylvania. The conference attendees placed all W.S.O. authority in the hands of five co-chairpersons, (1) for registration of groups, (2) for answering telephone and letter inquiries, (3) for outreach, (4) for managing the money and (5) for facilitating communication among these co-chairs and all appointed committees. W.S.O. committees were established to reexamine and officially file bylaws, develop a list of suggested literature, publish a newsletter, raise funds, and circulate announcements.

The early nonprofit incorporation of W.A. in Northern California continued in existence to provide meeting list updates and telephone listings of the ten meetings of W.A.'s only Intergroup. These meetings decreased in number until there were insufficient donations to pay for the services. The corporation was disbanded in the 90's and the small residual treasury was donated to the new W.A.W.S.O.

The effort to further the service structure refocused in the mid 1990's when there was a gathering consensus, from several members of W.A., for the fellowship to establish a home page on the Worldwide Web and start using email. At first a member of the Boston meeting made up an unofficial W.A. web page, put some of our published literature on it, and gave a reply address. This attracted interest, and newcomers occasionally used it to look for meetings and get other information, until it became too much for that one person to maintain.

Since 2002, W.A. has had a full Board of Directors in service. This renewed W.A.W.S.O. Board realized the Internet was a medium worth embracing, and, with the help of members of the Boston meeting and others, a URL was obtained and the web site was launched at **www.workaholics-anonymous.org** . Not only were Board members more easily able to communicate with each other via the website, but also the website became a valuable resource for suffering workaholics attracting interest from many parts of the world. It remains the official fellowship website today.

As of this printing, in 2005, the W.A. fellowship continues to grow. Our literature has increased in scope dramatically with the publishing of this book and we have plans to increase our website capacity as well as to undertake other literature efforts. Service to others and ourselves keeps our evolution as a fellowship progressing and our individual recoveries alive. Our fellowship history is made up of the collective effort of individuals performing acts of service for others, one at a time. Our fellowship's Higher Power helps guide us to serve in a balanced way. We are relieved one day at a time from the perfectionism, overwork, and procrastination of work addiction while carrying a message of hope to the workaholics who still suffer. We invite you to "take your turn" and join us in this service commitment, as doing so will help strengthen abstinence and insure that W.A. continues to be there for us and for all who wish to recover from workaholism.

Printed in Great Britain
by Amazon

24285952R00131